# Discovery Trips in

# Europe

By the Editors of Sunset Books and Sunset Magazine

# Lane Publishing Co.

## Menlo Park, California

**Book Editor: Cornelia Fogle**

Design: Joe di Chiarro

Illustrations: Rik Olson

Maps: Vernon Koski, Ells Marugg

**Acknowledgments**
We appreciate the assistance and cooperation of members of
the various European government tourist offices in preparing
and checking material for this book.

**Cover.** In Austria, balconied houses of Hallstatt climb wooded
slopes above deep blue waters of Hallstättersee southeast of
Salzburg (see page 74). Photograph by Fremdenverkehrs-
verband Hallstatt.

Sunset Books
  Editor: David E. Clark
  Managing Editor: Elizabeth L. Hogan

Fourth printing **(Updated)** March 1987

# Contents

# Discovery: The Essence of Travel

Travel has ceased to be a status symbol. It is an essential part of our personal education, a means of satisfying our needs and interests and learning more about ourselves and the world.

The journeys you make should be fun, not a test of endurance. They should provide personal satisfaction and a means of self-expression.

## Why do you want to travel?

People travel for different reasons. Many seek excitement and escape. Some want entertainment or an education. Others satisfy a passionate longing to visit faraway places.

Whether you travel for fun or stimulation, for relaxation or new adventures, your experiences will be richer if you combine your travels with personal interests.

*Discovery Trips in Europe* is a book filled with ideas to add an extra dimension to your travels. Many of the trips and destinations can be enjoyed in less than a day and can be fitted into a flexible itinerary on short notice. Others require more time and some planning. The book's features suggest some different experiences in transport— cycling, horse-drawn wagons, river and canal boats— and special interests that can enrich your holiday.

## Today's adventuresome travelers

People who venture far from home these days are more knowledgeable and curious than earlier innocents abroad. They put fewer limits on their experiences, and are more adventuresome in their personal explorations. They enjoy less-structured travel plans, spend more time in fewer areas, and are more venturesome in meeting local people and learning about their own origins.

Today's travelers usually combine city explorations with more leisurely journeys in the countryside, often departing the well-trodden paths for remote destinations. They search out the special pleasures awaiting those willing to try something unfamiliar. They bring along personal interests in music, crafts, or sports to enrich their travels.

## Europe still offers discoveries

Few places remain well-kept secrets any more. Yet you will still experience a personal thrill each time you happen on a special place—whether it is on your first trip to Europe or your 21st.

Well-traveled tourist routes are popular for good reason. For centuries their attractions have provided satisfaction to travelers. If you bypass all the popular places, you miss many memorable travel experiences.

To indulge your dreams, you must find new ways to experience these sites, to capture the fantasy still lurking there despite seasonal crowds. Visit these places in midweek and off-season. Stay overnight, and explore after the crowds depart and the town reverts to its inhabitants. A city best reveals its special delights in the early hours of evening and morning.

The most fascinating discoveries you'll make are those you find out about yourself. Travel provides an incomparable opportunity to learn about other cultures, to broaden our horizons in human as well as geographic terms.

When you travel with a relaxed attitude and a lively curiosity, each day brings new delights. Learn to recognize and respect differences. Explore contemporary living as well as the cultural life when you observe people and their customs.

## Joys of the countryside

Europe has been taking care of travelers since the great pilgrimages of the Crusades, and its fascinating cities have been a cornerstone of Western culture. Many of their special qualities remain, yet each year they become a little harder to discover. Modern cities are growing increasingly similar—hotels are larger and more impersonal, buildings of architectural charm are replaced by monoliths of steel and glass, traffic intensifies, and the number of people increases.

You discover the real Europe outside the cities as you wander through walled towns little changed from medieval days, prowl lively outdoor markets where village housewives buy their produce and household necessities, cruise inland waterways in pastoral stillness, sleep in a castle fortress or an ancient country inn.

In the countryside, the pace of life slows. Traffic diminishes, and you'll see more people walking or riding bicycles. Country people take time to talk with their neighbors, to chat with the postman or local shopkeeper, to pat a friendly dog.

There's a special charm in leisurely exploring off the main routes. Country byways follow the contours of the land. You rediscover small pleasures—the patterns of cultivated fields, mountains cleanly etched against the sky, the various local ways that grape vines are staked or hay is stacked to dry in the sun.

You become aware of an amazing variety of physical variation. Each region also has its own cultural distinctions—customs, festivities, often a distinctive apparel and dialect as well. Adaptable travelers enjoy and appreciate these differences, treating variations as pieces in a fascinating travel mosaic.

Outside the cities, sightseeing is less demanding. You can let each day's events unfold. Seek out country towns and little-known attractions. Stay in castle hotels, historic inns, or on working farms. Take a brisk walk, rent a bicycle, or shop for a picnic—and you'll open the way to more rewarding experiences.

## Put all your senses to work

Travel is more than a different setting, splendid scenery, unusual architecture, or a strange language. It is an experience of the senses, blending vivid impressions that you recall long after photographs have been put away. Cultural highlights are important, but you'll remember a riverside picnic beneath France's Pont du Gard or the night you spent singing in an Irish pub or dancing in a Greek *taverna* far longer than the year Westminster Abbey was built.

Sharpen all your senses. The visitor who is content to "see Europe" misses much of the fun. Enjoy its sights, but also taste its traditional dishes. Listen to the vegetable sellers call out their wares. Feel the uneven cobblestones beneath your feet. Smell the aroma of freshly baked bread or newly mown hay. Be a participant, not merely a spectator. If you're invited to join in activities, don't hang back; do so with a smile.

Many places are best explored on foot. Walk the cobbled alleyways where flowers cascade from stairs and balconies. Stride atop ancient ramparts encircling medieval towns. Linger near the harbor to watch as fishermen auction the day's catch. Stroll through rural fairs and markets. If you lose your way occasionally, consider it part of the fun.

Make history come alive as you seek out remnants of the past. Visit the homes where writers and artists and musicians lived and worked; then tour the countryside portrayed in their creative works. Collect new ideas as you visit European restaurants, gardens, and shops. Try your favorite sport in a new setting.

## Get the most out of your trip

With the escalating cost of travel, planning is more important than ever. You want full value from your travel dollars. Imaginative planning can still provide a memorable vacation at a reasonable cost.

The wise traveler mixes city and country life. You'll find stimulation and vitality—and high prices—in the cities. Country living is more relaxed and down to earth. You gain an appreciation of the country, its people, and the qualities that make each region unique.

**Go fewer places.** Minimize your travel as much as possible. Moving around costs time and money. Pick a single country (two or three at the most) and confine yourself to a few well-chosen cities or regions, but stay longer in each. Explore the cities you've chosen, then make day trips into the countryside.

**Use public transportation.** Europe excels in all phases of mass transit. You'll find trains, buses, ferries, lake steamers, and riverboats ready to transport you to your destinations.

In cities, keep public transportation in mind when you choose your hotels. Walking is often the most practical way to explore a city or town, but efficient subway, streetcar, and bus systems can be quickly mastered.

You'll want to explore farther, too. Economical trains and buses radiate into the countryside. On the scene, you can inquire about special tourist transportation tickets.

**Investigate package plans.** Organized travel packages can simplify many details of travel arrangements and save considerable money. You'll find many special-interest tours and short excursions that introduce you to a particular region and its people.

You don't have to tag along with a group. "Fly-drive" trips allow you to save money on both air and ground travel. Other travel plans provide both rental car and a choice of hotel accommodations, giving you plenty of planning flexibility yet allowing you to keep basic expenses within limited boundaries.

**Try alternative accommodations.** Seek out some of Europe's small hotels, inns, and pensions. Splurge with a night or two in a castle or charming country inn. Rent a cottage for a week, investigate bed-and-breakfast houses, stay with a farm family for a few days.

Make your first and last nights' reservations. Knowing where you'll stay on arrival and before departure simplifies travel planning. In summer, especially, make hotel reservations in major cities.

**Travel off-season.** Some of Europe's best weather occurs in spring and autumn. When you travel outside the busy summer months, you'll find fewer tourists. It's easier to find accommodations or make changes on short notice. Service personnel have more time to help you. Off-season prices are frequently lower.

**Use local information offices.** Cities and towns all over Europe have tourist information offices. Check with them about local attractions and excursions, accommodations, events, and special values.

## Obtain help from the experts

The days of uncomplicated travel are over. Yet all too often, a traveler's problems are brought on by inexperience, ignorance, or lack of preparation.

Each European government has tourist representatives in the United States to promote travel to its country. These offices can provide maps; city and regional brochures; hotel and restaurant listings in various price categories; information on special events, sports and entertainment, and special-interest touring; details of rail passes and other tourist travel bargains. They do *not* make reservations or plan individual trips.

A good travel agent can handle many of the details of your trip and save you time, money, and frustration. Travel agencies can provide information on tours, arrange for plane and train tickets, make hotel reservations, and arrange car rentals. If you wish, the agent can handle trip planning, including side trips and special events. Travel agencies do not usually charge for arranging transportation or for package tours, but they do charge for "custom" tour service. Be sure your agent understands clearly the type of accommodations and style of travel you desire.

# Government Tourist Offices in the United States

Below are addresses of European government tourist offices in the United States. Contact the regional representative nearest you for information on tourist travel within the country.

Addresses are updated each printing (see page 2) but offices do shift locations, and we suggest you re-check addresses before writing if possible.

## AUSTRIAN NATIONAL TOURIST OFFICES

New York, NY 10110: 500 Fifth Avenue, Suite 2009-2022
Chicago, IL 60611: 500 North Michigan Avenue, Suite 544
Houston, TX 77056: 4800 San Felipe
Los Angeles, CA 90025: 11601 Wilshire Boulevard, Suite 2480

## BELGIAN TOURIST OFFICE

New York, NY 10151: 745 Fifth Avenue

## BRITISH TOURIST AUTHORITY

New York, NY 10019: 40 West 57th Street, Suite 320
Chicago, IL 60611: John Hancock Center, 875 North Michigan Avenue, Suite 3320
Dallas, TX 75201-1814: Cedar Maple Plaza, 2305 Cedar Springs
Los Angeles, CA 90071: World Trade Center, 350 South Figueroa, Suite 450

## DANISH TOURIST BOARD

New York, NY 10017: 655 Third Avenue

## FINNISH TOURIST BOARD

New York, NY 10017: 655 Third Avenue

## FRENCH GOVERNMENT TOURIST OFFICES

New York, NY 10020: 610 Fifth Avenue
Beverly Hills, CA 90212: 9401 Wilshire Boulevard
Chicago, IL 60611: 645 North Michigan Avenue
Dallas, TX 75258: P.O. Box 58610, 2050 Stemmons Freeway
San Francisco, CA 94102: 1 Hallidie Plaza, Suite 250

## GERMAN NATIONAL TOURIST OFFICES

New York, NY 10017: 747 Third Avenue
Los Angeles, CA 90071-2997: 444 South Flower Street, Suite 2230

## GREEK NATIONAL TOURIST ORGANIZATION

New York, NY 10022: 645 Fifth Avenue
Chicago, IL 60601: 168 North Michigan Avenue
Los Angeles, CA 90017: 611 West Sixth Street, Suite 1998

## IRISH TOURIST BOARD

New York, NY 10017: 757 Third Avenue

## ITALIAN GOVERNMENT TRAVEL OFFICES—E.N.I.T.

New York, NY 10111: 630 Fifth Avenue, Suite 1565
Chicago, IL 60611: 500 North Michigan Avenue, Suite 1046
San Francisco, CA 94108: 360 Post Street, Suite 801

## LUXEMBOURG NATIONAL TOURIST OFFICE

New York, NY 10017: 801 Second Avenue

## NETHERLANDS BOARD OF TOURISM

New York, NY 10017: 355 Lexington Avenue
Chicago, IL 60601: 225 North Michigan Avenue, Suite 326
San Francisco, CA 94105: 605 Market Street, Suite 401

## NORWEGIAN TOURIST BOARD

New York, NY 10017: 655 Third Avenue

## PORTUGUESE NATIONAL TOURIST OFFICE

New York, NY 10036-5089: 548 Fifth Avenue

## SPANISH NATIONAL TOURIST OFFICES

New York, NY 10022: 665 Fifth Avenue
Chicago, IL 60611: 845 North Michigan Avenue
Houston, TX 77056: 4800 The Galleria, 5085 Westheimer
San Francisco, CA 94102: 1 Hallidie Plaza, Suite 801

## SWEDISH TOURIST BOARD

New York, NY 10017: 655 Third Avenue

## SWISS NATIONAL TOURIST OFFICES

New York, NY 10020: 608 Fifth Avenue
Chicago, IL 60603: 104 South Michigan Avenue
San Francisco, CA 94108: 250 Stockton Street

## YUGOSLAV NATIONAL TOURIST OFFICE

New York, NY 10111: 630 Fifth Avenue, Suite 280

# Rugged Corner of Historic Wales

Fortress castles, coastal resorts, mountain trails, and steam railways lure visitors to this remote region

The Welsh love their country with a fierce devotion. Pushed into the wild, western mountains during ancient battles with the Saxons, they defended their land passionately against all invaders, retreating to impregnable mountain strongholds. Still guarding the green valleys are the crumbling towers of battle-scarred fortresses like Harlech, Conway, and Caernarvon, built in the 13th century by English invaders.

In many ways, Wales remains a remote country within a country. Though part of Britain, it has kept a unique identity, clinging to an ancient Celtic language (whose literature goes back 1,400 years) and to many traditions. Place names with their complicated spellings may puzzle you, but you'll be relieved to know that everyone speaks English—with a charming lilt.

What does a visitor remember most about Wales? Probably the wild and wonderful beauty of the hills and the warmth of the people. The pace of life reflects a calmer, simpler era. Despite its mining and industry, Wales is still farming country. On market days farmers come to

town, some in horse-drawn carts, to sell their produce from outdoor stalls. You'll find warm conviviality in local pubs.

In the northwest corner of Wales, you discover a variety of attractions—historic castles, coastal resorts, charming villages, famous gardens, rugged mountains. Hills hide slate mines (tours available) and archeological remains.

Are you a rail buff? Narrow-gauge steam railways take you through wooded valleys, beside lakes, and up the region's highest peak. Interested in sports? You'll find diverse opportunities—from sailing and deep-sea fishing to mountain climbing and pony trekking. Want to know more about Wales first-hand? You can learn about its culture and traditions in local museums and see displays of Welsh crafts and textiles in workshops and craft centers.

## Exploring the countryside

Since Wales has few large towns, the best way to tour there is by car.

From English border towns, trains travel west from Chester along the north coast to Llandudno, Bangor, and Holyhead; and west from Shrewsbury to the central coast. The Cambrian Coast rail line curves along Cardigan Bay between Aberystwyth and Pwllheli. Eight narrow-gauge railways transport holiday travelers through the scenic countryside on weekends from Easter through September (daily in summer and during holiday periods); several offer extended schedules.

Local buses depart from the main towns, following roundabout routes through the countryside past farmhouses, grazing sheep, gray stone walls, and occasionally crossing a humpbacked bridge.

From the seaside resort of Llandudno, you can head inland or along the coast to explore Wales's northwest corner.

The daily life of a modern town goes on inside the medieval walls of Conway (Conwy in Welsh). A well-preserved castle dominates this fortress town, built in the 1280s by Edward I as a frontier post on the west bank of the River Conway. Immense circular towers rise above the thick curtain wall surrounding the town. To appreciate Conway's special appeal, explore the castle and walk along the town walls and Thomas Telford's famous suspension bridge. Discover old buildings and inns and unexpected touches of greenery. Along the ancient riverside quay, you'll mingle with anglers and yachters.

## The realm of Snowdonia

It's only 20 miles/32 km from the coast up the Vale of Conway to Betws-y-Coed, at the foot of Snowdon, yet you'll discover at least a half-dozen inviting places to stop.

Near Tal-y-Cafn, the spectacular displays of Bodnant Gardens slope down the eastern bank of the River Conway with Snowdonia's peaks as a backdrop. One of England's finest gardens, Bodnant is open from April through October. Seasonal exhibits of azaleas, magnolias, rhododendrons, and roses enhance its landscaped ponds, formal terraces, and rock garden.

A three-arch stone bridge spans the river at Llanrwst. You can obtain information about Snowdonia National Park at Tourist Information Centres in the region.

Once a natural fortress against invaders, the high rugged mountains are today a favorite destination for those who love the outdoors. You can tour parts of the park by car or mountain railway, picnic under the trees, or explore on foot. Nature trails leave from Beddgelert, Betws-y-Coed, Capel Curig, Maentwrog, and Pen-y-Gwryd.

Mountaineering, fishing, and pony trekking are other favorite park activities. Look for mountain climbers near Llanberis Pass.

## The great little trains of Wales

No visit to Wales is complete without a ride on at least one of the eight narrow-gauge steam railways that chug through some of the region's prettiest countryside.

In the 19th century, these small trains hauled slate, coal, and farm produce from remote communities to seaports. But the slate trade declined, passengers gravitated to buses and automobiles, and the little trains seemed destined for oblivion. Fortunately, hundreds of railway enthusiasts volunteered long hours restoring the trains, which now operate from Easter to late September. A railway museum is located in Porthmadog.

Trains depart from the following towns, listed north to south: Gilfach Ddu (Llanberis Lake Railway); Llanberis (Snowdon Mountain Railway); and Porthmadog (Festiniog Railway). Other narrow-gauge trains leave from Llanuwchllyn (Bala Lake Railway); Fairbourne (Fairbourne Railway); Llanfair Caereinion (Welshpool & Llanfair Railway); Tywyn (Talyllyn Railway); and Aberystwyth (Vale of Rheidol Railway).

## Lleyn Peninsula—a world apart

Facing a river estuary just south of Lleyn Peninsula is whimsical Portmeirion, an architectural fantasy of Italianate buildings and landscaped subtropical gardens.

"Land's end" of north Wales, Lleyn Peninsula thrusts westward into the sea. Its gorse-covered slopes and breezy headlands seem a world apart, and you'll delight in the old-world atmosphere of its small towns and old villages.

The main holiday centers are along the protected south coast—Criccieth, Pwllheli, Abersoch, and Aberdaron. Criccieth has a medieval hilltop castle. Pwllheli bustles with summer activity, particularly on Wednesdays when there's an open-air market in the town square. Yachters anchor in sheltered harbors at Pwllheli and Abersoch.

Churches along Lleyn's northern coast mark the route taken by ancient pilgrims to the holy island of Bardsey, just off the peninsula's tip. Narrow lanes wander down to long sandy beaches and secluded bays—smugglers' coves at one time—embraced by sheer cliffs. Massive stone ramparts more than 2,000 years old rise above wild heather near Llanaelhaearn, site of a large Iron Age stronghold.

Tower of 700-year-old Conway Castle offers visitors lofty view point over river sprinkled with pleasure craft.

Greenery and spring-flowering azaleas frame waterfall in famous Bodnant Gardens near village of Tal-y-Cafn.

One of Wales's main attractions is historic Caernarvon Castle, scene of the 1969 investiture of Prince Charles as Prince of Wales. Saturday is market day in the ancient walled town.

Across Menai Strait from Bangor is the Isle of Anglesey, joined to the mainland by bridge, rail, and ferry. The island is a favorite retreat for those seeking an informal, inexpensive holiday. The main road across Anglesey goes to Holyhead, terminus of the ferry to Ireland.

# Charming Villages Dot East Anglia

Sturdy churches, thatch-roofed cottages, and timbered inns delight back road explorers in Suffolk and Essex

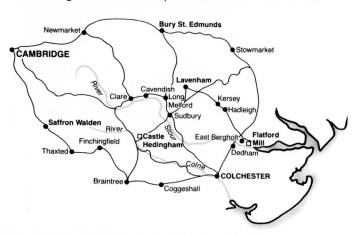

English country byways provide serendipitous discoveries for travelers willing to explore off the main routes. You'll enjoy the uncrowded English countryside at its best in East Anglia. Many villages preserve a rich legacy of timbered and thatch-roofed houses, oak-paneled inns, and solid churches.

The English wool boom of the 14th, 15th, and 16th centuries heaped prosperity on many towns and villages in Suffolk and Essex, as it did elsewhere in the country. Wealthy merchants and traders spent money freely on splendid houses and great parish churches. In each town the church is a focal point, its tower or spire rising prominently above the buildings and countryside.

When you venture onto East Anglia's back roads, you'll come upon such delightful hamlets as Clare, known for its ornamented houses; Cavendish, with thatched cottages facing the village green; Lavenham and Long Melford, noted for half-timbered buildings; Kersey, where a shallow stream crosses the main road; and Thaxted, on its hilltop. Depending on your interests, you can visit the Constable country or the horse-racing center of Newmarket.

You can travel to Cambridge or Colchester by train from London's Liverpool Street Station. Buses serve some towns, but you'll see the region best—stopping where and when you wish—by car. East Anglian inns offer pleasant hospitality, and you'll meet the English

Ornamental plasterwork, called pargeting, adorns many Suffolk houses. This Clare dwelling was built in 1473.

people in local pubs. Attractions are generally open daily from April to October, weekends only in winter.

## Byways wend through sleepy Suffolk

From Cambridge, drive southeast through the rolling Gog Magog Hills into quiet Suffolk. Some of the region's most delightful villages are sprinkled through the Stour valley. The meandering stream marks the boundary between the counties of Suffolk, north of the river, and Essex, to the south.

Clare contains delightful old houses displaying East Anglian pargeting, a craft where exterior walls are decorated with raised ornamental plasterwork. Cavendish has a wide village green and many attractive thatched cottages.

Dignified houses and attractive shops line Long Melford's long, wide thoroughfare. The town has a lovely church and two impressive mansions, Kentwell Hall and the Tudor brick Melford Hall.

Sudbury, a sturdy country market town, was the birthplace of painter Thomas Gainsborough. The family home is now a museum.

Lavenham's wool-trading ancestors built a magnificent perpendicular-style church, but the attractive town is best known for its wealth of black-and-white, timber-framed cottages and venerable inns, whose top stories often bulge over the lower ones.

Timbered and pastel-tinted cottages line the main street of Kersey, one of Suffolk's prettiest villages. Its church sits high above on a hill. Watch for ducks as you splash through the shallow, tree-shaded stream flowing across the main road. The wool town of Kersey gave its name to a coarse cloth; nearby Lindsey provided its name for linsey-woolsey, a fabric that clothed many American colonists.

In Hadleigh, townhouses and mansions from the Tudor, Elizabethan, and Jacobean periods mix with smaller houses and cottages built in half-timbered style.

Abbot's Hall Museum in Stowmarket depicts rural life in East Anglia, including traditional farming methods and country crafts. At roadside stands you may find plaited "corn dollies," decorative straw ornaments that originated as a post-harvest offering of thanks to pre-Christian gods.

## The Constable country

The lush valley near the mouth of the Stour is known as the Constable country, a region much painted by landscape artist John Constable.

Born in East Bergholt in 1776, he roamed these meadows, heaths, and woodlands as a youth. Near Dedham are two places associated with Constable that you can visit: Flatford Mill was once operated by the Constable family; Willy Lott's cottage, the subject of one of Constable's best-known paintings, looks much as it did in the artist's day.

Cross the wooden bridge and follow the towpath into a rural world of trees, meadows, and winding river.

## Exploring Essex back roads

You can loop back to Cambridge—or head south to London—through the farm lands and occasional woods of northern Essex.

Busy Colchester has deep roots in English history. It was the hilltop fortress of "old King Cole" (the ancient British chieftain, Cunobelin), the site of a great 1st century Roman city, and the target of invading Vikings and Normans. Cromwell's army besieged the town in 1648.

Colchester flourished as a great weaving center and is the hub of the British oyster trade (it holds an Oyster Feast in October). Part of the town's Roman walls remain, and main streets still follow the Roman plan. Impressive Colchester Castle, the largest Norman castle keep in Britain, is built on the site of a Roman temple and has a splendid collection of Roman artifacts.

Another medieval wool and lace-making town, Coggeshall has many attractive old buildings including the Woolpack Hotel and Paycocke's, a heavily beamed and richly ornamented wool merchant's house built about 1500.

The ruins of Castle Hedingham are visible long before you reach it. Huddling beneath the 12th century fortress are a Norman church and a Georgian squire's tower.

Country roads lead to photogenic Finchingfield. Attractive buildings from various periods and a curving street focus upon a sloping village green and duck pond. Rising against the skyline is the town's 11th century Norman church, topped by a small bell turret.

Many timbered and plastered houses line Thaxted's cobbled streets. Alongside the distinctive 15th century guildhall, a curving pedestrian lane ascends to a limestone church adorned with carved gargoyles, animals, and birds—a permanent reminder of the town's wealthy days as a wool center. Behind the church you'll see a double row of gabled, color-washed almshouses and a tower windmill.

Unspoiled Saffron Walden haphazardly combines ancient inns and modern shops, half-timbered houses and market stalls overflowing with farm produce. The town gained its wealth from wool and its saffron crop, once used both as a medicine and a dye. Outside town, a 17th century Jacobean mansion, Audley End House, stands in a large park.

## Horses race at Newmarket

If you enjoy horses, travel northeast from Cambridge to Newmarket, headquarters of British horse racing for more than 300 years. On race days this horse-crazy town is swamped by enthusiastic crowds. At other times, Newmarket is a staid, open-air country town strung along a wide main street.

Most of Britain's valuable racing thoroughbreds are trained here. Often you'll see lithe little jockeys and stableboys around the rambling stables, and elegant racehorses and their riders enjoying a practice trot on the rolling grasslands encircling the town. In autumn and early winter, you can attend the annual bloodstock sales at Newmarket's paddocks.

# Country Inns Offer a Friendly Welcome

*In family-operated rural hotels you find informal hospitality, regional cooking, moderate prices*

Venture off the well-trodden routes in Europe and you'll discover charming country inns and hotels where individuality is the key. Many are family-owned and operated hostelries whose proprietors take a personal interest in serving their guests. Inns offer both memorable experiences and excellent value.

You can choose among English thatch-roofed pubs and timbered inns, the simple *auberges* and provincial *relais* of France, Spanish *paradores* and Portuguese *pousadas,* the mountain chalets of the Alpine countries, country villas in Italy, and regional inns of Scandinavia.

In country hotels and inns, you meet interesting people in an informal atmosphere. Most inns have only a modest number of rooms, which are often decorated in regional style. Some country hotels offer praiseworthy cuisine; in small simple inns, the owner may also be the chef.

## Choosing inns with special appeal

Government tourist offices usually can provide information on country hotels and inns, though frequently you must ferret out the top choices yourself through supplementary reading and recommendations from other travelers. Many country hotels have banded together in national and international associations.

Write to the French Government Tourist Office for a copy of the "Relais et Châteaux" directory (see page 60).

tered over northern Europe and south to Spain and Italy. Its directory can be purchased in travel bookstores or through its representative (see page 41).

More than 75 excellent country hotels in Austria, Germany, Switzerland, and southern Scandinavia belong to the Romantik Hotels association. For a list, write to the German National Tourist Office. These small inns and restaurants are family owned and managed. Housed in historic buildings, they feature excellent cuisine.

## Britain's inns offer homey hospitality

You really haven't seen the English countryside until you sample a cross section of the delightful country hotels, inns, and pubs that pop up along its back roads.

Many visitors enjoy the informality of country pubs and inns where hospitality comes with a thatched roof, a resident ghost, or a tale of smugglers. Other travelers seek out gracious old country hotels or simple B-and-Bs (bed-and-breakfast houses).

Several excellent guides describe some of the best country inns and pubs. An invaluable companion to motorists is "Commended Country Hotels, Guest Houses and Restaurants," a British Tourist Authority publication listing more than 400 establishments recognized for providing outstanding service to visitors. For information on ordering publications by mail, see page 21.

## Ireland's country hotels

Charming country hotels are scattered across the Irish countryside—overlooking the sea, beside lakes and rivers, on wooded estates, in the beautiful Wicklow Hills. Many are family owned and operated. Some are small and elegant; many are informal.

You can choose historic mansions, country houses and lodges, and casual guest houses. Some feature Continental cuisine, but most serve traditional Irish country fare. Vacationers enjoy these country hotels as bases for outdoor activities—country walks, riding, salmon and trout fishing, golf, and boating.

## Gracious ambience in French country inns

Some travelers consider a French country inn akin to heaven. When you stay in a simple, family-run *auberge* or a charming *relais,* you'll enjoy country hospitality in the traditional French manner. Often your room will be furnished in provincial style with a bouquet of fresh flowers. From your window you may look down on a garden, vineyard, or a placidly flowing river.

Many French country hotels and inns pride themselves on their cuisine and wine cellars; others provide a pleasant springboard for great eating at notable restaurants in the area. Use your hotel as a base for leisurely country walks or for an excursion to a nearby town, where a historic church frequently rubs elbows with an equally distinguished restaurant.

## Cozy inns in Germany, Austria, Switzerland

Spread throughout the Alpine countries are family-owned inns and hotels that extend a warm welcome to travelers. Many have been operated by a single family for many years. Often you'll see *Zimmer frei* signs hanging above the doors of village inns and private houses, indicating that room is available.

**Germany.** You'll discover historic old coaching inns, country hotels in market towns, cozy forest inns and country guest houses, hotels near thermal springs, and accommodations in renovated farmhouses and breweries.

Each hotel has its own character and atmosphere. Some are furnished in regional antiques. Proprietors take pride in offering personal service, a relaxed and friendly atmosphere, and hearty food served in ample portions.

Many family-run hostelries belong to Ringhotels, an association of individually operated hotels. For a descriptive listing, write to the German National Tourist Office.

**Austria.** You'll find instant camaraderie in Austrian country inns, as proprietors strive to make you feel at home. You can choose a mountain inn serving Alpine hikers, a charming hotel overlooking the Danube, or lakeside inns for enjoying sailing and swimming.

Check with local tourist offices *(Verkehrsverein)* for suggestions on small places to stay. Countless private homes indicate lodging is available by posting signs—a green shield with symbolic bed or a *Zimmer frei* card.

**Switzerland.** Country inns abound in Switzerland—in the heart of small towns, on mountain slopes near skiing and hiking areas, in lakeside villages, amid hills and vineyards. Write to the Swiss National Tourist Office for a guide to small guesthouses and pensions.

Most Swiss country inns are relatively small, simple, and immaculate. A few are luxuriously appointed; others have baths down the hall. Most are family run. Some inns offer regional food specialties. Townspeople and inn guests gather for conversation and refreshment in the *stübli,* a casual publike room.

Write to the Swiss National Tourist Office for information on historic inns. You can stay in a large rustic wooden farmhouse that spreads beneath a broad gabled roof or choose among aristocratic mansions, old stagecoach inns, and Alpine chalets that have traditionally served travelers crossing mountain routes.

## Living the good life in Italy

Many old villas, mansions, and minor palaces have been converted into hotels, inns, and pensions in Italy. You'll find them throughout the country—overlooking lakes, in regional centers, and in the hills and mountains. They offer a warm welcome and gracious service that add pleasure to your holiday.

For a copy of the booklet "Hotels and Restaurants in Italy of Special Interest," write to the Italian Government Tourist Office.

## Iberian hospitality at its best

Travelers who seek out the comfortable *paradores* of Spain (see page 117) and the *pousadas* of Portugal (see page 125) enjoy the peninsula at its most gracious. Scattered across the countryside, these government tourist inns are renowned for atmospheric settings, warm hospitality, and regional menus.

Many are housed in restored and converted historic buildings; others are of modern construction.

## Staying in the Scandinavian countryside

You'll find an engaging informality and hospitality when you stay in country hotels in Scandinavia. Many enjoy scenic settings overlooking lakes, fiords, and other waterways. Travelers use them as a base for exploring and enjoying the outdoors.

In Norway, Sweden, and Finland, you'll find a number of mountain chalets and inns and lakeside hotels where guests enjoy accommodations on a pension basis.

Skåne, Sweden's southernmost province, has its own unique inns, built by royal command during the 17th and 18th centuries. About 25 of them still welcome guests. Food specialties of these traditional inns vary by season.

Tucked away in the rolling green hills and farms of the Danish countryside are many charming country inns (called *kroer*) that offer a hospitable welcome to travelers. Accommodations range from rustic-but-comfortable to luxurious. When you spend the night in a *kro,* you may be staying in a cheery roadside guest house that is hundreds of years old. Some have been operated by the same family for several generations.

# Scotland's Windswept Western Isles

Legends of Bonnie Prince Charlie and Highland clans add romantic appeal to the remote Hebrides

One of the last unspoiled parts of Britain, Scotland's Northwest Highlands and Western Isles contain magnificent mountain scenery.

In the Inner and Outer Hebrides, romantic legends enhance the islands' awesome beauty and historic ruins dating from the Iron Age. Small fishing villages huddle in sheltered bays along the coast. On remote islands, the old Gaelic way of life survives in language, music, and crafts.

Sundays are strictly observed. Most trains and ferries do not operate, petrol (gasoline) is not available, and shops and many restaurants and attractions are closed.

You can reach the islands of Barra and Benbecula by air from Glasgow. Trains and inter-city motorcoaches link the coast with Glasgow and other inland centers.

Inter-island car ferries and passenger steamers travel between the mainland and the Western Isles. Be sure to check current schedules in advance, since some vessels offer only seasonal service or do not operate daily.

Ferries depart Ullapool for the island of Lewis. Oban is the departure point for South Uist, Barra, Mull, and Iona. Ferries to Skye leave from Kyle of Lochalsh and Mallaig; you also reach several smaller isles from Mallaig. Ferries also link Skye with Harris and North Uist.

Passenger steamers link mainland ports with Portree (Skye) and operate between Oban and Iona in summer. Interisland ferries operate between Uig (Skye), Tarbert (Harris), and Lochmaddy (North Uist).

You'll find hotels in larger towns, but this is bed-and-breakfast country. Caravans (camper vans) are a popular way to explore without the bother of finding nightly accommodations. Motorists should be sure their cars are in good working order before leaving the main routes; repair shops and petrol stations are far apart.

Summer is the festive season. Highland Games and *ceiladhs* (pronounced cay-leys) are held at various sites. Sailing regattas and island celebrations take place during the tourist season.

## Through the scenic Highlands

From Inverness, follow the Great Glen southwest toward Loch Ness. You'll parallel the Caledonian Canal, a 60-mile/97-km waterway linking the Irish Sea and the North Sea.

About 1½ miles/2½ km southeast of Drumnadrochit, the ruins of Urquhart Castle stand on a promontory overlooking Loch Ness. Most buildings date from the early 16th century. Like most visitors, you'll probably scan the waters for the legendary Loch Ness monster. Anglers come to this district to fish lake and river waters. Pony trekkers and hikers head into the hills.

Fort William, an important touring center for the Western Highlands, lies at the foot of Ben Nevis, Britain's highest mountain. You can visit the West Highland Museum on High Street.

From the Great Glen, roads lead west toward the coast, through some of Scotland's wild back country. As you near the coast, scenery becomes more magnificent.

West of Kinlochewe, Beinn Eighe National Nature Reserve attracts hill-walkers, climbers, and anglers. Two nature tracks start at Loch Maree, a lovely inland lake set amid wild mountain scenery; you can picnic or camp here. Druids once worshipped on one of the lake's tiny islands.

The road linking Torridon and Kishorn opens up more spectacular mountain views. You veer inland around Loch Carron, then head west to the busy shipping and ferry port of Kyle of Lochalsh.

About 2 miles/3 km southeast of Glenelg, in Gleann Beag, stand two well-preserved Iron Age *brochs* (stone towers with double walls) probably built more than 2,000 years ago by the Picts for protection against raiders.

## Over the sea to Skye

Mist-shrouded Skye is an island of myths and legends. Largest of the Inner Hebrides, it contains some of the most glorious scenery in the Highlands. Though it's 50 miles/80 km long, no part of the irregularly shaped island is more than 6 miles/9 km from the sea. The stark, steep peaks of the Cuillin Hills dominate the landscape.

Ferries from Kyle of Lochalsh cross a narrow channel to Kyleakin on Skye. Island roads meet at Broadford. To the south lies Isleornsay, a sheltered harbor for yachters, and Armadale, a farm village. The island capital is Portree, an attractive town of whitewashed houses. It's situated at the mouth of a bay flanked by steep hills.

North of Kilmuir is the tomb of Flora Macdonald, the Highland heroine who aided Bonnie Prince Charlie's escape from British troops in 1746. Nearby is Isle of Skye Cottage Museum, a renovated, thatched croft house (open April to September).

The village of Uig is the ferry port for the islands of Harris and North Uist in the Outer Hebrides.

Dunvegan village grew up around Dunvegan Castle, seat of the chiefs of the Clan MacLeod. Dating from the 13th century, the fortress stands on a rock high above a sea inlet. Clan treasures kept there include the "Fairy Flag," a silken banner that reputedly protects the MacLeods. You can visit the castle from April to mid-October.

## Mull & Iona

Mull is a beautiful isle of heather and bracken-covered moorland, forest, and peaks. Steamers and freighters dock in Craignure's sheltered deep-water bay. Perched on a crag overlooking the water is Duart Castle, ancient home of the chiefs of the Clan Maclean.

At the north end of the island is Tobermory, the main town and fishing port. Brightly painted buildings overlook a natural harbor where yachts and cruisers call in summer. Thin waterfalls drop down sheer cliffs along Mull's southwest coast.

The small island of Iona lies off Mull's southwest tip. When he arrived from Ireland in A.D. 563, St. Columba established his abbey on this tiny island and sent his missionaries to convert Scotland to Christianity. The reconstructed cathedral dates from about 1500. Carved Celtic crosses dot the island. St. Oran's Cemetery was the burial place of 48 Scottish kings.

## The Outer Hebrides

Locally called the "Long Island," the Outer Hebrides are a wild and rugged group of islands stretching 130 miles/ 210 km from Lewis in the north to Barra in the south. Their western shores absorb the full pounding force of the Atlantic. Deep inlets mark the shores and scattered islets border the coast. Small houses built of stone or peat are traditionally topped by thatched roofs, held in place by ropes and weighted with stones. Most people here make a living by fishing or weaving; tweed weaving is still a cottage industry.

Largest of the islands is Lewis, 30 miles/48 km long. Simple cottages in scattered coastal villages are often painted in bright colors. At the northern tip, Butt of Lewis Lighthouse stands on rugged cliffs. Inland, small lakes speckle the rolling peat moors.

Stornoway, the island's unofficial capital, is an important herring port and the center of the Harris tweed

Stone ruins of 16th century Urquhart Castle overlook deep waters of Loch Ness south of Inverness.

Brightly painted buildings add color to Tobermory waterfront on island of Mull. Yachts anchor here in summer.

industry. In Arnol you can visit the Black House Museum, a traditional island dwelling.

Near Carloway is one of the best preserved Iron Age brochs in the Hebrides, standing about 30 feet/10 meters high on a hilltop; you can climb between its double walls. A ring of standing stones at Callanish, dating from about 2000 B.C., marks Scotland's Stonehenge.

Largest village on the island of Harris is Tarbert, standing on a narrow isthmus between bays. Cairns on the road to Luskentyre mark prehistoric funeral routes. The Toe Head Peninsula, stretching into the Atlantic, is a haven for sea birds. The village of Rodel is the site of St. Clement's Church, noted for its rich carvings.

Wild winds from the sea whip the tiny islands to the south, populated by families of crofters and fishermen. An island road circles North Uist's irregular shore, passing small lakes and standing stones and ruins dating from the Stone Age. More medieval ruins and nature reserves are located on South Uist, celebrated as the birthplace of Flora Macdonald. Barra's ancient castle, owned by the Clan Macneil, faces Castlebay.

# Hiking the Devon Coast

Explore seaside villages and visit cheery pubs as you follow clifftop paths above the Bristol Channel

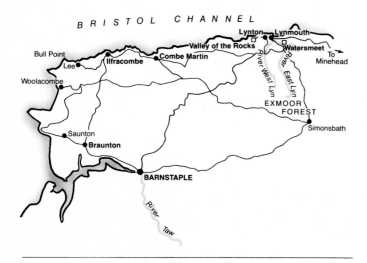

A favorite vacation destination for English families, the north Devon coast offers rugged scenery and inviting villages without the crowds that often take over popular port towns. Much of this dramatic seacoast belongs to the National Trust and is preserved for its great scenic beauty.

Whitewashed cottages with terraced gardens climb slopes from the water's edge. Hikers enjoy coastal footpaths—overlooking the Bristol Channel, along wooded river valleys, and through meadows and moorland dotted with grazing sheep.

In cozy pubs frequented by hearty fishermen, you can sample hard ciders made from local apples as well as regular pub fare. You may prefer to indulge in a Devon cream tea—a pot of tea accompanied by scones, butter, jam, and farm-fresh clotted cream. Fresh seafood from the channel is a treat at coastal inns.

You can reach north Devon by train from London's Paddington Station, changing trains at Exeter for Barnstaple. Local buses connect some of the region's larger towns.

## Along north Devon's seacoast

More than a thousand years old, Barnstaple sits at the head of the Taw estuary. Amble along Butchers' Row (an arcade of small shops) and Queen Anne's Walk. On Tuesdays and Fridays, produce sellers throng the covered Pannier Market. In summer you can take a guided tour of the Barnstaple pottery and watch potters at work.

A funicular railway links the twin towns of Lynton and Lynmouth. From Lynton, high on a cliff overlooking the Bristol Channel, you descend to Lynmouth, 430 feet/ 130 meters below where the rivers East Lyn and West Lyn meet and pour into the sea. Thatch-roofed cottages flank the small harbor, where colorful fishing boats anchor each evening.

It's a pleasant walk upstream from Lynmouth along wooded river banks—up the East Lyn through a rock-strewn valley to Watersmeet, and along the West Lyn to Glen Lyn. Another favorite route is the cliff path above the sea from Lynton west to the Valley of the Rocks. To sample the lonely moorland, head southeast into Somerset's Exmoor Forest.

Countryside surrounding Combe Martin typifies the varied charm of the Devon coast: rocky cliffs marked by occasional beaches and high rolling hills, including the area's famed strawberry fields.

A one-time bathing resort for wealthy Victorians, Ilfracombe has numerous cove beaches (including two reached by tunnels through rocks), a promenade, and public gardens for strolling. Local commercial fishermen and visiting yachters mingle around the harbor.

Superb coastal views await walkers on the zigzag Torrs Walk path west of town; it leads to Lee, a tiny village known for its fuschias. A more rugged path continues around Lee Bay to Bull Point, where a lighthouse guides boats rounding the coast into the Bristol Channel.

**High above Bristol Channel, hikers head west from Lynton along clifftop path to Valley of the Rocks.**

# Gentle Land of Robert Burns

In the peaceful Ayrshire countryside, retrace pathways followed by Scotland's most famous poet

**Whitewashed cottage in Alloway was birthplace of Robert Burns. Inside, you can peruse memorabilia of his Ayrshire days.**

The uncrowded and peaceful countryside of southwest Scotland is Robert Burns country, the gentle land that nurtured and inspired Ayrshire's famed "poet of the common man."

Born in Alloway in 1759, Burns immortalized many of the region's landmarks in his poems. You can trace his life and learn more about his work by visiting several towns and villages near Ayr.

An hour's train ride from Glasgow or a few minutes' drive south of Prestwick Airport, Ayr is the most popular holiday resort on Scotland's west coast.

## In the footsteps of "Rabbie" Burns

Begin your quest in Ayr, where Burns's statue stands outside the railway station. Nearby in the High Street is the thatched Tam o'Shanter Inn, named in honor of Burns's memorable poem; a brewhouse in the poet's day, it now houses a Burns museum. The 13th century Auld Brig of Ayr still spans the river.

The Burns story began south of Ayr in the village of Alloway, where he was born in a humble gardener's cottage on January 25, 1759. Preserved as a Burns museum, the small thatched house and its exhibits reflect his early life. At the nearby interpretive center, inquire about the regional Burns Heritage Trail.

Burns's father is buried in the churchyard of the ruined Auld Kirk of Alloway, where in "Tam o'Shanter" the inebriated Tam watched witches revel. Tam fled on his horse to the Brig o'Doon, a simple arched bridge now flanked by gardens, knowing that the witches chasing him would not dare cross the running stream. A Burns monument overlooks the bridge over the Doon.

From Alloway, head south along the coast to Culzean (pronounced "Cullane") Castle, an 18th century creation of Robert Adam set amid beautiful gardens in a country park. Opposite the castle entrance, a side road leads to Kirkoswald, where you can visit the house of Tam's crony, Souter Johnnie. The cottage is furnished as in Burns's day, and statues of the poem's characters stand in the garden.

More Burns museums are located north of Ayr at Irvine, Kilmarnock, and Lochlea Farm near Tarbolton.

Burns began married life in 1788 in Mauchline, where his Castle Street house is now a museum. You can stop for refreshment at Burns's favorite *howff* or inn, Poosie Nansie's, which has changed little since his time. A Burns memorial tower stands just outside town.

From 1791 until his death five years later, Burns lived in Dumfries. Here he wrote some of his most famous songs, including "Auld Lang Syne" and "Ye Banks and Braes of Bonnie Doon." In Dumfries you can view his statue in High Street outside Greyfriars Church, see manuscripts in his old home on Burns Street (formerly Mill Street), and visit his mausoleum in St. Michael's churchyard. Burns memorabilia are featured in the town museum, the Globe Inn, and the Hole in the Wa' Tavern.

# Pastoral Kent & the Sussex Coast

Loop southeast of London to enjoy Kent's fruit orchards and historic towns along the Sussex Coast

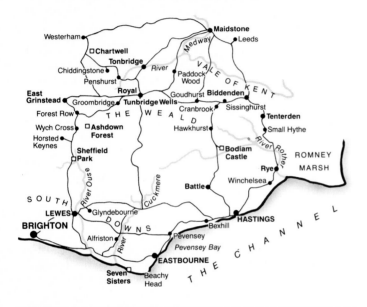

**Lone cyclist pedals down Chiddingstone's main street past rosy brick and black-and-white timbered buildings.**

England's historic southeast corner is an easy excursion from London. Brighton, Hastings, and other seaside towns are less than 2 hours by train from the capital.

The pastoral landscape, charming villages, and stately houses of Kent offer a pleasant change of pace. Called the garden of England, Kent is the country's fruit basket, where apple and pear orchards are a sea of blossoms in spring. Some of the magic of an ancient forest lingers in The Weald, a region once covered by thick forests. Deer still roam the woods.

Trains depart from London's Victoria Station for the Sussex resorts of Brighton, Lewes, Eastbourne, Bexhill, and Hastings. A coastal rail line connects these same towns. You board the train in London's Charing Cross Station to reach the Kent towns of Tonbridge and Royal Tunbridge Wells. Local buses fan out to smaller towns.

## Exuberant Brighton

Less than an hour from London by express train, Brighton is a lively town of delightful contrasts. Graceful Georgian and late-Victorian houses coexist with the riotously extravagant Royal Pavilion built in the late 18th century by the Prince of Wales (later George IV).

Pedestrians wander through a delightful maze of narrow streets called The Lanes, where restored cottages now contain antique shops. You can enjoy bracing sea air along the seafront promenade, watch dolphins at the Palace Pier aquarium, or ride the local railway to an open-air swimming pool.

At Lewes, a historic town on the River Ouse, you can visit Barbican House museum and the house given by Henry VIII to his fourth wife, Anne of Cleves, when he divorced her. Glyndebourne's opera season runs from late May to August. Once a smugglers' hideout, the Cuckmere valley town of Alfriston is full of old buildings.

## The historic Sussex Coast

The southeast coast has been the historic gateway to England. Romans landed here in A.D. 43, followed in the 5th and 6th centuries by Anglo-Saxon tribesmen. The Cinque Ports were established to repel Danish invaders. In 1066 William of Normandy and his troops landed at Pevensey and went on to conquer Saxon troops in a famous battle north of Hastings. Today a string of holiday resorts and historic towns mark this seacoast.

Hikers and pony trekkers enjoy superb, well-signed paths along the coast and the South Downs Way. This long-distance footpath begins west of Brighton and extends some 80 miles/130 km to Beachy Head. Mounds and earthworks along the track mark sites of Stone Age forts.

A branch of the South Downs Way runs along the chalk cliffs called the Seven Sisters, ending at Beachy Head. You can also reach this point from Eastbourne, an elegant resort that faces a long seaside esplanade; bands entertain summer visitors with bandstand concerts.

Quaint Pevensey is dwarfed by the immense Roman fortress of Pevensey Castle, now in ruins. Long ago, the boats of Roman legions and Norman troops sailed into Pevensey Bay, but the sea retreated in the 16th century, leaving this and other coastal settlements about 2 miles/3 km inland.

One of the original Cinque Ports, Hastings has been a fishing village since Roman times. At the east end of town, below the 13th century castle, fishermen pull their boats onto the beach to unload the catch. After 18th century doctors discovered the healthfulness of sea air, Hastings became a popular resort offering every type of holiday entertainment. Don't miss the Hastings Embroidery, a modern Bayeux tapestry depicting scenes from British history from 1066 to the present.

At the town of Battle, north of Hastings, an abbey stands on the site of the so-called Battle of Hastings.

In medieval times, Winchelsea and Rye crowned hillocks as fortified seaports, guarding the coast against attack by French warships. You'll enjoy a short stroll around peaceful Winchelsea, an orderly little town with its old church and white houses adorned with climbing roses and wisteria.

Historic Rye remains a lively, charming town. A steep cobbled street leads to the famous Mermaid Inn, which has served travelers since 1420. Town landmarks include the Church of St. Mary, dating from 1120; the 18th century Lamb House, home of novelist Henry James; the arcaded town hall, dating from 1742; and Ypres Tower, now a museum. You'll find many old houses in Mermaid Street, High Street, Church Square, and Watchbell Street.

The flat and misty Romney Marsh was the haunt of smugglers until the early 19th century. Now bird watchers come here to see migratory waterfowl and sea birds.

## Visiting some of Kent's villages

North of Rye, you can tour the home of actress Ellen Terry, who was a favorite of George Bernard Shaw. Located on the outskirts of Small Hythe, the half-timbered house contains many mementoes of her theater days.

Tenterden, an important wool-trading center in medieval days, has many attractive houses and old inns along its wide main street. The tall 15th century church tower is a local landmark.

Biddenden is proud of its medieval weavers' cottages and a seven-gabled cloth hall. The town sign commemorates the Chulkhurst sisters, Siamese twins joined at the hips, who lived here in the early 12th century.

North from Hastings, the route passes near the ruins of Bodiam Castle, a magnificent fortress built in 1386 to discourage invaders from sailing up the River Rother.

The gardens and buildings of Sissinghurst Castle, formerly the home of writer-poet Victoria Sackville-West and her husband, Sir Harold Nicholson, are open to visitors from April to mid-October.

Typical of the windmills once used in this region is the octagonal one at Cranbrook. It was built in 1814 and is kept in working order.

Goudhurst's medieval Star and Eagle Inn is renowned as a base of the Hawkhurst Gang, a band of 18th century smugglers who were finally routed by incensed villagers. The lovely village has old inns, a duck pond, and an ancient church with marks on its walls reputedly made by archers sharpening their arrows.

## The Medway valley

For centuries the River Medway played a major role in the history of Kent. River barges carried timber from Wealden forests and military supplies down through Maidstone to towns along the Thames estuary. After hops were introduced in the 16th century, the Medway provided water for Kent's brewing industry.

Today the Medway and its tributary, the Beult, wind peacefully through orchards, meadows, and hop fields. Anglers frequent the river banks, and walkers follow waterside paths. Pleasure boats cruise along the river.

Blossoming apple trees scent the air in mid-May in orchard country around Maidstone. From almost every road, you see old black-and-white timbered farmhouses.

Leeds has attractive houses and a church with a massive Norman tower, but it's best known for the medieval castle east of town. Built about 1120, the majestic fortress is surrounded by a wide moat. It was the home of Catherine of Aragon, first wife of Henry VIII. Elizabeth I was held prisoner here before she became queen.

Hop fields cover many acres in Kent, their vines growing up strings to a height of 20 to 25 feet/about 7 meters. Conical-topped oast houses, traditionally used for drying hops, are a familiar sight. You can see 25 of them at Beltring, about 2 miles/3 km north of Paddock Wood, a major hop-growing and marketing center.

## Through the hills of The Weald

Country lanes wind through the hills of The Weald, past fruit orchards and fields of hops and corn. Many families have farmed the same land for centuries. The Weald has its share of great houses, built or converted by wealthy families who preferred to live outside yet near London.

In Regency days, Royal Tunbridge Wells rivaled Bath as a fashionable spa. The Pantiles is the town's elegant colonnade of 18th and 19th century houses and shops. Lime trees shade the mall, where outdoor art shows are held in summer.

The village of Penshurst is dominated by Penshurst Place, an ancestral home on riverside parklands.

Chiddingstone is an Elizabethan village, preserved almost intact by the National Trust. You can see the original "chiding stone" where, according to legend, villagers chided any woman whose chatter annoyed them.

Chartwell, the country estate of Sir Winston Churchill, attracts many visitors. Inside the house, you'll see many mementoes of Sir Winston's life. A bronze statue of Churchill stands in Westerham.

From East Grinstead, a lively market town, country roads run south toward Ashdown Forest, a large tract of the once-vast oak forest that stretched across southeast England during the Roman era. The villages of Forest Row, on the River Medway, and Wych Cross are good centers for forest walks or drives. Tidy 18th century tiled cottages rim Groombridge's triangular village green.

Sheffield Park, a National Trust garden with five lakes linked by cascades, is open from Easter to early November. Nearby is the Victorian Railway, a short line running to Horsted Keynes.

# Footpaths Attract Hikers & Walkers

Inviting trails wind across rolling hills and mountain slopes, through forests, and along waterways

When you travel, you walk more than you do at home. Sightseeing on foot is the best way to explore—you study a town's architecture, stroll through its market or atop its ramparts, and feel the pulse of city life. In the countryside, you follow footpaths through woods and beside waterways, across moors and mountains.

Heed the oft-stated advice: Wear sturdy, comfortable footwear, well broken in. If you develop blisters, take care of them without delay.

### City walks add fresh perspectives

In cities, focus your energy on a particular district or pursue your own interest or hobby—visit literary or artistic haunts, ancient pubs or churches, or an area maintaining historic atmosphere. Inquire at city tourist offices about walking tours with local guides, or plot your own route with the aid of a good map and an informative guidebook.

If you enjoy variations in architecture, take a look at Dublin's elegant Georgian squares, the handsome canal houses along Amsterdam's waterways, or the old quarters of Swiss towns such as Lucerne and Berne. Discover the essence of Barcelona as you wander along the Ramblas, an ever-changing parade and open-air marketplace. For a personal look at the ruins of ancient Rome, take a Sunday morning walk on Palatine Hill.

London visitors can follow the footsteps of Sherlock Holmes, seek out the churches of Christopher Wren, or investigate the lively establishments sprouting on the former site of Covent Garden market. In Paris, explore the aristocratic Marais district, prowl the historic islands in the middle of the Seine River, or stroll the northwest slopes of Montmartre where you still can discover streets reminiscent of an Utrillo painting.

### Day excursions in the countryside

If you want to stretch travel-cramped muscles and get a close-up look at the countryside, take a day or afternoon walk. Routes can be as varied as your imagination and the topography allow.

If you're staying in an urban area, you can board a local bus or train to reach your starting point. In Alpine countries, hikers often ride a cable car, mountain railway, or chair lift up the mountains, then follow well-marked trails across the slopes.

Hikers can follow canalside towpaths, amble beside placid lakes, stroll above the sea, trek across lonely moors and mountains, or roam forested slopes and lush valleys. In your travels, you'll often see villagers mowing hay, gathering grapes, making cheese, or hanging up the wash against a backdrop of wooded hills or snowy mountains. Frequently, though, you'll have only a few inquisitive cows or a couple of sheep for company.

### Longer hiking excursions

Hiking is a popular pastime in Europe, and government tourist offices can provide extensive information on regional hiking areas and trails, guided or packaged excursions, and addresses of local hiking organizations.

On some Scandinavian and Alpine routes, hikers stop at trail huts spaced a day's hike apart. In more populated areas, walkers stay overnight in village inns, pensions, or private homes. Rainwear and good hiking boots are essential in any season. Detailed maps can be purchased from local hiking clubs or regional bookstores.

European hikers revel in a network of splendid long-distance footpaths that provide access to some of Europe's unspoiled countryside. Some routes wend through relatively flat country, others traverse hilly and mountainous areas.

The European Ramblers Association in Stuttgart, Germany, in cooperation with local and regional hiking clubs, is signing about 7,500 miles/12,000 km along six international hiking trails on the Continent. The trails stretch from the North Sea to the Mediterranean, from Austria to the Pyrenees, and from the Baltic to the Adriatic.

Britain has several lengthy trails; one is the Pennine Way, a 250-mile/400-km track along the Pennine Chain—the rugged backbone of England—to the Scottish border. Scandinavian long-distance trails include routes along the mountainous border between Norway and Sweden, and a 140-mile/225-km footpath across Lapland.

# special interests

# In Britain

## TOURIST INFORMATION CENTERS

Travelers in London can obtain detailed and up-to-the-minute travel information on all parts of Britain at the British Travel Centre in Lower Regent Street, just south of Piccadilly Circus.

Throughout Britain, a countrywide network of Tourist Information Centres (TICs) stands ready to assist travelers. TIC personnel provide holiday planning advice, directions to destinations, and information on regional travel and events. Many TIC offices can book accommodations for travelers. For a list of TIC addresses, write to the British Tourist Authority.

## INDUSTRIAL TRAILS

For a fresh perspective of Britain's diversity, include an industrial tour or two in your travels. Fascinating museums also focus on Britain's growth as an industrial nation. Tourist Information Centres can provide excursion ideas.

Here are a few possibilities:

The Industrial Revolution was born in the Severn valley, where the world's first iron bridge was built in the 1770s. Near Ironbridge Gorge you can learn about early china manufacturing at Coalbrookdale Museum and see 18th century industrial techniques at Blists Hill Open-Air Museum.

Before the modern rail and road network was established, working barges transported commercial cargo along Britain's waterways. Memories of the canal era are rekindled at the Waterways Museum at Stoke Bruerne in the Midlands and at the Llangollen Canal Exhibition in Wales.

In the Midlands you can visit the famous Staffordshire potteries of Wedgwood, Spode, and other manufacturers near Stoke-on-Trent. At the Gladstone Pot-

tery Museum nearby, you'll see old bottle kilns and workshops.

Among the offerings in Wales are mine tours and visits to mining museums. Watch the weaving of Welsh tapestry cloth at Meirion Mill near Machynlleth.

One of the most popular industrial routes is Scotland's Whisky Trail through the Spey valley, where travelers visit some of the famous distilleries dotting the hilly countryside of the Grampian Region.

## TRANSPORTATION TICKETS

Travelers in Britain can cut transportation costs with several passes and tickets.

Holders of BritRail Passes enjoy unlimited first or second-class rail travel in England, Scotland, and Wales for periods of 7, 14, or 21 days, or 1 month. Passes must be purchased outside Britain. Senior travelers (65 years and over) and young people (under 25 years) qualify for reduced fares.

Concentrating on Scotland? You can purchase a Highlands and Islands Travelpass, good for 10 consecutive days of unlimited travel on all trains and most bus and shipping lines of the region.

In London, travelers who purchase Go-As-You-Please Tickets from London Transport offices enjoy unlimited travel for 3, 4, 7, or 14 days on the city's red buses and Underground.

## GUIDES & MAPS

Tourist organizations in England, Scotland, and Wales publish a great variety of fascinating booklets. Among subjects covered are accommodations (including country inns and farm holidays); pubs and restaurants; castles, historic places, and gardens; museums and galleries; industrial tours and rural crafts; motoring trips; sports (angling, golf, cycling); and walks in London and the countryside.

Several firms in the United States sell many of these booklets by mail order; the British Tourist Authority will provide their addresses. You can also purchase guides at Tourist Information Centres throughout Britain. In London, you can obtain additional material at the National Tourist Information Centre, Victoria Station Forecourt, London S.W.1; and from offices of the London Tourist Board, Scottish Tourist Board, Wales Tourist Board, and Northern Ireland Tourist Board.

Many other excellent guides are pub-

lished by the Automobile Association (AA), London Transport, and commercial publishers. Excellent maps are available, including detailed Ordnance Survey maps and pictorial and historical maps. You'll find an impressive selection of British travel literature in major London book stores.

## OPEN TO VIEW TICKET

Travelers can see Britain's major historic sights with an Open to View Ticket, which admits the holder to more than 500 attractions.

Sold by BritRail Travel International offices, the ticket is good for 1 month. Purchasers receive a directory listing all locations covered by the ticket. For more information, write to the British Tourist Authority or a BritRail office.

## DAY TRIPS FROM LONDON

Travelers based in London can easily take day trips into the countryside. Private companies offer numerous guided motorcoach excursions. Your travel agent or the hall porter at your London hotel can make arrangements.

Britainshrinkers trips depart from London on day and overnight excursions to various regions. Accompanied by a guide, your group takes a fast train to the destination, where a motorcoach is waiting. After a day of sightseeing, lunch in a pub, and a look at the countryside, you return to London by train. Overnight trips include accommodation, dinner, and breakfast. Trips can be booked through your travel agent or BritRail offices.

## TRAVEL TO AIRPORTS

Heathrow Airport is directly accessible from central London by Underground (Piccadilly line). Trains leave frequently and service is fast (about 40 minutes from Piccadilly Circus to Heathrow Central).

Gatwick Airport also has a direct rail link with central London. It's a 40-minute trip by electric train between Gatwick and London's Victoria Station.

**For information on travel in Britain, write to the British Tourist Authority (addresses on page 7).**

REPUBLIC
OF
IRELAND
• Dublin

# Excursions from Galway

Sample the varied countryside of County Clare, fabled Connemara, and the windswept Aran Islands

A hearty hospitality prevails in Ireland's friendly and informal West Country, where people customarily greet you with a friendly wave and a smile. Stop at a pub and soon you'll be drawn into the conversation. Ask directions and you'll get a bit of history or folklore thrown in.

Lakes dot the verdant countryside, and ruins of ancient monuments and castles offer glimpses of the past. Artists and writers have long found inspiration here. Tradition is treasured. In Connemara and the Aran Islands, many people still use Irish (Gaelic) as their everyday language, though they speak English with visitors. You'll see handsome woven fabrics, hand-knit sweaters, and other regional crafts in local shops.

Galway, at the head of Galway Bay, is compact and easily explored on foot. Beginning at Eyre Square, you can stroll the narrow winding streets of the old "city of the tribes." Some of the ancient buildings recall Galway's trading days with Spain. In season, watch migrating salmon leaping upstream at Salmon Weir Bridge on the River Corrib.

From Galway you can venture south into County Clare or northwest to Connemara, fabled for its beauty. Motorists have little traffic to contend with, though farm animals occasionally stray onto the roads as they do throughout rural Ireland. CIE buses depart from Galway to serve country towns and villages. Regular steamer and air service links the city with the mysterious Aran Islands at the mouth of Galway Bay.

If you plan an extended stay in the West Country, you might enjoy renting a modern thatched cottage in a village or staying in a farmhouse with an Irish family. (For information on both, see page 29.)

## South into County Clare

A loop south of Galway follows the scenic coast of County Clare and returns through the bleak countryside known as the Burren. You can plan your excursion to sample local oysters, visit a Yeats museum, or banquet in a 15th century castle.

**Along the coast.** Clarinbridge is the place to stop for a platter of Galway Bay oysters (from September through April), accompanied by wholesome Irish bread and a pint of Guinness stout.

Overlooking an inlet of Galway Bay is Dunguaire, a beautifully restored 15th century castle north of Kinvara built on the site of a 7th century fortress. Visitors can tour the castle daily from April to September; from mid-May to mid-September, sumptuous medieval banquets are presented nightly, followed by lighthearted excerpts from the works of Synge, Yeats, and other Irish dramatists.

The main route follows the coast to the village of Ballyvaughan, then veers southwest over the Corkscrew Road toward Lisdoonvarna. An alternative road clings to the sea.

Ireland's favorite spa, Lisdoonvarna is liveliest following the harvest season. Southeast, you'll find the famed Cliffs of Moher, rising vertically from the Atlantic in a 5-mile/8-km wall. Best viewpoint is from O'Brien's Tower at the northern end, where the cliffs reach their maximum height of 668 feet/218 meters.

The coast road turns inland along the shore of Liscannor Bay. Golfers head for Lahinch and its championship 18-hole course near the sea.

**The Burren.** Inland, you enter a strange region of barren limestone hills called the Burren. Stop at the interpretive center at Kilfenora to learn about the area's unusual rock formations, rare plants, and other features.

Retreating glaciers of the Ice Age left great layers of bare gray rock over a wide area of northern County Clare. Numerous caves and passageways tunnel beneath the surface, and lakes appear and disappear mysteriously amid the limestone. Delicate wildflowers—normally found only north of the Arctic Circle—nestle between rocks. Prehistoric inhabitants left stone forts and a number of dolmens (two or more huge upright stones capped by one or more large ones); other antiquities date from medieval times.

**Thoor Ballylee.** One of Ireland's famous writers who loved the West Country was poet and playwright William

Butler Yeats, who spent his summers at Ballylee Castle (he called it "Thoor Ballylee") in the 1920s. From April to October you can visit this restored structure, located 4 miles/6 km northeast of Gort.

## Wild, lonely Connemara

Wedged between Lough Corrib and the Atlantic northwest of Galway, this sparsely settled countryside of green hills and rusty bogs has a special appeal.

Much of Connemara's charm lies in its lack of people. Scattered villages are small, tourist facilities rare, and horses and bicycles seem almost as common as automobiles. Often the only person you'll see for miles is a lone turf-cutter chopping bricks of dark brown peat and stacking them to dry in the wind and sun.

Your route to Connemara heads west from Galway, through its seaside suburb of Salthill and along the shore of Galway Bay. Small inlets and coves indent the rocky coastline. Inland, you pass through rolling, lake-studded moorland dominated by a range of conical peaks called the Twelve Bens. Heather and broom form patches of purple and gold. Fuchsia bushes edge many country lanes; stone-walled fields are bright with seasonal wildflowers.

Largest of the Connemara settlements is Clifden, site of the annual Connemara pony show in late August. Several small villages also accommodate visitors, who come here to enjoy invigorating walks, sea fishing, hill climbing, sailing, and other coastal activities.

Anglers head for island-dotted Lough Corrib, renowned for its excellent salmon and trout fishing. At Oughterard and other fishing centers, you can hire a boat for a day on the lake, fishing or exploring some of the lake's 365 wooded islets. Inchagoill Island contains the ruins of several small churches.

## The mysterious Aran Islands

The bleak and rugged Aran Islands lie at the mouth of Galway Bay, some 30 miles/50 km west of Galway. A place of mystery, these windswept isles leave a deep impression on visitors.

The three rocky islands are home to independent subsistence farmers and hardy fishermen who cling to the Irish language and many ancient customs and superstitions. Their songs and stories are filled with folklore. Fishermen sail the cold Atlantic in the traditional *currach,* a fragile craft of lath and tarred canvas that easily rides the waves. John Millington Synge immortalized these rugged men in *Riders to the Sea* and *The Aran Islands.*

Island dress has not changed in centuries. Almost every man wears a *bawneen* jacket of white homespun, heavy tweed trousers, and *pampooties* (heelless shoes made of rough hide). Women still spin wool and weave their own fabric. Home knitters fashion heavy Aran sweaters and other garments from unbleached wool, knitting in decorative motifs and folk symbols.

Ferries from Galway and Rossaveal dock at the village of Kilronan on Inishmore, largest of the islands. Voyagers to the two smaller islands are rowed ashore in a currach. Aer Arann planes from Galway land on grass

Greenery frames stately Kylemore Abbey, now a boarding school, near Letterfrack. Anglers fish nearby Kylemore lakes.

Aran Islanders launch small currach. These traditional boats are used for fishing and interisland travel.

airstrips on Inishmore and Inishmaan. Small guest houses offer overnight accommodations.

The islands have several attractive villages, good sandy beaches, and dramatic scenery. Archeologists are drawn to the stone forts and other monuments left by prehistoric inhabitants. Most famous is Dun Aengus on Inishmore, a massive 1st century fortress clinging to the edge of a 300-foot/100-meter cliff. Hermit monks came here to meditate in the early centuries of Christianity, and you can explore the remains of several monastic settlements.

REPUBLIC OF IRELAND

Dublin

# Linger Awhile by Dingle Bay

Explore the seacoast and enjoy small daily pleasures when you settle in to relax in County Kerry

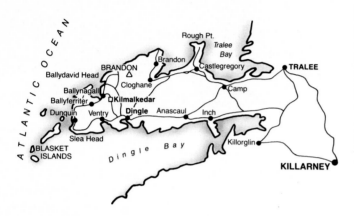

**Farmer guides horse-drawn hay wagon on slope above Dingle Bay. Magnificent views abound along coastal road.**

If you enjoy the idea of snuggling down for a few days in an Irish village, take a look at County Kerry. Jutting into the Atlantic off Ireland's southwestern coast, a half-dozen peninsulas offer glorious scenery, homey villages, and interesting ruins. Here, folk customs, crafts, and lore are still passed from generation to generation.

There's an engaging lack of hustle in Irish villages. Mailing a letter in the grocery store or asking route directions often takes more time than you expect. Weather can be as changeable as a leprechaun's mood, though the Irish accept the frequent "mist" with good humor.

Once you settle into village life, you'll have time to relish small pleasures—lingering over a hearty Irish breakfast, watching raincoated women bicycling to market, sharing ideas over a glass of Guinness or Irish coffee, sampling freshly caught salmon and local scallops, joining an evening songfest in a local pub.

The most relaxing way to explore the region is by rental car (available in Killarney, Tralee, and other major centers). It's a half-day train trip from Dublin to Killarney and Tralee, where government-operated C I E buses depart for the larger Kerry settlements.

## A look at the Dingle Peninsula

Northwest of crowded Killarney is the Dingle Peninsula, renowned for the sweeping grandeur of its coast and the archeological remains scattered over its slopes.

Mountains of the Slieve Mish range stretch west from Tralee, giving way to the wild, lake-dotted hill country of the central peninsula and a magnificent coastline. Folk customs still thrive in the Irish-speaking hamlets of the west.

A narrow road leads into the shop and pub-lined main street of Dingle, the peninsula's chief settlement. Situated on the north side of Dingle Harbour, the town has a quaint Irish charm. Blooming flowers brighten the plain houses, and tall-masted fishing boats bob in the harbor. You can rent a motorboat or rowboat for a fishing excursion or coastal exploring. Dingle was the chief Kerry port in the Spanish trading days, and it was a walled town during the reign of Queen Elizabeth I.

Beautiful beaches rim the rocky promontories, though you may have to clamber down a steep footpath to reach the golden sand. Walkers and hikers find no lack of scenic routes.

Studding the green slopes are archeological ruins—stone and earthen-ring fortifications, standing and inscribed stones, and other remains. Most unusual are the numerous *clocháns*, unmortared beehive-shaped stone huts reputedly built more than 1,000 years ago. Ancient church buildings are well preserved at Kilmalkedar and 2 miles/3 km south at 1,200-year-old Gallarus Oratory.

Magnificent coastal views abound on the road to Slea Head, Ireland's westernmost point; offshore, the Blasket Islands gleam like emeralds in the blue Atlantic. Fishing villages are worth a stop, and you can watch the building of the traditional high-prowed rowboats called *currachs* at Ballydavid.

# Cruising the River Shannon

Enjoy Ireland's pastoral countryside and waterside towns as you navigate this ancient river highway

Pink-cheeked Limerick schoolboys pose politely. Meeting local people is a benefit of leisurely boat travel.

Of all the ways to tour Ireland, few are as relaxing and reveal the countryside as well as a cruise on the River Shannon. Several companies operate cruises on the river, or you can charter a boat for a week and explore at your own pace. Country roads border stretches of the river.

Rising in the northern highlands of County Cavan, the slow-moving Shannon flows diagonally across Ireland, linking a series of shallow lakes and emptying into the Atlantic near Limerick. Boats can navigate upstream above Carrick-on-Shannon. Ireland's longest river is also its oldest highway, used hundreds of years ago by marauding Danes who sailed upstream to plunder the prosperous countryside.

Along the river's 140 miles/225 km of cruising waters, you'll see sheep and cattle grazing knee-deep in grassy meadows, haughty herons standing half-hidden in thick reeds beside low banks, an occasional fisherman or tidy stone cottage. Small islands and riverside ruins invite exploration.

Main bases for Shannon cruising are Carrick-on-Shannon, Athlone, and Killaloe; you can charter all types of vessels, from sailing dinghies to fully equipped eight-berth cruisers. Your travel agent or the Irish Tourist Board can provide information on boat excursions and charter firms.

## Life along the river

Not the least of the Shannon's delights are the people you meet in towns and villages along the way. Shopping in small towns gives you a chance to talk to some of them. Lock keepers mix helpful advice with jovial messages to be passed on to friends up or down the river. At night, strangers find a warm welcome at the local pub.

Athlone, "capital" of the midlands, sits astride the Shannon. On the eastern bank, narrow streets approach the river and its bridge. A 13th century castle rises on the west shore.

South of Athlone, the Shannon meanders through flat green fields to Clonmacnois, Ireland's most famous monastic settlement and medieval university. The once-walled city was founded in 548 and became the object of numerous plundering raids. Set on a high treeless plain, it contains ruined churches, round towers, Celtic crosses, and many monumental slabs. Still in use is the ancient Pilgrims' Road, which approaches the settlement from the northeast; traces of an 11th century cobblestone causeway connect the broad path with the cemetery.

A few miles downstream is Shannonbridge, a village with a single street and an impressive stone bridge spanning the river. Shannon Harbour, the river's link with Ireland's Grand Canal, is a favorite meeting place for yachting people. Banagher, located midway between lakes Ree and Derg, is the heart of the angling country. From the west shore of Lough Derg, you'll have fine views south to Killaloe.

Finally, you come to Limerick, a 9th century settlement of Viking raiders that today is a busy regional industrial center.

REPUBLIC
OF
IRELAND
●Dublin

# The Garden of Ireland

Wooded glens, tumbling streams, and ruins of a great monastic city await you south of Dublin

**Glendalough's historic Round Tower watches over tombstones, Celtic crosses, and other ruins of ancient monastic city.**

The Irish call County Wicklow "the garden of Ireland." Wooded glens and dark lakes lie tucked between its domed granite mountains. Streams tumble down hillsides and cut through unspoiled valleys. In the foothills, peaceful villages tempt you to linger. Anglers test their skills against brown trout in the clear streams; hikers and horseback riders explore quiet trails.

You'll enjoy the Wicklow Mountains best on a leisurely car trip. Distances in the region are relatively short, the countryside invites leisurely touring, and roads are well marked and lightly traveled.

Since accommodations in Ireland are limited outside the capital, plan ahead if you want to stay in a country hotel. For assistance in making reservations throughout the country, stop at the tourist information office in Dublin.

From Dublin, local buses serve the main towns; in summer, sightseeing buses travel to Glendalough and Avoca. Trains follow the coast from Dublin to Wicklow, veer inland along the River Avonmore, then return to the sea at Arklow.

## Into the Wicklow Mountains

Roads fan southward from the capital—along the coast, into the mountains, toward inland towns.

Driving south from Dublin, you'll come upon the Wicklow Mountains in less than an hour. This is a region of wild grandeur and haunting beauty. Generations of painters have tried to capture the changing colors of the hills—shades of brown flecked with the grayish white of granite outcrops, the many greens of forest and field, purple heather, and golden gorse. Home weavers there capture these subtle hues in their fabrics.

**Enniskerry.** One of Ireland's most attractive villages, Enniskerry lies about 12 miles/19 km south of Dublin in a wooded hollow among the Wicklow foothills. About a mile east, the waters of the Dargle River enter a thickly wooded ravine that restricts them to a rushing torrent.

From Easter to October, you can enjoy the terraced gardens and ornamental lakes of Powerscourt, an elegant estate along the Dargle near Enniskerry. Follow the main drive along the river through a deer park to the Powerscourt Waterfall, a 400-foot/120-meter cascade.

**The Military Road.** From Enniskerry the Glencree road climbs west to connect with the north-south Military Road, built by the British after the Insurrection of 1798. For centuries the Wicklow Mountains were the stronghold of the unsubdued O'Tooles and O'Byrnes. British redcoats pursued the Wicklowmen across these mountains in an effort to suppress the uprising and control the territory.

Today this route opens up for motorists the lonely and mysterious moorlands, several mountain lakes, and the summit of Kippure. You pass near the source of the River Liffey, then cut through the Sally Gap. Loughs Tay and Dan lie below in a deep eastern valley.

Bleak and lonely moorlands suddenly give way to the untamed, dramatic valley of Glenmacnass, walled in by towering mountains. You follow it to Laragh, gateway to Glendalough.

The Military Road continues south, climbing again into the hills, then dropping down into Glenmalure and ending 5 miles/8 km south at Aghavannagh. Narrow side roads follow the Avonbeg and Aughrim rivers downstream toward Avoca.

## Historic valley of untamed beauty

West of Laragh stretches Glendalough, the "Valley of Two Lakes," famed both for its scenic pleasures and its historical and archeological interest. Good walking trails traverse the valley and its slopes.

Lying around the lakes' shores are the remains of a great monastic city, once renowned as one of the great learning centers of Europe. You can trace the glen's history from its ruins—from the monastery founded by St. Kevin in the 6th century, through the city's scholarly golden age, to its plundering by the Vikings and later invaders. In 1398 English troops burned the settlement and left it deserted.

You enter through a gateway that was the original entrance to the monastic city. Though the cathedral is now in ruins, several structures are well preserved. St. Kevin's Church, topped by a steeply pitched stone roof, is typical of early Irish barrel-vaulted oratories. The 110-foot/33-meter Round Tower is still in almost perfect condition after more than 1,000 years; monks reached the small doorway high above the ground by ladder, which was drawn up behind them in time of attack.

## Tranquil glens, tumbling rivers

Clear streams course down the Wicklow hills, draining Lugnaquilla Mountain and other lofty peaks. Dense greenery edging the rivers provides a backdrop to tidy villages, white houses, and stone bridges.

From Laragh, follow the River Avonmore south through the wooded Vale of Clara and the little town of Rathdrum. Many travelers stop at the small riverside park about 3 miles/5 km north of Avoca at the confluence of the Avonmore and Avonbeg rivers, a sylvan setting made famous by Thomas Moore in his poem "Meeting of the Waters."

The Vale of Avoca is at its prettiest in late spring, when white blossoms of wild cherry trees stand out against the green foliage. The River Aughrim flows into the Avoca at the village of Woodenbridge. Gold found near here led to a "rush" in 1796; other ore deposits in the district—copper, lead, zinc, and sulphur—were known in Roman times.

## Sampling the seacoast

Coastal resorts, each with a distinct identity, border the Irish Sea southeast of Dublin.

A flourishing amusement center, Arklow lies at the mouth of the River Avoca. You can enjoy its beach, visit the maritime museum, check out regional pottery, or rent a boat for a trip on the bay or up the river. The coast road passes fine beaches at Brittas Bay and Silver Strand and cuts across lonely headlands south of Wicklow.

Overlooking a wide bay of the Irish Sea, Wicklow town is popular for the sailing and fishing it offers. Though considerably modernized, the old town of narrow streets retains a pleasing early-day character.

The coast road continues north to Greystones, Bray, and other resort towns, but our route turns inland, up the valley of the River Vartry.

Ashford is the site of the Mount Usher Gardens, open weekdays from 10 to 5:30 all year, and Sundays from May to September. Many rare trees and shrubs are planted in natural settings near the river.

## A look at western Wicklow

To enjoy the western side of County Wicklow, return to Laragh and drive west through the Wicklow Gap and scenic Hollywood Glen. A dam holds back the waters of the River Liffey to form Pollaphuca Lake, a tree-rimmed reservoir holding Dublin's water supply. Anglers come here for brown trout.

Built in the late 17th century, Blessington typifies the restful rural charm of Ireland's small towns. Dignified Georgian façades line its single long, wide, tree-lined main street. In the days of horse-drawn mail coaches, Blessington served as a staging post on the route from Dublin south to Carlow, Kilkenny, and Waterford.

Near Blessington you can visit Russborough, an elegant country house built in the 1740s. It is open for guided tours on weekends from Easter through October, and on Wednesday afternoons from June to September. It houses an art collection including paintings by Vermeer, Goya, Rubens, and Velasquez. A woodland garden is open when plants are flowering.

# Plan a Trip by Horse-drawn Wagon

When you travel by "gypsy" caravan, you meet local people and get a close-up view of country life

What better way to get acquainted with the countryside than to travel through a region at a leisurely pace in a horse-drawn "gypsy" caravan? Though not for every traveler, these wagons offer a close-up view of rural life and many opportunities to meet local people.

Although you must harness and drive the horse yourself, you don't have to be an accomplished equestrian. Before you start out, the operator will instruct you on the care, feeding, and harnessing of your horse; the operation of wagon equipment; good travel routes; and places where you can stop along the way.

### Tracking down the wagons

One of the best countries for traveling in this style is Ireland, where there's no language barrier when you stop to chat with farmers and join in the evening conviviality in a village pub. Operators of horse-drawn caravan trips are based in counties Cork, Kerry, Limerick, and Wicklow. In Britain you can travel by this mode in Norfolk, on the Isle of Wight, and in central Wales.

If you speak a bit of French or German, you can look into renting a *barouche* or *roulotte* (horse-drawn trailer) in France or a *Zigeunerwagen* (gypsy wagon) in Austria, Germany, or Switzerland. Horse-drawn wagons are pop-ular in various regions of France—Brittany, Burgundy, Limousin, Lorraine, Normandy, and Provence. In Germany, covered wagons follow roads through the Hunsrück region near the Mosel River or in the Allgäu Alps. Wagons are available in the Swiss Jura and central Switzerland, and in Austria's Burgenland. Carriage and wagon trips are also popular in Denmark.

Write to the appropriate government tourist office (see page 7) for more information and addresses of operators.

If you prefer to ride a horse instead of drive it, ask the tourist office for information on equestrian holidays. Many Europeans enjoy horseback touring and riding holidays; equestrian packages are available in some countries.

### Planning your trip

Weather is usually warm enough for caravan touring from April through September, though rain showers are always possible. Wear comfortable clothes, and don't overlook light rain gear.

The rental company will suggest itineraries which avoid heavy traffic and steep hills, and can advise you of farms and roadside inns where you can purchase food or arrange to pasture or stable your horse for the night.

The gaily painted wagons are usually rented by the week, though some operators rent for shorter periods. Your rustic home-on-wheels may not have all the conveniences of a modern house trailer, but you'll find its facilities reasonably comfortable and adequate to your needs.

On many caravan trips, you sleep aboard in narrow berths; on others, you spend the night in small roadside hotels along planned routes. Most wagons are equipped with a two-burner gas stove and a small sink for washing dishes. Water is drawn from a refillable plastic container. Ample bedding, dishes, and kitchen equipment come with the wagon; check to see if you'll need to bring towels. Provisions and dishes are fitted into cupboards, bedding is stored under bunks, and storage shelves and closets are included wherever there's room.

Before you start out, purchase a detailed road map of the area through which you'll travel. The operator will introduce you to your horse (each animal has its own personality) and instruct you in procedures. The horses are completely familiar with traffic, but they understand directions only in the local language, so you must remember to translate "giddy-up" and "whoa" into the vernacular.

### On the road

As your horse plods along peaceful country roads, you pass through simple villages. Plan to cover only about 12 miles/19 km a day.

When you see the countryside at a horse's pace, you notice little things: wind rippling across a wheat field, a small stream gurgling over rocks, the smell of freshly cut hay. You'll stop at midday for a roadside picnic. Evening meals can be cooked in your wagon or taken in a wayside inn or hotel.

# special interests

# In Ireland

## CENTRAL RESERVATIONS BUREAU

For information on accommodations, ranging from castles and stately houses to country hotels and farms, write to the Irish Tourist Board.

Your travel agent can book your hotels, or you can write to the Irish Tourist Board's Central Reservations Service, 14 Upper O'Connell Street, Dublin 1, Ireland. Enclose an international postal reply coupon with your reservation request.

## SUGGESTED SCENIC DRIVES

Ireland's uncluttered roads invite leisurely touring. When you drive through wild glens, across undulating green hills, or along the rugged coast, you'll touch the soul of Ireland. For suggested scenic drives in various parts of the country, write to the Irish Tourist Board.

## RENT AN IRISH COTTAGE

If you want to live the easy-going Irish way, then rent a whitewashed, thatch-roofed cottage in the West Country. Cottage rentals are popular with visitors who want to experience life in a small rural community. You stay near the village, shop for food in local stores, have a drink in the village pub, and relax in front of your own fireplace at night.

Cottages are located near small communities in countries Clare, Donegal, Galway, Kerry, Limerick, Mayo, and Tipperary. Though traditional in design, they have all modern facilities including central heating. Each cottage is built around a large,

modern kitchen with beamed ceiling and open fireplace; they accommodate up to eight people. Rates vary by the season.

For information and reservations, see your travel agent or write to the Irish Tourist Board.

## STAY ON A FARM

Dozens of farm families all over Ireland offer a warm country welcome to visitors. You can stay overnight or make the farmhouse your headquarters for a longer stay. Farmhouses approved by the Irish Tourist Board are identified by a sign.

Buildings vary from renovated old-style farmhouses to elegant Georgian manor houses. Clean and homey accommodations, hearty cooking, and informal hospitality are offered at moderate cost. Many farms have ponies or horses for children.

For more information on farmhouse holidays, write to the Irish Tourist Board. Local tourist offices can assist you in making arrangements for farm accommodations.

## IRISH ENTERTAINMENT

Theater is available the year around in Dublin—plays by Irish authors, international classics, Irish cabaret, revues, and other entertainment. Cork and Galway also offer theater throughout the year. In summer, performances are presented all over the country.

Strangers find a convivial welcome at singing pubs, where you enjoy Irish ballads along with a pint of Guinness. You'll find these pubs throughout Ireland.

In recent years, entertainment featuring traditional music, dance, and folk customs has flourished. Most performances are held between June and September. The Irish Tourist Board can provide information on locations and dates.

## A TASTE OF OLD IRELAND

Enjoy historic Ireland when you attend a banquet in a medieval castle or spend a traditional evening in an Irish cottage.

Medieval banquets and entertainment are staged nightly at three 15th century castles: Bunratty, on the Limerick-Shannon road; Knappogue, at Quin north

of Shannon; and Dunguaire, at Kinvara on the shore of Galway Bay. Entertainment features Irish music at Bunratty, a dramatic pageant of Irish history at Knappogue, and the works of Synge and Yeats at Kinvara.

Banquets are presented the year around at Bunratty, mid-May through September at Dunguaire, and May to October at Knappogue.

For a glimpse of Irish folk life, attend an Irish *ceili* at Bunratty Folk Park. After a simple meal of Irish stew, soda bread, and apple pie, you'll enjoy a fiddler, storyteller, and other folk entertainers. The Shannon Ceili is presented nightly from mid-May through September.

Reservations are essential for these popular evening programs, and can be made through a travel agent, by toll-free phone 1-800-343-6472, or by writing to Shannon Castle Tours Desk, Shannon International Free Airport, County Clare, Ireland.

## SPORTS & HOBBY HOLIDAYS

You can golf on 240 scenic courses, rent a horse-drawn caravan, trace your ancestors, or ride horseback on country trails during your holiday in Ireland.

For information on these and other sports and hobby vacations—such as fishing, cycling, backpacking, boating, archeology—write to the Irish Tourist Board.

## RAIL & BUS TICKETS

Within Ireland, the Coras Iompair Eireann (known as CIE) national transportation company operates all trains and buses. Services connect most cities and towns.

Rambler Tickets (available in the United States or at the Dublin, Limerick, and Cork railway stations) provide bargains in unlimited rail, or combined rail and bus, travel throughout the country. Tickets can be purchased for 8 or 15 days. Children under 15 years are charged half-fare.

Overlander Tickets provide unlimited travel for 15 days on CIE, Ulsterbus, and Northern Ireland Railways.

Rambler and Overlander tickets are available from CIE Tours, 122 E. 42nd Street, New York, NY 10168, or at CIE offices in Ireland.

**For information on travel in Ireland, write to the Irish Tourist Board (addresses on page 7).**

# Follow the Meandering Dordogne

Visit cliffside villages, prehistoric art caves, and castle fortresses as you savor the heart of central France

One of the longest rivers in France, the Dordogne is considered by many travelers to be the loveliest as well. From high in the Massif Central, it cuts diagonally southwest through France's unspoiled heartland, past cliffside villages and castle fortresses.

In ancient caves you gaze at prehistoric wall paintings drawn by Cro-Magnon man, or you can explore subterranean caverns hollowed out of limestone by underground rivers. At small comfortable hotels you'll savor Périgord cooking, frequently flavored by bits of elusive black truffles.

Quiet, flower-filled towns built of yellowish stone dot the Périgord region. Castle-lovers find a rewarding number of châteaux (many are open to visitors); most of them were built as early fortresses dominating river valleys. As elsewhere in France, everything closes between noon and 2 P.M., and some castles and caves also close on Tuesdays.

Though few Americans travel deeply into central France, the Dordogne valley is only a few miles off one of the main routes to Spain, just east of the Bordeaux wine district.

Fast trains speed south from Paris (Gare d'Austerlitz) to Brive-la-Gaillarde, where you continue on to Souillac or Rocamadour. Local trains and buses provide limited service to riverside towns, but a car offers opportunities for more comprehensive and slower paced touring.

## Follow the scenic river road

The lovely heartland of the Dordogne valley extends from Castelnau to St–Cyprien. Roads parallel the river, occasionally crossing from one bank to the other.

Red stone towers and ramparts of Castelnau Castle rise above the trees to command the confluence of the Dordogne and Cère rivers. Built in the 11th century, the large walled fortress is a superb example of medieval military architecture.

Houses roofed in brown tile cluster around Carennac's old priory. At Creysse, you climb flights of steps to reach vine-covered houses; a steep passageway leads to a church and castle ruins above the town. Reflecting the era of Louis XIV is graceful La Treyne Château, perched on a cliff above the Dordogne.

## South of the Dordogne

On a loop south of the river, you can visit the pilgrimage village of Rocamadour and go cave exploring. In autumn, bright foliage accents the grayish stone with splashes of red and gold.

Hanging from the cliffside above the winding Alzou valley, the buildings of Rocamadour appear to defy the force of gravity. Since the Middle Ages, religious pilgrims have traveled here to honor the Black Madonna. From the settlement at the base of the cliff, you climb the great stairway to the ecclesiastical city; many pilgrims kneel at every step. If you prefer, you can ascend by elevator. A path marked by Stations of the Cross leads up to the castle ramparts atop the cliff.

Canyons and caverns riddle the vast limestone plateau of central France; many of the caves are open to visitors during the tourist season.

One of the best is the Gouffre de Padirac, where you explore underground galleries and a subterranean river on foot and by boat. Descend by elevator and stairways into the wide, deep chasm, then board a flat-bottomed boat to float along the placid underground river.

Other nearby caverns include Lacave Caves, northwest of Rocamadour, where a small railway transports visitors along part of the route; and the Cougnac Caves north of Gourdon, which contain both limestone formations and prehistoric cave paintings. More fine cave art can be seen farther south at Pech-Merle Cave, northeast of Cahors.

## Castles overlook the river

The Dordogne meanders through hills and woodlands, between cliffs crowned with castles, past lovely cliffside villages at Domme, La Roque-Gageac, Castelnaud, and Beynac-et-Cazenac.

The district's largest towns are Souillac, which grew up around an ancient abbey, and Sarlat, the capital of the district. Sarlat's fascinating old section is ideal for strolling. Mellow ocher-colored stone enhances the subtle beauty of the architecture. Some of the handsome gabled houses are ornamented with turrets, carved facades, and mullioned windows. On Saturday mornings, open-air market stalls sprout in the Place des Oies.

Along this river route, you can visit a pair of castles: Fénelon's 15th century military fortress, and restored Veyrignac, a 17th century château. Montfort Castle (not open to the public) clings to a sheer rock above a deep bend in the river.

Attractive Domme crowns a rocky promontory on the river's south bank. Balconies, outside stairways, and climbing vines ornament the ocher stone buildings. Bright flowers bloom everywhere. From a clifftop belvedere, the Dordogne valley spreads like a green carpet cut by a blue ribbon of river.

Along the north shore, La Roque-Gageac and Beynac-et-Cazenac have awesome perches, clinging to cliffs that drop vertically to the Dordogne River. The ruins of Castelnaud fortress and several smaller castles rise on the south bank.

Late afternoon sun illuminates La Roque-Gageac's cliff face; its houses are mirrored in the calm waters below. Passageways lined with pretty houses lead to the church on the rock, where you have an excellent view over the meandering river.

Beynac-et-Cazenac's stern 13th century castle looms atop a sheer cliff, overlooking the river and village below. You can reach it by climbing the town's narrow streets or by taking the road that begins west of the village.

St–Cyprien's massive church hangs onto the side of a hill near the river.

**Medieval bastion at Beynac-et-Cazenac offers panoramic view over cliffside village and Dordogne River.**

## Prehistoric art in the Vézère valley

One of the world's richest prehistoric sites is the region around Les Eyzies-de-Tayac, along the Vézère River and its tributary valleys.

Neanderthal tribes roamed these hills and valleys some 150,000 years ago. Much later, Cro-Magnon man, representing a new stage in the evolution of man, emigrated here. Some 25,000 years ago, these hunting tribes found shelter in caves pitting the cliffs above the river valleys. And in these isolated caves, they drew pictures of the animals they stalked—horses, deer, bison, mammoths—and left remnants of tools and bones for modern archeologists to discover.

Begin your explorations with a visit to the National Museum of Prehistory in the cliffside castle overlooking Les Eyzies. Diagrams explain prehistoric chronology, and you'll see objects and works of art discovered locally.

The outstanding Lascaux Cave is closed to visitors, due to deterioration of the paintings, but splendid examples of cave art can be seen at Font-de-Gaume and at Les Combarelles. Earliest known drawings are at Bara-Bahau—animal outlines carved by sharpened flints. You'll explore galleries at Rouffignac by electric railway. Other caves are also open to visitors.

**Flowers grace many of the golden buildings of Domme, high above the river in the heart of the valley.**

# Brittany's Prehistoric Monuments

Ancient stone markers recall a long-lost culture along the lonely Atlantic coast of northwest France

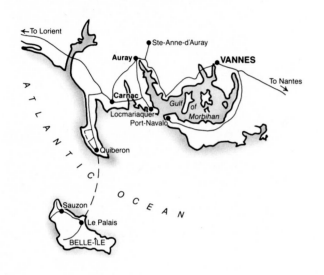

Brittany's rugged coast lures travelers who love the sea. Lonely headlands jut into the cold Atlantic, and deep bays indent the shore. Beneath an often-overcast and always-changing sky, life along the coast is governed in large part by the moods of the sea and the rhythms of the tide. Legends thrive in this lonely land. Religious fervor is intense, and a mystical faith in the supernatural pervades daily life.

Summer is the holiday season in Brittany; off-season visitors find many hotels and tourist attractions closed. At *pardons* (religious festivals), open-air markets, and other festive events, you'll still see Breton women wearing traditional white starched *coiffes* (headdresses).

Among Brittany's most distinctive attractions are the great prehistoric monuments scattered over the countryside north of Vannes. More than 3,000 giant stones can still be seen around Carnac and Locmariaquer, placed by a little-known race between 3500 and 1800 B.C.

## Upright stones mark the countryside

Single stones (called *menhirs*), often over 20 feet/6 meters high and weighing up to 350 tons/317 metric tons, were set up near ancient tombs and on slopes of hills. Largest was the Great Menhir, in the village of Locmariaquer, now broken in several pieces but once some 75 feet/23 meters long.

*Dolmens* were probably burial chambers, circular or parallel rows of upright stones topped by a flat slab. Originally they were buried under mounds of dry stones or earth, called *tumuli.* In the same clearing as the Great Menhir, you'll see the Merchants' Table dolmen, partially covered by a tumulus, with carved designs on the inside walls.

Lines of menhirs are probably the remains of ancient religious monuments. The greatest display is north of Carnac, called the Alignements of Ménec. More than a thousand upright stones were arranged in parallel rows, covering an area 100 yards/90 meters wide and 3/4 mile/1 km long. Running from east to west (apparently placed to coincide with the lines of sunrise and sunset at the summer and winter solstices), they end in a semicircle of giant stones.

Attractive towns are scattered along the Brittany coast. The charming old quarter of Vannes is grouped around the cathedral and partly enclosed by ramparts. Auray has links with Benjamin Franklin, who landed here in 1776 when his ship was unable to sail up the Loire River to Nantes.

South of Vannes, the Gulf of Morbihan cuts deeply into the coast. Many fishing boats and pleasure craft sail among its islands, for the best way to enjoy this small, island-studded inland sea is by boat. In summer, excursions depart from Vannes.

On the Quiberon Peninsula, walk or drive along the rugged western shore. Steamers leave Quiberon for scenic Belle-Île, largest of the Breton islands.

**Golden gorse ornaments lichen-covered megaliths near Carnac. Rows of upright stones were probably religious monuments.**

# Pérouges Waits to be Discovered

Northeast of Lyon, this fortified village sits on its isolated hilltop, watching the busy world pass by

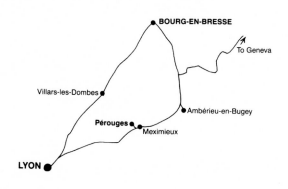

A pocket of tranquillity bypassed by the 20th century, the walled village of Pérouges is a French medieval fortress—intact, inhabited, waiting to be discovered. It crowns a hilltop some 22 miles/35 km northeast of Lyon. To reach it, turn off Route N84 just west of Meximieux and climb the slope that gave the tiny fortified town its strategic site.

During the Middle Ages, Pérouges was a fief of the Dukes of Savoy, a settlement of farmers and crafts people, primarily linen weavers. During war between France and Savoy, the town was overrun and sacked; rebuilt after the siege of 1468, it has a unity of architecture undisturbed by more modern structures.

When the factory age arrived, highways and the railroad bypassed the walled town. From its hilltop, Pérouges watched the world go by. Since its weavers could not compete with the mills, the town's prosperity declined and most of its inhabitants moved away. Buildings fell into disrepair. By 1909 Pérouges was virtually dead and scheduled for demolition.

To rescue the town, a conservation committee was established. Under an innovative plan, old houses are leased at nominal rent to new owners who agree to restore them as residences. Exteriors retain their 13th to 15th century façades while interiors are refitted with electricity, modern plumbing, and other conveniences.

You enter through the town's massive Upper Gate, its heavy wooden door now permanently ajar, into a walled village little changed in 500 years. From ancient stone ramparts, you gaze over rich farm lands toward the Rhône valley and snow-clad Alps. Fitted into the wall is the fortress Church of Ste. Marie-Madeleine; gunports, instead of windows, look out on its valley side.

## A stroll through old Pérouges

Activity in Pérouges centers around the Place du Tilleul, a cobbled square faced with vine-draped stone buildings and dominated by a huge linden tree. One of the 13th century houses now serves as an inn, the renowned Ostellerie du Vieux Pérouges; its cuisine rates a coveted Michelin star and draws many of the town's visitors (reservations recommended).

Across from the Ostellerie, another restored house contains a small but fascinating museum displaying historic documents, Renaissance furniture and household utensils, and coats of arms of the town's leading families. Adjoining the museum is the house of the princes of Savoy; it opens into a courtyard where medieval gardens have been re-created.

The only way to explore Pérouges is on foot, ambling along its cobbled lanes. Curving within the town's perimeter is the pebbled Rue des Rondes, a water trough marking its center. Narrow alleys branch off at odd angles. Lining the streets are beautiful old houses, some still awaiting an owner with enough francs to restore them.

As you walk along, perhaps you'll follow the local mail carrier or pause to admire a sleek cat basking in the sun. You can watch several crafts people who now work here. The smell of baking pastry may entice you to try a wedge of *galette pérougienne*, a local specialty. Few sounds disturb the peaceful town, though occasionally you may hear the shouts of children playing in the schoolyard or church bells calling the faithful to services.

**Bypassed by industrial age, walled medieval town of Pérouges sits on hilltop. Many of its buildings have been restored.**

# Hill Towns Perch above the Riviera

Visit museums of modern art and explore walled villages on slopes high above the lovely Côte d'Azur

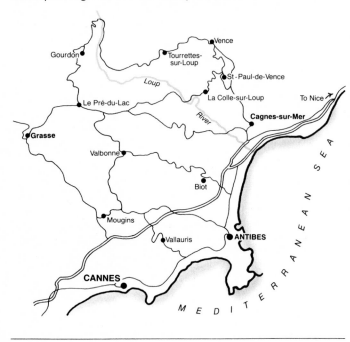

**Morning sun warms stone buildings in Vence, as women set out on day's chores. Drying laundry hangs from upper window.**

Behind the French Riviera's narrow strip of seaside resorts rise the undulating hills of the Maritime Alps. Walled towns and villages cling to the slopes and perch on the hilltops, vestiges of the days when Saracen pirates and medieval mercenaries invaded and plundered southern France.

The coastal towns seem to live for the tourist, but the inland villages preserve a Provençal character. Built with stones from the hillsides, they blend with the land. Tall, narrow houses lean protectively against one another, clustering around a town's castle or church. Winding cobbled lanes and steep alleyways often must be covered on foot. Men of the village meet in the central tree-shaded square for a leisurely afternoon game of *pétanque* (outdoor bowling).

Hotels and restaurants often have garden terraces where you can linger over lunch or sip an apéritif of anise-flavored *pastis*. Art lovers discover an impressive array of excellent museums. Handicrafts also flourish in the hill towns.

Fast trains link Paris with the Riviera resorts, where you can rent a car or learn about bus service to the hill towns.

## A treasury of modern art

Since the end of the 19th century, many artists and crafts people have settled here, bringing artistic vitality to the

**Modern paintings, sculptures, and other art works are displayed in indoor-outdoor setting at Maeght Foundation.**

region. Today the Côte d'Azur is a veritable treasury of modern art. Some of the best works remain in towns where the artists lived and worked.

**Maeght Foundation.** Calder mobiles hang in pine trees and Giacometti figures stand amid visitors at the Maeght Foundation, situated on a hillside outside the village of St-Paul-de-Vence. Open daily, the galleries and tiered gardens show off works of art in an indoor-outdoor setting. The superb collection includes paintings, graphics, mosaics, and sculptures by Braque, Léger, Bonnard, Matisse, Tal-Coat, Chagall, Miró, Calder, Giacometti, and other 20th century artists. Original signed lithographs and limited-edition print reproductions may be purchased in the salesroom.

**Chagall.** Located above Nice in the elegant suburb of Cimiez, the Chagall Museum contains ceramics, sculptures, gouaches, and etchings by Marc Chagall—all illustrating scenes from the Bible.

**Léger.** Bright colors adorn both the outside and interior of the Musée Fernand Léger (open daily) in Biot. Paintings, sculptures, ceramics, and collages by this prolific artist are arranged to illustrate his evolving art from an impressionist period into a uniquely stark and powerful style of cubism.

**Matisse.** Located in the Nice suburb of Cimiez, the Musée Matisse contains paintings, drawings, lithographs, sculpture, ceramic panels, and stained glass work showcasing the varied talents of Henri Matisse. The museum is open daily except during the month of November and Mondays in winter.

Matisse designed and decorated the Chapel of the Rosary in Vence—a simple, dignified chapel used by Dominican nuns. Visiting hours are restricted to Tuesdays and Thursdays. Large black-line murals decorate the chapel's white walls, and light filters in through vividly colored stained glass windows. Sketches by Matisse, on which he based finished designs, are displayed in an adjoining gallery.

**Picasso.** Paintings, ceramics, drawings, and lithographs by Pablo Picasso during his Riviera period (beginning in 1946) are displayed with paintings of that same era and tapestries in the Musée Grimaldi in Antibes. The museum is open daily, except during November and on Tuesdays in winter.

In Vallauris you can see Picasso's *Man with a Sheep* sculpture dominating the town square. His *War and Peace* chapel is located nearby in the thick-walled Château de Vallauris; two massive paintings cover the walls and arch up to the midpoint of the ceiling.

**Renoir.** Above Cagnes-sur-Mer at Les Collettes is the house where Auguste Renoir spent the final years of his life. Set amid olive groves and orange and lemon trees, the Musée Renoir is open afternoons daily except Tuesdays, holidays, and from October 15 to November 15.

## Exploring the hill towns

To visit some of these museums, you ascend into the pine-clad hills behind the Mediterranean. Attractive towns perch on hilltops and tile-roofed villas grace the slopes.

Breezes pick up the scent of lavender, wild thyme, and flowers—carnations, jasmine, mimosa, orange blossoms, roses—cultivated for the perfume industry in Grasse.

**Mougins.** An old fortified market town set atop a hill, Mougins has won recent renown for its excellent restaurants. Pablo Picasso lived here until his death in 1973. The town has a 15th century gateway and traces of the old ramparts. From the church belfry, there are good views over the countryside from Grasse to the Mediterranean Sea.

**Vallauris.** This town owes its fame to its unique clay deposits—known even before the Roman era, and used in making cookware and pottery. After settling in the area following World War II, Picasso became involved in ceramics and triggered renewed interest in the local craft. Numerous potters now work here, and shops sell local pottery and ceramics.

**Biot.** An attractive village, Biot is also an important craft center. Although best known for its pottery, it has an interesting glassworks *(verrerie)* where you can watch glass blowers in action.

**Cagnes-sur-Mer.** Set in a flower-decked countryside, this hilltop town is a favorite haunt of artists. The old town, called Haut-de-Cagnes, is dominated by a medieval castle; nearer the sea is the fishing village and beach resort of Cros-de-Cagnes. The upper town retains its ramparts, gates, and old streets and houses. The castle now contains a museum; from the castle tower, there's a splendid panoramic view.

**St-Paul-de-Vence.** One of the most charming walled hill towns, St-Paul has a pleasing medieval atmosphere. An arched gateway frames the worn stone fountain in a tiny plaza. Flowers tumble over iron balconies. Pedestrians take their time along intriguing cobbled lanes and the ramparts.

Art lovers will want to stop at La Colombe d'Or inn to dine amid a valuable collection of paintings—some acquired in trade for room and meals by the art-conscious proprietor—from artists who stopped here and later became famous.

**Vence.** Set atop a rocky promontory, Vence is surrounded by cultivated flower fields. You can stroll its interesting old quarter or relax under plane trees in the square.

## The Loup valley

Northwest of Vence, a scenic loop drive follows the gorge-like valley of the Loup River. Strike out toward the fortified village of Tourrettes-sur-Loup, home of several artists and crafts people, where outer walls of the houses form the town ramparts.

Paralleling the river gorge, the road heads north from Pont-du-Loup past several waterfalls cascading over the limestone cliffs. When your route intersects road D3, turn sharply south toward the perched village of Gourdon. You'll have magnificent views over the mountains and the Loup gorge. From atop Gourdon's lofty site, you can see all the way to the sea.

# Savoring Europe from the Water

Take a leisurely look at Europe's inland waterways from the deck of a hotel boat or self-drive cruiser

One of the most pleasant ways to see the European countryside is from the water—sailing along rivers and canals, through farm land and forests, past waterside villages and sturdy castles. You see farmers working in the fields and hikers striding along the towpaths.

Informal "hotel boats"—river barges or English canal boats—carry small groups of passengers along the inland waterways of Britain and northern Europe. Larger steamers cruise the Rhine and Danube rivers and sail along Norway's fiord coast.

If you prefer to pilot the boat yourself, you can rent a fully equipped "self-drive" craft and tour the waterways as you wish, navigating canal locks and tying up at inviting spots along the way. Otherwise, you can charter a boat with crew for your holiday.

Boats operate from April through October or early November; peak season extends from mid-May through mid-September. In early spring and late autumn, some firms offer lower rates. Your travel agent and government tourist offices can provide information on hotel boat cruises, charters, and self-drive rental boats. These are some of the leading operators:

*Boat Enquiries Ltd.,* 7 Walton Well Road, Oxford OX2 6ED, England (hotel boats and self-drive boats in England and Wales).

*Continental Waterways,* 11 Beacon Street, Boston, MA 02108 (hotel barge trips in France).

*Floating Through Europe,* 501 Madison Avenue, New York, NY 10022 (hotel barge trips and self-drive boats in France, England, and Holland).

*Quiztours,* % C.I.R., 310 Madison Avenue, New York, NY 10017 (hotel barge cruises and self-drive cruisers in France).

*Skipper Travel Services Ltd.,* 210 California Street, Palo Alto, CA 94306 (barge cruises and self-drive boats in England, Scotland, Ireland, France, and Holland).

*Waterways of France,* 12 rue du Helder, 75009 Paris, France (hotel barge trips in France).

Most European cities originated as coastal ports or were built along large rivers or lakes. So even if your itinerary doesn't allow enough time for an extended boating or shipboard holiday, you can still explore some of the Continent's waterways on day excursions.

## Hotel boats cruise rivers & canals

An increasingly popular mode of tourist travel, the hotel barge trip offers a leisurely look at the countryside. You glide serenely along at about 4 mph, stopping occasionally to explore small towns or waterside shops and pubs or to go through a navigation lock. Surprises lie around many turns—anglers sitting on the bank or errant cattle wading into a canal. As the countryside changes elevation, waterways are regulated by a series of locks.

In England, hotel barges navigate the River Thames and the Norfolk Broads, but you must board a "narrow-boat" to explore the maze of canals. In France boat trips through Burgundy and Champagne are popular, but you can also cruise through Brittany and Anjou, along the Charente River in the Cognac region, through Alsace and France-Comte, and on the Canal du Midi. In Holland, hotel barges ply the canals and rivers lacing the western windmill and bulb country; some trips extend south to Ghent and Bruges in Belgium.

Travelers sleep and eat most meals on board; the crew handles navigation and meal preparation. Boats vary in size and accommodate from 6 to 28 passengers. Some barges have bicycles aboard or a mini-bus available so passengers can explore nearby villages and castles. Each night the boat ties up at a different town.

## Self-drive rental boats

If you're happiest handling the wheel yourself, why not hire a boat for a holiday afloat? You can rent cabin cruisers, narrow canal boats, or yachts by the week and sail the inland waterways of Britain, Ireland, the Netherlands, and France. Boats vary in size, with berths for 2 to 8 people. If you prefer, charter a boat with crew for your party of family or friends. Sailing schools at home and abroad provide expertise and confidence for beginning yachters.

In Britain, boaters cruise along the River Thames or probe the vast network of canals on a "narrow-boat." Sailors head for the Norfolk Broads, where yachts and cruisers crowd the maze of waterways in summer.

For an Irish boating holiday, you can cruise on the River Shannon (see page 25), the River Erne, or the Grand Canal and River Barrow.

In the Netherlands you can hire cruisers, yachts, or canal boats for sailing on Dutch lakes, canals, and estuaries. The Friesland lake district attracts many sailors, but boats can also be rented in North Holland, Zeeland, North Brabant, Limburg, Utrecht, and Gelderland provinces.

You can explore French waterways by rental boat in three scenic areas: along Burgundy's rivers and canals, in Brittany, and in southwestern France on the Canal du Midi.

## Cruising on the Rhine, Mosel & Danube

Europe's oldest highways are its rivers. Today, large floating hotel ships cruise the Rhine and Danube from April through mid-October, carrying passengers along these historic routes. You can cruise the Mosel as well.

**Rhine River.** Rising high in the Alps, the Rhine River curves through Switzerland before taking a northwesterly route to the North Sea. A highlight of the upstream trip is the approach from Strasbourg to Basel, where the river rises 410 feet/126 meters by a series of locks.

Several German and Dutch operators offer trips along the Rhine and Mosel rivers, cruising through the waters of the Netherlands, Germany, France, and Switzerland. The Köln-Dusseldorfer German Rhine Line also offers theme and holiday cruises.

On the popular Rhine River cruise, passengers disembark at several stops along the river—usually Cologne, Koblenz, Rudesheim, Mannheim, and Strasbourg—for wine tasting and excursions to shore attractions.

**Danube River.** A riverboat cruise down the Danube from Vienna becomes an international adventure, as you pass through the waters of six nations—Austria, Czechoslovakia, Hungary, Yugoslavia, Romania, and Bulgaria—on its route through Central Europe to the Black Sea. The river cuts through the Carpathian Mountains at the historic Iron Gate (see page 109). You cruise through rural Balkan countryside and stop occasionally for shore excursions.

Austrian, Russian, and Romanian vessels depart from Vienna on round-trip cruises to Budapest (4 days), Belgrade (7 days), and the Black Sea (15 or 16 days).

### Two classic Scandinavian cruises

Step aboard a Norwegian coastal steamer or a Swedish canal boat and turn back the clock to an earlier, more leisurely era. These sturdy vessels allow travelers unusual glimpses of Scandinavian life. Passengers ride along with mail and cargo to Norwegian fishing ports north of the Arctic Circle or cruise across the rural heartland of Sweden.

**Norway's fiord coast.** Coastal express steamers and luxury cruise ships sail along Norway's spectacular western coast, venturing into narrow fiords that knife deeply between wooded mountains that ascend steeply from the water's edge. You dock at remote Norwegian coastal ports, where townspeople often line the dock and children wave as you arrive. Ships cruise far above the Arctic Circle, past the majestic North Cape promontory to Kirkenes near the Russian border.

Ships of the Bergen Line transport cargo, mail, and passengers on informal 11-day voyages from Bergen north to Kirkenes and back, throughout the year. For many small coastal ports, these ships provide the primary means of communication.

Passenger ships of several cruise lines follow the fiord coast to North Cape in summer; your travel agent has information on ships and schedules.

**Sweden's Göta Canal.** From mid-May to early September, small steamers transport passengers through the scenic lake district of Sweden on 3-day trips along the Göta Canal. The route links Gothenburg, Sweden's second city and largest seaport, with the capital city of Stockholm. Boats also cruise the reverse direction.

About one-third of the 347-mile/655-km route is through manmade canals, where 65 locks raise vessels more than 300 feet/90 meters above sea level, then gradually lower them as the end of the trip approaches. On the remainder of the route, boats cruise through natural waterways—rivers, lakes, and island-studded sea.

You pass old castles, waterside villages, and anglers along the water's edge. The canal cuts through forests of beech, birch, and pine, where branches occasionally brush the boat as you pass. Cruising through Swedish farm land, you'll see workers in the fields. You can walk along the towpath, watch action at the locks, or just sit in a comfortable deck chair and enjoy the scenery.

# Along the Alsatian Wine Road

Delightful winemaking towns nestle among the vineyard-covered foothills of the Vosges Mountains

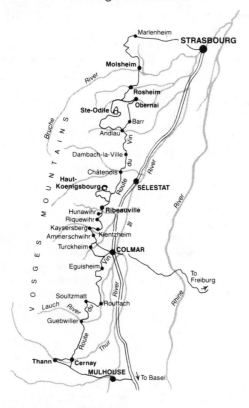

The peaceful vineyards of Alsace cover the eastern flank of the Vosges Mountains, rising above the flat Rhine plain. Small winemaking towns huddle around steepled churches amid the vine-covered foothills. Lonely ruins of feudal fortresses crown the high rocky outcrops, and trails wind across the wooded slopes.

For centuries Alsace has been the buffer between warring powers on opposite banks of the Rhine River. A hybrid civilization has grown, combining a Gallic culture with Teutonic influences in language, architecture, and even cuisine.

Many of the region's attractive wine villages are linked by the Route du Vin, which winds for some 75 miles/120 km through the Vosges foothills. It begins west of Strasbourg at Marlenheim and meanders south to Thann. Grapes have been cultivated here since Roman times, and the vineyards still provide the livelihood for many families in the region.

You probably won't need an excuse to try the light and fruity Alsatian wines. Some vintners have small tasting rooms where you can stop to sample wines and buy a bottle for a picnic; look for *dégustation libre* (free tasting) signs. You'll enjoy the golden Rieslings and Sylvaners in any season, but it's at harvest time—usually around the middle of October—that you catch activity at its peak.

Perhaps your visit will coincide with one of the local festivals. These are much enjoyed by Alsatian villagers, who gather to parade in traditional dress, dance to lively melodies, and taste the local wine.

South of Strasbourg, express trains stop in Sélestat, Colmar, and Mulhouse. Local trains and buses serve some small towns, but you'll enjoy the region best by car.

## Driving the wine road

The Alsatian wine road is a route to be savored. Winding your way along it, you come upon one enchanting town after another, each with its own character.

Fortifications from the Middle Ages still surround some towns. Medieval and Renaissance churches and timber-framed buildings crowd together on narrow, curving streets. Plump eiderdowns hang out of gable windows, soaking up the fresh morning air. Ancient gateways, decorated fountains, and charming old inns await discovery. Occasionally you may spot a stork's nest, though few of these birds now return to Alsatian river valleys to raise their young.

From Marlenheim the road winds south through vineyards on the eastern slopes of the Vosges. Facing Molsheim's central square is the Metzig, a gracious Renaissance building dating from 1525 and decorated in Alsatian style (high steep roof, multistoried, much ornamentation).

Rosheim contains some of the oldest ruins and ramparts in Alsace. Old houses along the Rue de General-de-Gaulle date from the 12th century, as does the Church of St-Pierre and St-Paul, built in the characteristically sober and unornamented Rhenish style.

Multistoried gabled houses rise along Obernai's small winding streets, and 13th century ramparts surround the town. On an easy walking tour, look for the attractive market square, belfry, six-bucket well, and 16th century town hall. Paths wend through the hills.

Roads climb west to Ste-Odile, an ancient pilgrimage town and convent honoring the patron saint of Alsace. From the summit of Mont Ste-Odile, you have a broad view over the plain.

Barr is a major wine-producing center below the fortified castles of Landsberg and Andlau. Overlooking acres of vineyards, it boasts handsome old houses and a 17th century town hall with decorated loggia and sculpted balcony.

Three ancient gateways breach the fortifications of Dambach-la-Ville, a seductive Renaissance town. Dambach's pride is St-Sebastien Chapel with its ornate 17th century baroque altar.

## Lofty hilltop fortresses

On the hilltops between Châtenois and Ribeauvillé, castles stand like sentinels: Haut-Koenigsbourg, Kientzheim, Frankenbourg, St-Ulrich, and Girsberg.

A winding mountain road climbs southwest of Châtenois to Haut-Koenigsbourg, a massive 15th century fortress commanding the Rhine valley from a lofty, isolated site. In the early 20th century, Kaiser Wilhelm II restored the feudal stronghold as a summer retreat. After touring its magnificent halls and apartments, climb to the keep to see the memorable view of the Rhine valley with the Black Forest in the distance. Marked paths descend the wooded slopes to valley towns.

Among other well-preserved ruins are those of St-Ulrich, reached by trail (about 2 hours) northwest of Ribeauvillé. From its site you enjoy a panorama over the valley, the ruins of Girsberg Castle, the town of Ribeauvillé, and the Alsatian plain.

## Heart of the wine country

Many of Alsace's premier winemakers have settled in towns southwest of Sélestat.

Narrow cobbled alleys branch off Ribeauvillé's main street. As you approach the town's 13th century clock tower, you pass an attractive Renaissance fountain. Just south of Ribeauvillé is the attractive little village of Hunawihr, where vineyards surround the 15th century fortified church and cemetery.

In Riquewihr, surprises await you around each curve and corner. Spared by World War II, this charming 16th century village is a feast of beautiful timbered Alsatian houses, ancient fountains, and curving streets. Flowers spill from window boxes and over balustrades. Vineyards climb the hills behind town. You can learn about Alsatian folklore in the Dolder (gate) museum and look at postal stamps in the PTT museum.

The Route du Vin passes through the streets of Mittelwihr, Bennwihr, and Sigolsheim—all rebuilt since World War II. The small fortified town of Kientzheim has typical gabled houses and an Alsace wine museum.

Albert Schweitzer was born in 1875 in Kaysersberg, a town that, in the Roman era, controlled passage between Gaul and the Rhine valley. The Weiss River flows through town below the fortified castle. Charming and medieval, Kaysersberg has several handsome churches, a Renaissance town hall, and a 15th century fortified bridge.

One of the prettiest Alsatian towns, Ammerschwihr was burned by incendiary bombs during the winter of 1944–45 and has been rebuilt in modern Alsatian style. It still has a tall 13th century gateway and fortifications.

## South of Colmar

Smaller and less crowded than Strasbourg, the old Alsatian town of Colmar is a favorite center for exploring the wine villages. Afoot through its inviting streets, you'll happen upon impressive early buildings such as the old Douane (customs house), and many restored wooden

Bright red geraniums adorn hexagonal town fountain and window boxes along main street of Ribeauvillé.

Vineyards cover slopes surrounding Hunawihr and its fortified 15th century church. Post supports each grapevine.

Renaissance houses including the Maison Pfister and the Maison des Têtes. In the quiet district called Little Venice, old houses and overhanging trees border placid canals. A former convent is now the Unterlinden Museum.

Back on the Route du Vin, the small village of Turckheim guards its Renaissance character. A wall and three ancient gates enclose the town square, fountain, and timbered old houses.

Surviving intact since the 16th century, Eguisheim is built around an ancient castle and surrounded by vineyards. After you've explored the attractive little village, take a forest drive along the Route of the Five Châteaux to the hilltop ruins of Hohlandsbourg Castle.

Old churches, dating from the 12th century, are highlights in the towns of Rouffach, Soultzmatt, and Guebwiller. Rouffach's Church of Notre Dame is the oldest Gothic building in the Upper Alsace district.

At the south end of the wine road, Cernay has medieval fortifications and a small historical museum in the Porte de Thann. Towering over Thann are the castle ruins of Engelsbourg. Thann boasts the Collégiale St-Thiébaut, richest in Gothic details of all the churches in Alsace. A museum of Alsatian and local history is housed in the town hall.

# Normandy's Captivating Honfleur

A favorite of painters, this historic port charms you into exploring its cobbled streets and attractive harbor

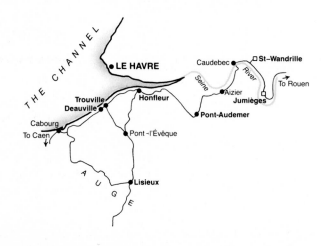

For more than a century, Honfleur has captivated artists. Handsome Norman buildings line the quays rimming the town's enclosed harbor basin, where painters and photographers still attempt to capture Honfleur's character and charm on canvas and film.

During the 1860s, Eugène Boudin encouraged his fellow painters—among them Courbet, Monet, Jongkind, and Daubigny—to join him on the Normandy coast, where they recorded their impressions of the region's changing moods of light and nature. They gathered for conversation and fellowship at the St–Simeon inn on the Côte de Grâce.

Spared from major war damage, Honfleur has changed little in appearance since the 17th century. Mirrored in the old harbor are colorful boats and tall, slender houses topped by steep slate roofs. Commercial fishermen mend their nets along the river quay, where fishing boats tie up in the tidal estuary. Narrow, wood-frame dwellings huddle side by side along cobbled streets leading off the harbor basin.

Frequent trains leave Paris (Gare St–Lazare) for Normandy. In Lisieux, Caen, Deauville, or Le Havre, you can board a bus at the Gare Routière (bus station) and continue on to Honfleur.

## Rambling around Honfleur

Activity in Honfleur centers around the colorful port and the marketplace.

From Quai St-Étienne you look across to narrow, slate-faced façades reflected in the water. Fishing boats and pleasure craft rock gently at their moorings. St-Stephen's Church now houses an Ethnographic and Norman Folk Art Museum.

At the entrance to the old basin is La Lieutenance, the 16th century house of the King's Lieutenant, the governor of Honfleur. A nearby plaque commemorates Samuel de Champlain, who sailed from Honfleur early in the 17th century to found Quebec. Narrow cobbled streets lined by typical Norman houses (wood-frame buildings roofed in slate) branch off the harbor quays.

Stroll up the Rue des Logettes to Place Ste-Catherine, which brims with activity on market days. Facing the marketplace is Ste-Catherine's Church, constructed entirely of wood by ship-building carpenters; its interior has twin naves that peak to resemble ships' hulls. Bells ring out from the nearby church belfry.

You can see some of the luminous seascapes and pictures of Norman peasant life painted by Boudin and his contemporaries in the Eugène Boudin Museum on Rue Albert 1er (closed Tuesdays and in winter). The museum also displays traditional Norman apparel.

Above town on the quiet Côte de Grâce, you can visit a small, tree-shaded chapel and enjoy the view from Mont Joli over the town and Seine estuary.

From Honfleur, you can make a variety of excursions. Follow the Seine upriver to the abbeys of St-Wandrille and Jumièges and the cathedral city of Rouen. Pont-Audemer has numerous old Norman houses. To the south lies the pastoral Auge region—land of cheese, cider, and Calvados. The coast road heads southwest to the resorts of Trouville and Deauville.

**Narrow quayside buildings and moored boats are reflected in quiet waters of Honfleur's enclosed harbor basin.**

# special interests

# In France

## FRANCE ON TWO WHEELS

Cycling is a popular pastime in rural areas. You'll see housewives cycling home with bread and groceries and groups of long-distance cyclists wheeling along country roadways.

If you prefer leisurely pedaling—down tree-lined lanes, beside the coast, along old canal towpaths—why not rent a bicycle for a day or half-day excursion? Rentals are available at more than 80 stations of the French National Railroads and at other sites. For more information, write to the French Government Tourist Office.

Summer bicycle tours are organized by the Bicy-Club de France, 8 place de la Porte Champerret, 75017 Paris. Other cycling itineraries are published by the Fédération de Cyclotourisme, 8 rue Jean-Marie-Jégo, 75013 Paris.

Parisians and other visitors to the vast Bois de Boulogne in Paris can rent bikes by the hour or day at a kiosk at the park operated by the Bicy-Club de France.

## HIKING PATHS

One of the best ways to enjoy the French countryside is on foot, traveling on trails far from major highways, delighting in sites and villages that the motorist frequently misses.

You'll discover a vast network of trails that passes through rural farm lands and wooded mountains and alongside waterways. Signposts and red-and-white markers guide you along the *sentiers* (footpaths). The local Syndicat d'Initiative (tourist office) can direct you to the best local routes for day trips.

Serious hikers can purchase "topoguides" (in France) published by the Comité National des Sentiers de Grande Randonnée (National Committee of Hiking Routes), 9 avenue George V, 75008 Paris. The guides contain maps, detailed route descriptions, and practical advice. The organization also issues itinerary suggestions and a hiker's guide containing information on preparation and equipment needed for a holiday on foot.

## CASTLE HOTELS, INNS, FARMS

In France you can fit your accommodations to your travel style and budget by staying not only in conventional hotels but also in castles, country manor houses, *auberges* (country inns), or on farms.

Many interesting hostelries belong to the Relais de Campagne et Châteaux-Hôtels organization (c/o David Mitchell & Company Inc., 200 Madison Avenue, New York, NY 10016) or Hostelleries d'Atmosphère (Château de Pray, 37400 Amboise). Included among these hotels are former castles, abbeys, and manor houses that have been converted into comfortable accommodations.

There are also many excellent country hotels and inns that belong to the Logis de France federation (25 rue Jean-Mermoz, 75008 Paris) or to the Petits Nids de France (Hôtel du Mouton-Blanc, 33 avenue Alsace—Lorraine, B.P. 132, 59403 Cambrai Cedex).

If you want to stay on a farm, you can live with a farm family and take your meals with them or rent a country cottage (*gîtes ruraux)* and do your own cooking. For more information on various accommodations, write to the French Government Tourist Office.

## SKIING IN THE FRENCH ALPS

Skiers flock to major ski resorts such as Courchevel, Val d'Isère, and Chamonix in mountain valleys near France's southeast border. Skiing continues through the summer at some alpine resorts.

Various ski packages are available containing accommodations, lift passes, and other features such as instruction, some meals, and transportation between airport and resort. For more information on skiing in France, write to the French Government Tourist Office.

## MAPS AND GUIDEBOOKS

Many travelers in France rely on the renowned guides and regional road maps published by the Michelin Tire Company.

Revised annually, the red, hard-cover book rates the country's best hotels and restaurants and provides detailed maps of the larger towns. Michelin red guides are also available for Great Britain-Ireland, Germany, the Benelux countries, Italy, and Spain-Portugal.

Soft-cover Michelin green guides provide information on main points of interest (especially museums and churches), tourist routes and walking tours, and city maps. English versions are available for Paris, Normandy, Brittany, the Loire valley, Périgord, and the Riviera. Also available in English are green guides to Austria, Germany, Italy, Portugal, Spain, Switzerland, and London. Guides covering other regions are published in French.

If you have a reading knowledge of the French language and a strong interest in French food and restaurants, take a look at several other respected guides—the *Guide Kléber* and *Le Nouveau Guide Gault-Millau*—in French bookstores.

## FRANCE RAILPASS

If you plan to travel by train, check the advantages of the France Railpass, issued by the French National Railroads. It offers 4, 9, or 16 non-consecutive days of first or second-class train travel within a specific period. (The 4-day pass must be used within 15 days, the 9-day or 16-day passes within 1 month.) All three provide travel bonuses and discounts on admission fees, tours, accommodations and car rentals throughout the country.

Winter travelers can purchase the France Saverpass, available for first or second-class train travel from October through March. Priced for two persons traveling together, it offers the same benefits, at a discount, of the 9-day France Railpass. For more information, see your travel agent or contact an office of the French National Railroads.

## HOBBY AND STUDY VACATIONS

During your holiday in France you can explore rivers and canals by boat, take classes in French cooking, visit art museums and festivals, join wine tasting or food tours, take French language classes, ski at alpine resorts, relax at a spa, cycle through the countryside, or spend a holiday on horseback or aboard a horse-drawn "gypsy wagon."

For information on enjoying your own favorite interest or hobby, write to the French Government Tourist Office.

**For information on travel in France, write to the French Government Tourist Office (addresses on page 7).**

# Historic Towns Recall a Golden Era

Ramble through gracious old towns and ports that once thrived beside the fabled Zuider Zee

During the 17th century, Holland was one of the world's foremost maritime powers. From thriving ports rimming the Zuider Zee, Dutch ships sailed forth on voyages of exploration and trade. Fishing and whaling fleets roamed the northern seas.

Echoes of this golden age linger in the towns of North Holland. Tradition remains strong—most visibly in the colorful summer "folklore" markets and in villages where townspeople still wear traditional dress.

Trains from Amsterdam serve the larger towns; infrequent buses transport passengers between country villages and small towns. Driving is particularly enjoyable—you can explore inviting back roads, stopping as often and as long as you wish. Dike-top roads are narrow, so be alert for bicyclists.

## Country fairs & markets

Traditional markets are one of North Holland's attractions. Best known is Alkmaar's Friday morning cheese market, held weekly from mid-April to mid-September. At local weekly markets, residents exchange news and gossip while purchasing food, clothing, and other supplies.

Villagers often don regional dress for summer country fairs. Costumed dancers frequently perform, and handicrafts of bygone days are demonstrated—you might see a sheep shearer at work, a basket weaver plaiting supple twigs, or a carver using hand tools to shape wooden shoes from a block of willow. At food stalls you can sample tiny pancakes (*poffertjes*) flavored with orange liqueur, herring with chopped onions, local cheeses, or cooky specialities.

Midsummer folklore markets are held weekly in several North Holland towns including Hoorn, Medemblik, and Schagen. Alkmaar and Purmerend feature weekly cheese markets. The Netherlands Board of Tourism (see page 7) and local VVV offices (tourist information centers) can provide a list of dates and times.

## The Zaan district

During the 1600s, Zaandam was the center of the important Dutch shipbuilding industry. Russia's Peter the Great was one of many who came from other countries to study the Dutch methods.

Hundreds of windmills pumped water from the lowlands. Other industrial mills ground grain and sawed wood for the shipbuilding industry. Most of the mills are gone now, but you'll still see some along the waterways. A merchant's house in Koog aan de Zaan has been converted into a windmill museum with exhibits focusing on mill history and construction.

**It's quite a show: colorful, traditional cheese market is the big draw each Friday in summer in Alkmaar.**

Near Zaandijk, typical houses and mills of the district have been grouped into a small village called Zaanse Schans along the east bank of the Zaan River. Buildings facing the cobbled mall have been converted into small shops, museums, and a restaurant. Compact green-painted houses border nearby canals; arched bridges and narrow paths invite you to explore.

At Uitgeest you can head north for Alkmaar, past yacht-dotted Alkmaarder Lake through Akersloot.

If time permits, follow the coastal road northwest behind the wooded dunes bordering the North Sea. Local buses link the small settlements. Spur roads branch west about 2 miles/3 km to simple family seaside resorts. Bergen, a few miles inland at the edge of the woods, is a favorite of walkers and artists.

## Traditions continue in Alkmaar

From mid-April to mid-September, tourists converge on this North Holland town for the Friday morning cheese market. When the clock in the Weighing House strikes 10, Alkmaar's marketplace comes alive to follow a 300-year-old tradition. Hundreds of Edam and Gouda cheeses are piled in the square, where buyers inspect them for age and quality. After buyer and seller seal the price with a slap of hands, the round golden balls and wheels are piled into wooden cradles. Then costumed teams from the cheese carriers guild go to work, transporting the cheese-laden cradles to the scales to be weighed.

Besides this colorful spectacle, Alkmaar offers many delights for the visitor who allows time for a walking tour; you can pick up a map at the VVV office (tourist information center) opposite the Weighing House. Quiet canals encircle and interlace the heart of the old town, with its gabled houses, churches, and almshouses. Drawbridges span the placid waterways.

On Friday mornings enjoy the activity at the fish market near the Mient. Stroll along the tree-lined Oude Gracht. Seek out the 18th century windmill, still used as a flour mill, on old ramparts near the Ritsevoort bridge.

Walk north to the Great Church, noted for its impressive interior and fine organs (recitals on Friday mornings during July and August). On weekdays you can visit the town hall, whose rooms are decorated with antique furnishings.

From Alkmaar, drive eastward across the polder country (land reclaimed from the sea). Many windmills still mark the flat landscape. In spring, blooming bulb fields and fruit orchards brighten the countryside.

## Sleepy ports recall a golden age

Quiet towns dotting the shore of the old Zuider Zee are reminders of Holland's great seafaring days. Three centuries ago, Dutch navigators explored the earth's oceans, colonists emigrated to America, and a trading empire took shape in the East Indies. Fishing, whaling, and trade brought the country vast profits. Industry and the arts flourished.

Today, though, the Zuider Zee has been closed off from the sea to become a lake—the IJsselmeer. Racing yachts have replaced fishing boats and merchant ships, and old towns struggle to adjust to a changing economy.

Traveling to the West Frisian port towns, you'll pass through a rich agricultural area supporting fruit orchards, vegetable districts, and fields of flowers grown for seed.

**Medemblik.** A small old town, Medemblik is proud of its restored 13th century Radboud Castle, the mighty 15th century church, and the attractive gabled houses of the inner town. Parks, campgrounds, and a large yacht harbor offer recreation opportunities. An ancient steam train links Hoorn and Medemblik from May through August.

**Enkhuizen.** Pride of this once rich trading town is the fascinating Zuider Zee Museum, an open-air village where visitors learn how families lived and worked in Zuider Zee fishing towns from 1880 to 1932. Open daily from April to mid-October, the museum also contains old sailing ships, traditional costumes, and other historic exhibits.

Also worth exploring are the town's twisting alleyways, attractive canals, and large yacht harbor. Enkhuizen's noteworthy buildings include the twin-towered Drommedaris, a handsome town hall, 16th century Weighing House, Koeport gate, and several churches.

**Hoorn.** Once one of the most powerful towns in Holland, Hoorn still revels in its colorful past. On Wednesdays the town takes on a festive air as shoppers stroll amid open-air market stalls and pavement displays. In summer, market days are enlivened by the performances of costumed dancers and demonstrations of old crafts.

The sturdy Hoofdtoren, part of the town's 16th century defenses, now marks the harbor entrance for recreational sailors. Renovated houses and old warehouses border quays surrounding the inner harbor. Along narrow streets, brick houses appear to tilt forward; hooks on the upper gables are used to hoist furniture up from the sidewalk.

Hoorn's main square, the Rode Steen, lies several blocks inland from the harbor. Here you'll find the tourist information office, the impressive 1609 Weighing House, and the 1632 West Frisian Museum. Coats of arms of the seven cities of West Friesland decorate the museum's ornate gable; inside you'll see furnished interiors of regional dwellings, local costumes and folk art, and other excellent exhibits associated with Hoorn and the region.

**Other towns.** Bordering the IJsselmeer just north of Amsterdam are several interesting towns. Each is compact enough for strolling and offers insights into Dutch customs and architecture of an earlier era.

Just opposite Edam's stately town hall is its best-known building—the Captain's House, renowned for its floating cellar, built-in furniture, and period furnishings.

Tourism provides the chief source of income for Volendam and Marken, whose residents often wear traditional dress and encourage visitors to take pictures. In both towns, activity is centered around the waterfront. Walk along the top of the dikes for intimate glimpses of neat cottages and gardens inside the breastworks. The island of Marken will be absorbed in the new Markerwaard polder.

You return to Amsterdam through the tidy village of Monnikendam and the cheese-making settlement of Broek in Waterland.

# Cycling Excursions Add Zest to Travel

Rent a bicycle for a day or a week and pedal along the scenic rural roads of northern Europe

You need an adventurous spirit, a bit of energy, and ample time—but if you have all three, consider making part of your European tour by bicycle. You'll see European cyclists everywhere, pedaling to work, school, and market.

You can rent a bike for an afternoon cycling excursion, or pedal with friends for a few days on a prearranged itinerary. Dedicated cyclists often spend their entire holiday touring by two-wheeler.

Astride a bicycle, you not only see the countryside and its people, you hear birds singing and smell flowers and new-mown hay. You have freedom to pedal at your own pace, stopping to enjoy a view or picnic under a tree.

### Short-term rentals and package trips

It's easy to rent a bicycle for a day excursion or a longer regional trip. In many countries you can obtain bicycles at the railroad station; sometimes you'll get a discount if you show a valid rail ticket. You can also hire bikes at bicycle rental firms and some bike repair shops, through local tourist offices, and at some hotels and resort centers.

In summer it's a good idea to reserve a bicycle, particularly in popular areas. You will probably be asked to show identification, and a deposit may be required.

On most package trips, you cycle with friends at your own pace along a prearranged itinerary. Bike rental, accommodations, and meals are arranged in advance. Some cyclists bring their own bikes. Trips range in length from a 3-day weekend to about 2 weeks, but most last about a week to 10 days.

Write to the government tourist offices (addresses on page 7) for general cycling information. Once you're in Europe, local tourist offices can direct you to the nearest rental outlet and suggest regional cycling routes.

You also can get information on European cycling and tours from hosteling organizations or from the International Bicycle Touring Society, 2115 Paseo Dorado, La Jolla, CA 92037.

### Cycling through Europe

Almost anywhere north of the Alps, you can roam over paved, traffic-free back roads where cycling is still a joy.

**Austria.** From April through October, rental bicycles are available at 95 stations of the Austrian Federal Railways and can be returned at other stations. The Austrian National Tourist Office can provide a list; further information is available in Austria at any rail station or at local tourist offices. Resort towns in all of Austria's provinces have created a network of bicycle paths and routes.

**Belgium.** Bicycles can be rented at about 20 Belgian railroad stations and returned at other stations. You can follow scenic routes through the countryside or along the coast. On a short trip from Bruges, follow the tree-lined canal west to Damme.

**Britain.** Write to the British Tourist Authority for cycling information and for suggested itineraries with terrain to suit cyclists of different abilities. Local Tourist Information Centres can also direct you to rental companies and suggest routes through scenic regions such as the Lake District, East Anglia, the Cotswolds, the Kent countryside, and the south coast.

**Denmark.** Flat countryside and scattered islands make Denmark an ideal cycling country, and you'll see many Danes on bicycles. Rental two-wheelers are available from bike shops and many railway stations. Many cycling tours are available. You'll find excellent bicycle routes on Funen and the southern islands of the archipelago, on the Jutland peninsula, in the countryside around Copenhagen, and on the island of Bornholm.

**Finland.** Bicycles can be rented at some tourist offices and at many hotels, holiday villages, and hostels. Check with the local tourist office for the nearest rental firm. The Finland Tourist Board can provide information on cycling tours organized in several centers. There are plenty of country roads ideal for cycling and special bike trails in some areas. Pleasant routes parallel Finland's south coast both west and east of Helsinki. You'll also find good cycling in the lake districts and on the Åland islands.

**France.** You can rent bicycles for day or half-day trips at more than 200 stations of French National Railroads and at other sites. You can cycle over old towpaths beside canals or pedal down tree-lined country lanes. You can explore river valleys and quiet villages, skim along sections of the coast, pedal from château to château, or cycle through vineyards. Local Syndicats d'Initiative (tourist offices) can provide route suggestions.

**Germany.** Travelers can rent bicycles at more than 300 railway stations in scenic areas of Germany; usually you can arrange to return your vehicle at another station if you wish. Rentals are also available at many cycle shops.

Local tourist offices can suggest scenic routes along back roads and special bicycle trails. If you travel through the Neckar valley, stop at the German Bicycle Museum in Neckarsulm, southeast of Bad Wimpfen.

**Ireland.** More than 60 railway stations and many bike shops rent 3-speed bikes with carrier bags for touring. Cyclists should always carry raingear, since weather changes frequently and quickly. Many scenic routes show off the best of Ireland's green countryside, such as the central lakes region, the coast of County Cork, or south-west peninsula routes near Killarney.

**Luxembourg.** Check with local tourist offices for the nearest place to rent bicycles. You can cycle along a pleasant track connecting Diekirch, Echternach, and Vianden.

**Netherlands.** You'll find no better place for cycling than Holland. The countryside is flat yet varied, attractions are close together, and a network of bicycle paths links villages and towns.

Bicycles can be rented at many stations of the Dutch National Railway (and returned at other stations), and at numerous cycle stores and repair shops. Write to the Netherlands Board of Tourism for "Cycling in Holland," a booklet describing independent touring routes and a number of regional cycling packages that include bicycle and equipment, accommodations, meals, and other features.

Local VVV tourist offices have cycling maps (see page 53) at nominal cost outlining scenic routes. Bike trails wind through woods and moors, polders and dunes, past castles and windmills, and through towns and villages.

**Norway.** Many local tourist offices and numerous hotels and guest houses have bicycles for rent by the day. You can enjoy Norway's spectacular scenery on back roads of the Oslomarka district, along the south coast, and beside lakes and fiords.

**Sweden.** Local tourist information offices will help you rent a bicycle. Organized cycling trips are also available. One of the most pleasant regions for cycling is the southern-most province of Skåne, renowned for its sunny "Swedish Riviera" coast and fishing villages, castles and manor houses, orchards and country inns. You can cycle along the Göta Canal towpath or pedal around the flat and friendly islands of Öland and Gotland.

**Switzerland.** Bicycles can be rented at most stations (and returned at other stations) of the Swiss Federal Railways and many private railways, and also at other cycling centers. Reserve your vehicle a day or two in advance, if possible. A cycling leaflet available at Swiss rail stations gives additional information. Many local and regional tourist offices organize cycling weeks.

You can pedal through rural districts such as the Emmental or follow the curving shores of Swiss lakes. Bicycles can be transported on lake steamers or postal buses (advance arrangements necessary) to your destination, then you can bike back leisurely to your starting point.

### If you bring your own bicycle

When most of your holiday will be spent astride a bicycle, you may prefer to bring your own or purchase a new one in Europe.

Most transatlantic airlines allow U.S. and Canadian passengers to take one suitcase and one bicycle on flights to Europe without charging extra for the bicycle, providing it has been properly packed. If you take two suitcases plus the bicycle, you'll be charged extra for the bike. On most flights, the bicycle must be boxed with pedals removed and handlebars parallel to the frame; most airlines provide free bike boxes. Consult the airline for shipping information and excess baggage rates.

If you're bringing your own bicycle, check with appropriate government tourist offices regarding import regulations and required safety equipment.

In Europe, you can arrange to transport your cycle at nominal cost by train; you look after the loading and unloading of the bike. Some postal buses and river, lake, and coastal steamers also transport cycles. It's best to make all arrangements at least a day in advance.

# Zeeland Battles the Sea

Historic merchant towns, water sports, and a fascinating reclamation project draw visitors to the southwest

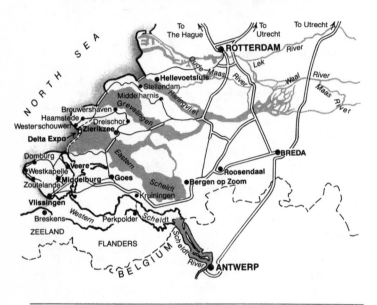

Long arms of the North Sea cut deeply into Holland's southwest coast, leaving Zeeland's lowlands exposed like narrow fingers surrounded by water. For generations, the region's hard-working farmers and fishermen pursued a relatively isolated and independent life, subject to the whims of weather and sea.

Disastrous floods in 1953 triggered a massive hydraulic engineering project that is shutting out the North Sea and gradually transforming some of the wide estuaries into vast fresh-water lakes. This has turned Zeeland into one of Europe's outstanding water sports areas and an increasingly popular destination for family holidays.

Yet tradition remains strong. At festive weekly markets in the larger towns, you'll often see Zeelanders in regional costume strolling amid the stalls. You can join the shoppers on market day—Tuesday in Goes, Thursday in Middelburg and Zierikzee, and Friday in Vlissingen (Flushing).

A pastoral region enhanced by a rich maritime history, Zeeland is accessible by road or rail west from Breda or by road southwest from Rotterdam. Paved highways—some built atop dams and dikes—and long bridges link Zeeland's scattered islands.

From Roosendaal, frequent trains depart for Goes, Middelburg, and Vlissingen; buses link these towns with outlying villages. Ferries cross the Western Scheldt between Vlissingen-Breskens and Kruiningen-Perkpolder. In summer Netherlands Railways operates independent day excursions to Zeeland. Group trips to the Delta Works depart in season from Rotterdam.

Since accommodations are limited, you might settle in one of the larger towns and make day excursions into the countryside. The mild coastal climate attracts visitors from May through September; reservations are essential during July and August, peak season in the beach resorts.

## A continuing struggle against the sea

Over the centuries, the Dutch have labored to reclaim their land from the sea. One of the most ambitious and extensive hydraulic engineering projects ever undertaken is now nearing completion in southwest Holland near the delta of the Rhine, Meuse (Maas), and Scheldt rivers.

Following the tragic Zeeland floods of 1953, all plans for protecting the southwest against future floods were merged into a single encompassing plan called the Delta Project. When the final barrier across the Eastern Scheldt is completed, massive dikes connecting the western tips of land will shorten the Dutch coastline some 425 miles/ 700 km and close out the North Sea. Lakes formed behind the dams are gradually changing to fresh water, increasing Zeeland's water sports attractions. Waterways leading to the ports of Rotterdam and Antwerp will remain open to ship traffic.

You can learn more about this massive project—both the background and the work involved—at the Delta Expo exhibit near Westerschouwen, at the mouth of the Eastern Scheldt. Open from April to mid-October, the exhibit is located on a large work island constructed during the final phase, the building of a 9-km/6-mile storm surge barrier across the mouth of the Eastern Scheldt. Film and slide presentations, models, and photographs give the visitor a broad picture of the plan's scope.

## Exploring the island of Walcheren

Many of Zeeland's attractions are located on Walcheren, an island commanding the entrance to the Western Scheldt and the port of Antwerp. Occupied and fortified by the Nazis in 1940, the Walcheren coast later was bombed by the Allies so the sea would breach the dikes and flood the Germans out. Reclamation was a tremendous task, but finally the land was made productive again—until the floods of 1953.

**Middelburg.** Badly damaged by bombs during World War II, this provincial capital has been rebuilt and restored. Middelburg's impressive town hall, one of the best in the country, faces the market square.

Allow time to walk around. Handsome old buildings reflected in placid canals and the gateways looming above curving streets recall Middelburg's past as a wealthy merchant city. Regional exhibits are displayed in the Zeeland Museum at Abdij 3.

A favorite attraction for both children and adults is Miniature Walcheren (open from early April through September), where you stroll amid small replicas of the island's towns and landmarks.

**Veere.** On the island's northeast rim is historic Veere, now an important yachting and water sports center. Families sail, fish, and water-ski in the Veersemeer, a former estuary now enclosed to form a fresh-water lake—one of the largest lakes in Holland.

Veere acquired most of its wealth during the 15th and 16th century wool trade. Raw wool was shipped here from Scotland, then sent on to Flemish merchants in Bruges, Belgium, to be made into fine cloth. The town hall was built by the wealthy Van Borselen family, who had exclusive rights to the Scottish wool trade; they decorated the exterior with life-size statues of family members. They also began construction of the huge church, later used by Napoleon in 1811 as a hospital for his troops.

Since 1961, yachts have replaced the fishing boats that formerly tied up in Veere's harbor. Breathe in the brisk North Sea breezes as you stride along the dike to the Campveerse Toren, a medieval tower (now a small restaurant) marking the harbor entrance. Continue your walk alongside the yacht harbor to the small museum housed in De Schotse Huizen (Scotch Houses), once used by the guild of Scottish merchants.

**Beach resorts.** On a coastal circuit of the island, points of interest include the family resort of Domburg, the reminders of the Nazi occupation and bombing at Westkapelle, and a series of small beach resorts along the "Zeeland Riviera" facing the Western Scheldt. You can walk along the wide sandy beaches and through the woods sheltered behind the dunes.

Largest of the summer coastal resorts is the port of Vlissingen (Flushing), a shipbuilding and fishing center. Along the promenade, you'll enjoy a good view of shipping traffic plying the Scheldt between Antwerp and the North Sea.

## Other Zeeland landmarks

Main city of South Beveland, Goes is surrounded by farms and fruit orchards. The town's most impressive and historic buildings face a large central square, scene of the Tuesday market.

Continue north across Holland's longest bridge—the Zeelandbrug—to Zierikzee, largest town on the island of Schouwen-Duiveland. A 16th century mood permeates this slumbering old port. High sea walls flank the harbor entrance, and a stately four-spired tower looms above the drawbridge. Impressive gateways mark medieval entrances to the canal-enclosed town, and handsome old buildings border its cobbled streets. In the municipal museum at Meelstraat 8, you'll learn more about Zierikzee's history.

A loop around the island takes you through several villages. Dreischor has one central building containing town hall, school, church, and fire station. The port of Brouwershaven has a noteworthy town hall. On the western tip, Haamstede and Westenschouwen are starting points for brisk walks in the wooded dunes and on quiet beaches.

Veere's town hall was financed by one family's profits from wool trade. Statues commemorate those merchant princes.

Stunning, brilliant color doesn't faze these field workers—they're just checking for diseased tulips.

# Touring the Arnhem Countryside

In the country's heartland, explore attractive towns, visit museums, and follow woodland trails in a national park

**Shallow canals lace Giethoorn, so villagers get around by boat. Attractive houses sit on individual islands.**

Located about 60 miles/100 km southeast of Amsterdam, Arnhem is an excellent base for touring central Holland. Trains serve most of the larger towns, and buses depart in all directions from Arnhem's main station. Walkers and cyclists enjoy trails through the district's wooded parks and along waterways.

Completely rebuilt since World War II, Arnhem is a busy modern city noted for its parks. However, most of the region's attractions lie outside the town. Of special interest are the Netherlands Open-Air Museum (see page 132), landmarks and a museum associated with the Battle of Arnhem (see page 53), and Hoge Veluwe National Park.

## Riverside towns & villages

To see more of this scenic countryside, follow dike-top roads north from Arnhem along the broad IJssel River. Old towns and attractive villages dot the river route, and you'll pass an occasional windmill or castle.

Zutphen's old town is a delightful maze of curving streets and gabled houses. Deventer has developed into an industrial center, yet it retains some handsome old buildings and has an excellent municipal museum in the Weighing House.

Continue north along the IJssel's west bank to Zwolle, an old Hanseatic town at the crossroads of ancient trade routes. Canals outline the boundaries of the medieval city, but most of the ramparts have been replaced by lawns and flower beds. The old town, centered around the Great Church and market square, has an intimate character. Landmark buildings and fortifications date from the early 14th century. The Overijssel Museum faces the Melkmarkt.

Zwolle's Friday morning market draws villagers from outlying agricultural districts. Another lively market is held Thursdays in Meppel; during July and early August, costumed dance groups add a festive air.

West of the main road is Staphorst. Besides its colorfully painted farm buildings, this village is noted for its costumed residents, who follow strict Calvinist religious beliefs and unusual customs. Photographers are resented; visitors are particularly unwelcome on Sundays.

Rustic Giethoorn is unique—a village where nearly all traffic goes by boat. This charming hamlet has no streets, only shallow canals shaped by peat diggers three centuries ago. Houses topped by thatch roofs sit among trees on individual islands, each reached by boat or wooden footbridge. Flat-bottomed boats called "punts" transport cows, villagers, and supplies. You can arrange for a boat ride through the maze of waterways or stroll leisurely along the narrow path beside the main canal.

On your return trip to Arnhem, you'll pass through the rolling farmlands and wooded parks of the Veluwe. Apeldoorn is a lavishly landscaped garden city, encircled by charming villages. The Rijksmuseum Paleis Het Loo is open daily except Monday throughout the year.

Walkers and cyclists enjoy trails through the woodlands and heather-covered moors of Hoge Veluwe National Park. Just east of Otterlo, on a quiet forest road in the park, is the Kröller-Müller art museum, renowned for its outstanding Vincent Van Gogh collection.

# Stroll through Old Bruges

Prosperous merchants shaped this handsome, canal-laced town into a leading medieval trading center

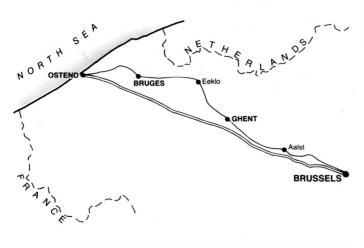

Ornamented buildings and outdoor cafes rim Markt square in Bruges. For this lofty view, climb to top of belfry tower.

A sleepy ambience today pervades the Belgian city of Bruges, one of the great trading centers of Europe in the 14th and 15th centuries. Canals meander through the old Flemish town, and narrow cobbled streets lead past façades little changed in hundreds of years. Art museums display paintings from the city's golden age.

You can reach Bruges in less than an hour by train from Brussels; by road, it's about 60 miles/100 km northwest of the capital.

## An unhurried look at Bruges

In medieval days merchants traveled to Bruges from all parts of the world, sailing up the Zwin River with rich cargoes—wool from Britain, silks from Asia, and spices from the Middle East. Vast fortunes were made in the sea trade and in the manufacture of woolen cloth. Merchant guilds built impressive meeting halls. Prosperous burghers converted their wealth into handsome houses, monuments, and churches, and they encouraged and supported Flemish artists.

But in the 16th century the Zwin silted up. Merchants and bankers moved on to Antwerp, and Bruges became a neglected backwater.

The heart of any Flemish town is its market square.

In Bruges, outdoor cafes and ornamented buildings rim the Markt. Here you'll find the tourist information office, the city's covered market, and the most famous landmark in Bruges—the belfry. If you feel energetic, climb the 365 steps to the top of the tower for a spectacular view.

A side street leads from the Markt to the Burg square. The 14th century Stadhuis contains a colorfully decorated Gothic hall used for weddings and important civic events. Other governmental buildings and the Chapel of the Holy Blood also border the Burg.

Follow the canal southwest to the art treasures of Bruges. Among the old aristocratic houses bordering the water is the Groeninge Museum, containing masterpieces by many of the Flemish painters who contributed to the city's renown. Nearby is the Gruuthuse Museum, former palace of an aristocratic family; it's furnished with decorative and utilitarian objects of the Renaissance. Major works by Hans Memling are housed in the former Hospital of St. John.

Cross the canal bridge leading into the Begijnhof, a secluded compound of small whitewashed houses and a chapel bordering a large parklike square. Founded in the 13th century, it once served as a refuge for devout women whose husbands were off fighting the Crusades. Today Benedictine nuns occupy the convent buildings.

Just beyond is the Minnewater, the busy inner port of Bruges during medieval days. Greenery and massive stone towers of the old city walls frame this peaceful vista.

To learn more about the history and traditions of Bruges and its people, walk northeast from the Markt to the Folklore Museum (Volkskunde) on Balstraat. Across the street at Kantcentrum Brugge, students still learn the fundmentals of lacemaking, a skill practiced in Bruges for hundreds of years.

On pleasant days, small open boats depart from docks along the Rozenhoedkaai and Dyver for half-hour tours of the *reien* (canals). Overhanging willows shade the waterways as you cruise past medieval buildings and beneath arched bridges. Houses of several early merchants have been converted into small hotels.

# Luxembourg— Green Heart of Europe

Uncrowded roads make it easy to enjoy this small country's forested hills, waterways, and pleasant towns

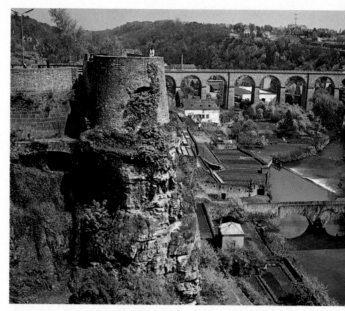

**Ramparts of Luxembourg's capital overlook dramatic bridges and riverside farm plots of deep Alzette valley.**

**Fortified gateway guards entrance to Mersch. Medieval bastions still command views over many towns and river valleys.**

Tucked between Belgium, France, and West Germany in the peaceful green heart of the Continent, the Grand Duchy of Luxembourg is small enough to see in 2 or 3 days of touring. Too often bypassed or visited only briefly by travelers, it can be a restful stopover or a base for leisurely sightseeing.

Uncrowded, well-marked roads lead to medieval towns guarded by ancient fortresses, to rugged forested hill country, and to hillsides covered with vineyards. Posted hiking and cycling paths encircle lakes and wind through valleys and wooded mountains.

The country has only one sizable city: the 1,000-year-old hilltop fortress of Luxembourg City. Perched atop a rocky cliff, this ancient citadel dominates the river valley and newer town below. At night, floodlights illuminate the fortifications, towers, and pointed roofs of the old town.

Until the 19th century, this bastion was stormed repeatedly by nearly every invading army sweeping across the Continent. In 1867 the European powers guaranteed the perpetual neutrality of the Grand Duchy, and now Luxembourg is the center of peaceful endeavors toward a united Europe.

## Stroll around Luxembourg City

Luxembourg City's central gathering spot is the Place d'Armes, the main square of the old town. Here you can sit at outdoor tables, sipping refreshments while watching passers-by or perhaps listening to a band concert. On Wednesday and Saturday mornings, market stalls crowd the Place Guillaume (Kneudler) Square. Cathedral bells echo across the valley on Sunday mornings.

On a stroll around town, you'll pass impressive religious and secular buildings, including the residential palace of H.R.H. the Grand Duke. The promenade around the city's ramparts offers good views over the valley and its striking bridges.

Most of the old fortifications have been transformed into attractive parks, particularly around the lower town. However, you can still visit the Bock Casemates, a network of underground passages hewn from solid rock commanding the Alzette valley.

Outside the city is an eloquent reminder of World War II—the immaculately groomed U.S. military cemetery. Here lie more than 5,000 American soldiers, many of whom died during the Battle of the Bulge in the winter of 1944–45. The grave of their renowned commander, General George S. Patton Jr., is at the top of a grassy slope.

From Luxembourg City you can make a circuit of the small country, sampling its varied landscapes—the vineyard district along the Moselle (Mosel), the wild rocky region known as "Little Switzerland," and the forested mountains and swift rivers of the Ardennes.

## Vineyards & wooded ravines

Neatly tended vineyards cover the hills along the Moselle River on the country's southeastern border. From spring through autumn, you can visit wine cellars between the towns of Remich and Grevenmacher, perhaps buying a bottle of the delicate white wine to go with a picnic lunch of smoked Ardennes ham.

Along the Moselle, strollers enjoy tree-shaded walks. You'll see anglers casting from the shore, and chugging canal boats transporting freight.

Echternach and Berdorf are favorite summer resorts near the entrance to "Little Switzerland," an area of wooded ravines and unusual rock formations. Echternach's medieval buildings form the backdrop for the town's festive Whit Tuesday dancing procession. The ruins of two castles tower over Larochette, a charming old market town set in a narrow wooded valley.

"Little Switzerland" is a hiker's paradise. Dozens of footpaths crisscross its wooded hills and quiet valleys, and lead to waterfalls, rocky areas, and scenic view points. Many visitors come here for fishing, canoeing, and rock climbing. One scenic route follows the valley of the Ernz Noir River through the Mullerthal.

## Delightful Vianden

The ruins of an immense feudal fortress loom over Vianden, a charming town on the Our River near Luxembourg's northeastern border. Below, ancient ramparts with their watchtowers still encircle the town, whose origins go back to the 9th century.

One of the country's beauty spots, Vianden provides a good base for exploring the Ardennes, the rugged forested strip extending across northern Luxembourg and eastern Belgium. The town's diversions are quiet ones—strolling through narrow curving streets or along the Our River. A chairlift provides access to a view point high over the valley. One of numerous forest paths leads upriver to the castle ruins of Stolzembourg and Falkenstein.

Victor Hugo lived at Vianden during his exile from France, and a small but interesting museum is housed in his former home near the bridge.

## Relaxing in the Ardennes

Fast-moving rivers cut the forested hills in the northern part of the country. The Ardennes region was the scene of fierce fighting during the last winter of World War II, culminating in the famous Battle of the Bulge.

Today this hilly, wooded countryside draws vacationing families, who enjoy the region's recreational attractions. Marked walking paths follow waterways and wind through the forested hills. Lakes and rivers attract anglers and boaters. Campgrounds mushroom with brightly colored tents.

Diekirch is a favorite waterside resort for fishing and canoeing on the Sûre River. You can see well-preserved Roman mosaics here and the Celtic dolmen called "Devil's Altar."

In Clervaux, a modern abbey rises alongside the 12th century castle, the latter heavily damaged during the Ardennes offensive in 1944. Clervaux's museum of World War II memorabilia is overshadowed by the town's magnificent permanent collection of photographs by the late Edward Steichen, a native of Luxembourg.

Follow the Clerve River south to the village of Kautenbach, a good starting point for excursions into the western valleys. In the spring you may see canoe competitions on the Clerve and Wiltz rivers.

A medieval castle dominates the whitewashed city of Wiltz and its surrounding countryside. This Ardennes tourist center contains a museum commemorating the Battle of the Bulge. (Another war museum lies across the Belgian border in Bastogne.)

An impressive setting distinguishes the small market town of Esch-sur-Sûre. Surrounded by steep hills and almost encircled by the Sûre River, the town's houses cluster around a high rock crowned by ruins of a once-mighty castle. The lake of the upper Sûre attracts water sports enthusiasts.

Both Ettelbruck and Mersch are important crossroads towns. You can return to the capital through the Mamer valley via Kopstal, starting point for visits to nearby prehistoric caves, Celtic shelters, and the remains of a Roman temple.

# Getting to Know Some Europeans

Learn about other countries and their customs from new acquaintances along your route

Travel can be a real adventure when you reach out to meet new people. Yet all too often, travelers return from abroad having seen the sights but without getting to know any local people. Whether you rely on an informal network of personal contacts, participate in sponsored "people-to-people" programs, or stimulate informal conversation with people you come across, making new friends enriches your travels.

Even people who don't share the same language can communicate surprisingly well with smiles and gestures. A warm handshake, a shared bottle of wine, and mutual enjoyment of an experience give a feeling of contentment.

Sincere and obvious interest in another person's way of life can help you to really learn about a country and its customs.

## Personal contacts

Your friends or relatives may have acquaintances abroad whom you can call upon. When you bring greetings from a mutual acquaintance, you'll usually find a cordial reception. If you're contacting the friend of a friend, you may prefer to introduce yourself ahead of time by letter. Once you're on the scene, invite the person to join you for coffee or drinks at your hotel or a nearby spot.

Wait to establish a first-name basis, taking your cue from your new acquaintance. Some nationalities are rela-

tively reserved, others more spontaneous and friendly.

If you're invited to a home, don't be certain that the invitation includes a meal unless it's specified. It's customary to take along a small gift or a few flowers and to arrive promptly. If you're in doubt about local customs, inquire at the tourist information office.

## People-to-people programs

Various government-sponsored programs and unofficial service, educational, and social organizations match travelers with residents having similar careers, interests, or affiliations.

Before you leave home, check with the appropriate national tourist offices to learn about opportunities for meeting local people. You can "Get in Touch with the Dutch" in Amsterdam, "Meet the Swiss" in Zurich, "Know the Norwegians" in Oslo, "Meet the Danes" in Odense and Århus, and "Meet the Irish" in various cities. Some German cities also sponsor introductory contacts. (For other countries, you can inquire locally if similar programs are available.)

Through these free programs, visitors can meet a family at home for an evening of conversation, seeing how they live and exchanging ideas over a friendly cup of coffee or tea. Neither meals nor lodging is included. Some programs do not operate during the summer.

When you arrive, check in with the local tourist office in the participating city. Within 24 to 48 hours, the office arranges for you to visit a local English-speaking host family whose background and interests are similar to yours. To learn more about Ireland's hospitality program, write to the Irish Tourist Board well in advance of your trip.

## Informal meetings

You don't have to be a linguist to meet people, though even a few phrases in the local language will bring pleased smiles. But you'll feel more confident if you know something about local customs and have a bilingual dictionary handy.

**Talk to strangers.** Pull out your map and ask local people for directions. Once you've made contact, ask about places to visit or a good restaurant for dinner. Children may be shy, but braver ones enjoy practicing English.

**Share your table.** When a European restaurant is full, diners often share tables with strangers. If you see others doing it, indicate your willingness to the management. On a train, share a bag of candy with others in your compartment. Eating with strangers can be a highlight of your trip.

**Stay in small hotels.** When you stay longer than overnight in a small hotel, you mingle with the same people. In many small English hotels, guests gather in the bar before dinner and converse after dinner over coffee in the living room.

**Live with a family.** Spending a few days with a family as a paying guest, you experience a foreign life style firsthand. Several countries have programs where visitors stay with a farm family (see page 140).

# In the Low Countries

## BATTLEFIELD MEMORIALS

Many famous battles of World Wars I and II have been fought in these countries.

In central Holland, landmarks and memorials recall the Battle of Arnhem, World War II's greatest airborne operation. You can visit a museum housed in the former Hotel Hartenstein, Allied headquarters during the battle. A detailed brochure is available from the Netherlands Board of Tourism or at local VVV (tourist information) offices.

The Battle of the Bulge was fought in the Ardennes Mountains spanning eastern Belgium and northern Luxembourg. The Bastogne Historical Center in Belgium, and Luxembourg museums in Wiltz, Clervaux, Diekirch, and Ettelbruck, recall this famous conflict.

## LUXEMBOURG MINI-TRAIN

Learn about Luxembourg's dramatic history on a 45-minute mini-train ride through the Petrusse Valley. Trips depart from the center of Luxembourg-City and pass the old fortification walls and remnants of the medieval city.

## DUTCH FOLKLORE & CRAFTS

In summer, market towns throughout the Netherlands sponsor folklore markets. Costumed residents perform country dances, and crafts people demonstrate traditional skills such as shearing sheep, hand-carving wooden shoes, and weaving willow twigs into baskets. You can sample Dutch cheeses, *poffertjes* (tiny round pancakes), *stroopwafels* (syrup waffles), and local cookies and breads.

Watch artisans at work, view displays on traditional Dutch crafts, and purchase handcrafted items at Amsterdam's Dutch Art Centre, located at Nieuwendijk 16 in the heart of the old city. You can visit daily from 10 a.m. to 5 p.m. from February through September (closed Mondays in February and March).

## EUROPE'S FLOWER GARDEN

Holland's floral calendar peaks in spring, when vast bulb fields brighten the countryside and fruit orchards burst into bloom. Also in spring, the Keukenhof exhibition garden near Lisse (a day trip southwest of Amsterdam) presents a breathtaking floral display. Flower pageants continue through the summer and into early autumn.

For a list of floral events and locations of outstanding displays, write to the Netherlands Board of Tourism.

## ART MUSEUMS

The Low Countries have a rich artistic heritage. The work of master painters—old and new—can be seen and savored at museums throughout the region.

More than 100 museums in the Netherlands display paintings by Rembrandt, Van Gogh, Vermeer, Hals, Mondriaan, and other renowned Dutch artists.

Belgium takes enormous pride in its great masters—Memling, Van Dyck, Brueghel, Rubens, Van Eyck—and modern surrealists such as Delvaux and Magritte.

Works by Luxembourg artists such as Kutter hang with art by painters from abroad in Luxembourg's State Museum.

## RAIL TRAVEL

Netherlands Railways offers 3-day and 7-day passes entitling the holder to unlimited first or second-class rail travel on all Dutch railways. Single-day excursion fares feature many of the country's attractions. Also available are 3-day and 7-day passes on trams and buses. For information contact the Netherlands Board of Tourism.

Belgium's Tourist Pass can be purchased for first or second-class travel for 5, 10, or 15 days. Weekend tickets and other rail travel concessions are also available. You can obtain information on rail tickets and excursions from the Belgian Tourist Office and at railroad stations in Belgium.

Luxembourg National Railways offers weekend and holiday return tickets, as well as 1-day, 5-day, and 1-month network tickets valid for unlimited rail and bus travel. Travelers over 65 years of age qualify for reduced fares. For information on various tickets, write to the Luxembourg National Tourist Office.

## TOURING AIDS

Automobile club members can purchase detailed regional motoring and cycling maps issued by the ANWB, the Dutch Automobile Club. (Membership card must be presented at time of purchase.) Available at ANWB offices in Amsterdam (Museumplein 5 and Surinameplein 33) and around the country, the maps indicate locations of windmills, castles, bulb fields, view points, hiking trails, and other points of interest.

Information on motoring and cycling in Holland is available from the Netherlands Board of Tourism.

## ENJOY THE OUTDOORS

During your holiday in the Low Countries, you'll find marvelous opportunities for water sports, hiking, fishing, cycling, horseback riding, golf, tennis, and other activities.

Write to the appropriate government tourist office for information on your favorite sport. After you arrive, check with local tourist information offices about organized walking trips, cycling routes, and other specific and timely information.

## HOLLAND CARDS

Non-residents of the Netherlands can purchase two special cards, the Holland Culture Card and the Holland Leisure Card, that offer discounted or free benefits on specified travel, tours, restaurants, shopping, entertainment, and attractions. The Culture Card includes a National Museumcard, covering entry to more than 300 museums.

For information describing the features of each card and how to order, contact the Netherlands Board of Tourism.

**For information on travel in the Low Countries, write to the Netherlands Board of Tourism, the Belgian Tourist Office, and the Luxembourg National Tourist Office (addresses on page 7).**

# Bavaria's Royal Castles & Cozy Towns

Visit extravagant castles built by an eccentric king, and relax in Germany's alpine vacationland

Eccentric European monarchs have added a colorful touch to the history and landscape of the Continent. Among the strangest was King Ludwig II of Bavaria, who erected a trio of fanciful castles in the foothills of the Bavarian Alps.

After becoming king at the age of 19 in 1864, Ludwig soon became notorious for his theatrical and bizarre behavior. He had two great passions: the building of extravagant castles and a lifelong infatuation with composer Richard Wagner and his music. Ludwig's ambitious projects depleted the royal treasury and ultimately caused him to be deposed in 1886. Three days later, he died under mysterious circumstances in Starnberger See near Berg.

On a loop south of Munich, you can visit four royal castles: Hohenschwangau (the country palace of the Bavarian royal family) and Ludwig's three exuberant structures (Neuschwanstein, built atop a mountain; Linderhof, nestled deep in the forest; and Herrenchiemsee, rising on an island in the middle of an Alpine lake).

Ludwig's mountain kingdom is now Germany's Alpine playground. Snowy peaks form an awesome backdrop to mountain lakes and chalet villages. In Bavarian towns, attractive old houses with wide eaves and flower-filled balconies line the streets; paintings depicting religious or folk scenes adorn many façades. Slim belfries rise above stately churches.

The Bavarian Alpine resorts are at their busiest in winter, when crowds flock to Garmisch-Partenkirchen and smaller towns for skiing, skating, and other winter sports. In summer the mountain towns attract hikers and mountaineers. Trains on the Munich-Innsbruck line serve several of the larger Bavarian resorts.

## Ludwig's magnificent castles

As you drive south through the Lech valley toward Füssen, the spurs of the Alps provide a magnificent vista.

Begin your journey at Hohenschwangau, once the rural retreat of the Bavarian royal family. Young Ludwig spent his summers here, dreaming of Teutonic legends. The castle, rising on a wooded spur, overlooks a small lake rimmed by mountains.

**Hohenschwangau.** Built in the 1830s by Maximilian II of Bavaria, Hohenschwangau has the warmth of a lived-in castle. Its walls and ceilings are elaborately decorated; many murals portray medieval heroes. The family's swan motif appears frequently.

Ludwig II was an admirer and patron of composer Richard Wagner, who visited Hohenschwangau many times. Mementoes of their long association are displayed in the music room on the second floor. From his bedroom window at Hohenschwangau, Ludwig could watch through a telescope the building progress at Neuschwanstein.

**Neuschwanstein.** Perched on a craggy rock above dark green pines, Neuschwanstein exemplifies a child's fantasy of a fairy-tale castle. Grayish white towers and turrets give the feudal-style keep a dreamlike appearance.

As you walk up the long approach road, you begin to appreciate the difficulty of constructing such a massive project on this isolated site. (Tired sightseers can arrange to ride up the hill in a horse-drawn cart.)

Neuschwanstein's interior is equally remarkable: rooms decorated with marble, gilded paneling, heavy tapestries, magnificent chandeliers and candelabras. You'll see Ludwig's artificial grotto and the great Singer's Hall (a pair of triumphant shrines to Wagnerian heroes), the unfinished throne room, and the castle kitchens.

**Linderhof.** Built in the 1870s, this small creamy white villa nestles in a wooded valley west of Oberammergau. Although it was used primarily as a royal hunting lodge, Linderhof is a palatial gem combining Italian Renaissance and baroque styles. Opulent decorations adorn the interior.

Surrounding the castle is a magnificent park containing formal gardens, fountains, and pools. Don't miss the Moorish pavilion and artificial grotto that Ludwig used whenever he decided to play Oriental potentate.

**Herrenchiemsee.** Ludwig's last palatial indulgence was Herrenchiemsee, built on a wooded island in the Chiemsee, largest of the Bavarian lakes. Visitors reach the island by boat from the Prien-Stock dock.

Inspired by a visit to the palace of Versailles, Ludwig began construction on this castle in 1878. In the next seven years he spent 20 million marks, virtually exhausting the royal treasury.

Herrenchiemsee's royal apartments are lavishly decorated. On Saturday evenings in summer, chamber music concerts are presented by candlelight in the magnificent Hall of Mirrors as giant fountains play on the terrace.

## Relaxing in the Bavarian Alps

Ludwig's castles are only one of Bavaria's attractions. All around are charming villages to explore, Alpine trails to hike, and snowy peaks to climb. Chair lifts and aerial tramways provide access to the heights.

Garmisch-Partenkirchen, site of the 1936 Winter Olympics, is Germany's leading winter sports center. Its excellent skiing and skating facilities attract a fashionable international crowd. Life is quieter in summer, when days usually are spent outdoors—in the mountains, by the lakes, or strolling around the twin towns.

If time limits you to a single mountain goal, it might as well be the highest one around—the 9,731-foot/2,966-meter Zugspitze. Its spectacular panorama has been called the finest in Europe. A large deck offers you a quick tan in the clear, thin air and a view of the skiers on the slopes below. If the weather turns cold or windy, you can retreat to the glass-enclosed restaurant. You can make the ascent in two ways: by narrow-gauge cog railway from Garmisch or by aerial tram from the Eibsee.

If you want to do some hiking, take the cable car from the village of Partenkirchen up the Wank, a lower peak (5,840 feet/1,780 meters) traversed by Alpine footpaths. You look down on lovely towns snugly encircled by great peaks. Another excursion leads up the Partnach gorge south of Partenkirchen. Take along a raincoat to visit the Partnachklamm; the rocky path crosses the gorge in two narrow places where spray from the waterfalls drops on hikers.

Mittenwald nestles in a valley near the Austrian border, protected by the rocky wall of the Karwendel. An array of colorful houses brightens the town; many of them are painted with historical or Biblical scenes. Skilled craftsmen have made stringed instruments here for nearly 300 years, and a museum shows the evolution of the craft.

Attractive Oberammergau is known both for fine woodcarving and for its Passion Play, presented every 10 years (next in 1990). A Biblical atmosphere pervades the town; many façades display murals with Biblical scenes, and streets bear names from the Bible. Originating in 1634, the Passion Play fulfills a vow by the people of the village to present a play depicting the Passion of Christ once each decade if the ravages of a widespread plague were ended. All of the participants come from the town, and more than a half-million spectators witness the all-day performances each decade.

Northwest of Oberammergau, off the main roads, you'll find the exuberantly adorned church of Wies, considered by connoisseurs to be the most beautiful rococo church in Germany. Its simple exterior contrasts with the rich but harmonious decorations found inside.

Wooded mountains rise dramatically behind Linderhof Castle, a palatial villa built by Ludwig II as a hunting lodge.

Balconies, flowers, and frescoes brighten chalets in Mittenwald. Violin making is a 300-year-old tradition here.

FED.
REP.
OF
GERMANY
Bonn

# Scenic Routes through the Black Forest

Folk traditions and rural crafts linger in the wooded hills and valleys of southwestern Germany

Lush field at edge of Black Forest keeps cows satisfied. Large farmhouse shelters family and animals under same roof.

## Scenic roads link forest towns

Three north-south routes connect Baden-Baden with Freudenstadt. The Black Forest High Road cuts south through forest and mountain landscape and charming villages; the Black Forest Low Road follows the Murg valley through Gernsbach and Forbach; and the Baden Wine Road links wine villages of the western foothills.

No single route dominates the country south of Freudenstadt, though main roads follow the valleys of the Kinzig and Gutach rivers. Allow at least a full half-day for driving between Freudenstadt and Freiburg. Many forest roads are narrow and winding, and main routes are often crowded. Marked trails lead into the woods from villages and forest car parks.

Hikers work off hearty meals roaming countless miles of well-maintained trails—through woodlands, across lush meadows, up winding ridges, and down wild gorges. Southern mountain lakes attract swimmers and sailors. When snow falls, ski-touring and sleigh riding dominate winter activity.

On weekdays you can watch craftsmen blow glass and cut crystal by hand at the glassworks in Wolfach.

In Triberg's Heimatmuseum you can learn about Black Forest history, customs, folk dress, and crafts. Or you might follow the path from the Gutach bridge up the shaded ravine to beautiful Gutach Falls. Old Black Forest farm buildings have been assembled in the Gutach open-air museum.

Furtwangen's clock museum displays cuckoo clocks and other historic timepieces. West of Furtwangen, up the Katzensteig valley, you can visit the source of the Danube River.

From Freiburg, a road leads east through the wild and rocky Höllental (Hell Valley) to Titisee, a jewel-like lake set in a mighty forest.

Though its name may sound foreboding, the Black Forest is no more sinister than the cuckoo clocks it produces. Nestled in Germany's southwest corner in the elbow of the Rhine River, it stretches for more than 100 miles/160 km north to Karlsruhe. Dark evergreens cover the slopes of the smoothly rounded mountains, giving the region its name, but the valleys are green with open fields.

For more than a century, visitors have come to this year-round holiday area to enjoy bracing air, mountain scenery, and rustic charm. Small family-owned hotels and pensions house the out-of-towners.

Dotting the countryside are large wooden farmhouses, each sheltering people and animals under a single roof. In some areas, such as the Gutach and Kinzig valleys, villagers still don traditional dress for church and local festivals. Hand-carved cuckoo clocks have been made here for more than 200 years.

FED. REP. OF GERMANY

Bonn

# Along Germany's Romantic Road

Walk the ramparts and cobbled streets of these enchanting medieval towns

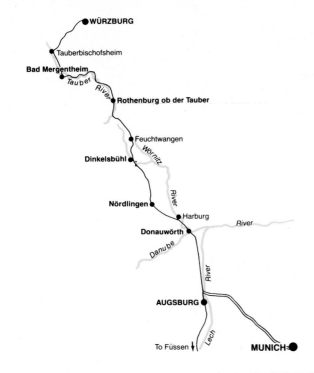

WÜRZBURG
Tauberbischofsheim
Bad Mergentheim
Tauber River
Rothenburg ob der Tauber
Feuchtwangen
Wörnitz
Dinkelsbühl
River
Nördlingen
Harburg
Donauwörth
River
Danube
River
AUGSBURG
To Füssen
Lech
MUNICH

Strollers in Rothenburg enjoy town ramparts, sturdy buildings enhanced by flowers, wrought iron signs and lanterns.

Romantics with a passion for the past will want to take their time exploring along Germany's delightful *Romantische Strasse* (Romantic Road), which wends south from Würzburg through farm lands to the Austrian border.

Along this ancient route are venerable walled towns that escaped destruction during the devastating Thirty Years' War (1618–1648) and survived World War II bombing raids nearby. High ramparts studded with gates and watchtowers surround the towns. You pass through thick gates into a medieval world of gabled buildings and cobblestone streets. Wrought iron signs announce shops.

This is a route for lingering and dreaming. You'll enjoy the region best if you travel by car, stopping where and when you like. No trains reach these towns, but buses operate daily from late March to early November between Würzburg and Augsburg; stops are brief, so you may wish to plan at least one overnight stay.

## A trio of medieval gems

Highlights of the Romantic Road are three walled towns—Rothenburg, Dinkelsbühl, and Nördlingen. Each is a large, open-air medieval museum of gabled buildings and ancient squares, cobblestone streets and twisting alleys. Obtain a town map at the local tourist office, then let your whims guide your explorations.

Captivating Rothenburg ob der Tauber has been called Germany's best-preserved medieval town. (It's a popular stopping place, however, so traffic and crowds can be a nuisance in summer and on weekends.) Facing the Marktplatz is the imposing town hall and the Ratstrinkstube tavern, where carved characters in the gable clock enact the local wine legend hourly between 11 A.M. and 3 P.M. Gabled mansions built by prosperous burghers line the Herrngasse, which leads to a garden overlooking the valley. Allow time for a leisurely walk along the ramparts surrounding the town. The St. Jakob-Kirche contains a magnificent carved altarpiece by Tilman Riemenschneider.

Quiet waters of a reed-bordered moat reflect Dinkelsbühl's walls and watchtowers. Inside the ramparts, tall gabled buildings brightened by blooming flowers face the main square. You can climb to the top of the church bell tower for a view over the town.

Nördlingen's remarkable perimeter wall completely encircles the town; many of its fortified gateways and towers are topped by helmet-shaped roofs. Another striking asset is the baroque 15th century church, whose majestic tower rises nearly 300 feet/100 meters above the red roofs. Narrow cobbled streets stretch like spokes from the Marktplatz to various old market districts and craftsmen's quarters. Buildings reflect Nördlingen's medieval wealth and local pride.

# Through the Fairy-tale Countryside

Folk tales and legends abound in the Weser valley hills and the thick forests of the Harz Mountains

Village, woods, and green Diemel valley are the scenic reward for a climb up tower of 12th century Trendelburg Castle.

In old brewery town of Einbeck, many wooden buildings are enhanced by carved and painted ornamentation.

Brave princes and captivating golden-haired princesses, mean stepmothers and wicked witches, industrious dwarfs and bewitched animals—these characters popularized by the brothers Grimm originated in the folk tales of central Germany.

In the early 19th century, Jacob and Wilhelm Grimm lived in Kassel, working as court librarians while gathering legends and traditional stories in the surrounding villages. They collected some 200 tales, including such classic characters as Hansel and Gretel, Snow White, Rumpelstiltskin, and Little Red Riding Hood. Kassel's tribute to this illustrious pair is the Brothers Grimm Museum, where their manuscripts and mementoes reintroduce you to your childhood memories.

A pleasant loop through this unspoiled region begins by following a section of the German Fairy-tale Road (*Die Deutsche Märchenstrasse*), a route that meanders from the brothers' birthplace of Hanau (east of Frankfurt), north about 350 miles/600 km to Bremen.

In this land of once-upon-a-time, it's often uncertain where history ends and legend begins. However, you'll find much more than fairy tales in the rolling hill country of the Weser valley and the thick forests of the Harz Mountains. You can wander on foot through medieval towns, stay in country castles or historic hotels, explore forest trails and mountain ravines.

Trains and buses serve the large cities and towns, but you'll find motoring the best way to enjoy the area. In summer, passenger boats cruise the Weser between Hann.-Münden and Hameln.

## Elegant houses & hilltop castles

In its upper reaches, the Weser River is a scenic stream, bordered by charming towns and villages that resemble illustrations in a children's storybook.

Towns large and small boast lovely old houses—elegant timber-framed buildings (*Fachwerkhäuser*) as well as sandstone ones built in the local architectural style (known as Weser Renaissance) with characteristic scroll-work and pinnacles on the gables. Gray slate or weathered pink limestone tiles cover the roofs. Frescoes or folk sayings sometimes ornament the façades.

Hann. Münden lies at the confluence of the Fulda and Werra rivers, which join to form the Weser. After a look at the gabled Rathaus (town hall), stroll through the old section to admire some of the town's 450 half-timbered houses and a 14th century bridge across the Werra.

Follow the Weser river north toward Karlshafen. If you like, veer northwest from Veckerhagen into the wooded Reinhardswald toward a pair of medieval castles (both are now hotels). Twin black-domed towers rise above romantic 14th century Sababurg (locally called "Sleeping Beauty's castle"), deep in the forest northeast of Hofgeismar off the main road. Even older is 12th century Trendelburg Castle, perched on a wooded hilltop above its village and the Diemel valley. The ruins of Krukenburg overlook the town of Helmarshausen.

From Karlshafen continue downstream to Fürstenberg, famous for its porcelain.

The pleasant riverside town of Höxter is a stroller's delight. It's filled with colorful houses ornamented with decorative woodwork; many have folk sayings or proverbs inscribed on their façades.

In Bodenwerder, a museum displays mementoes of the town's best-known resident, the legendary Baron Hieronymus von Münchhausen, renowned for his tall tales of adventure.

A special place in German folklore belongs to Hameln and its famed rat catcher, the Pied Piper. Townspeople dramatize the legend on summer Sundays at noon in the old town. (Rat-shaped souvenirs are a local specialty.) Clustered around the medieval town center are many handsome old houses.

East of the Weser, you'll enjoy a stop in Einbeck, famed in the Middle Ages as the home of 600 breweries. Carvings touched with color brighten the 16th century wooden houses grouped around the Marktplatz. Many houses have large attic vents, indicating that hops and barley were probably stored there. Facing a pedestrian mall are more attractive old structures; they include the Rathaus with its pair of unusual conical projections, and the Ratswaage, its wooden façade festooned with carved ornamentation.

## A visit to medieval Goslar

Of the many towns at the foot of the Harz Mountains, the most important is the imperial city of Goslar, more than a thousand years old and one of Germany's classic medieval cities. You can easily spend a full day exploring this fascinating place.

Once a favorite residence of the emperors of the Holy Roman Empire, Goslar began to boom when rich ore deposits were discovered in the Harz. In the early 16th century, prospering merchants and skilled craftsmen built an impressive town hall, mighty churches, richly decorated guildhalls, and timber-fronted houses ornamented with elaborately carved oriel windows (*Erker*). Moats and high walls, marked by sturdy towers and gates, encircled the town. Goslar began to decline about 1550, and it remained substantially undisturbed for several hundred years.

Begin your exploration at the dignified Marktplatz, the town's central gathering place. Here you'll find the arcaded Rathaus, the spire-topped Marktkirche, and the traditional old (1494) Hotel Kaiserworth, one of several historic structures now housing travelers.

Stop at the tourist office for a map and sightseeing information, then set out on foot. Intricately designed houses framed in timber and roofed in slate face the central square and line narrow side streets. Models of medieval Goslar are displayed in the Goslarer Museum; historic paintings and imperial mementoes can be seen in the Kaiserpfalz (Imperial Palace). One of the most pleasant walks parallels the Gose stream that flows through the old town.

## Hikers enjoy the Harz Mountains

If you enjoy the outdoors, you may wish to join those who have made the Harz a popular holiday area. Visitors flock to its resorts and spas and hike through the pine forests. Biking and hiking paths link towns and villages, and many mountain trails begin and end at car parking areas. Miniature cottages in wooded glens remind you of Hansel and Gretel. In winter, snow blankets the hills.

Rugged, wooded hills rise suddenly out of the north German lowlands, topping all the surrounding foothills and straddling the border between West and East Germany. Highest point is Mount Brocken in East Germany; according to legend, witches astride broomsticks gather on Brocken's summit on Walpurgis night (April 30) for revelry until dawn.

Clausthal-Zellerfeld was once the mining capital of the upper Harz Mountains; the Zellerfeld museum illustrates some unusual local mining methods. From here you return to Goslar through the Oker valley, one of the most scenic of the Harz ravines. On sunny days sailboats glide across the broad Oker reservoir.

# Live Like Royalty in Castles & Mansions

Hilltop fortresses and stately country homes open their doors to guests as historic hotels

As you travel in the European countryside, you'll discover many ancient castles, baronial mansions, and old monasteries that have been transformed into delightful hotels.

Crossing the narrow bridge over the old moat to reach a castle's inner courtyard, you enter another era. Your imagination is quickly captured by the fairy-tale aura of these buildings, where you dine and rest in settings once reserved for nobility. From your tower room, you can gaze in a lordly fashion over village, fields, and vineyards.

Castle hotels and stately homes have diverse charms, but they reflect a certain style in appointments and way of living. A romantic air lingers. Some historic hotels serve their guests fish or game from the estate and wine made from grapes grown in the castle vineyards.

Frequently your host is also the owner. Some buildings have housed family members for many generations. Many accommodations have been opened to the public to supplement funds needed for costly repairs, maintenance, and taxes.

Not all accommodations are grandiose: some lodgings are relatively intimate. Rates vary, from surprisingly reasonable at some hotels to expensive at those offering elegant appointments and cuisine. Some castles close for brief periods in late autumn and winter.

Government tourist offices can provide information on castle hotels, and several books describe these historic hostelries. Some airlines and travel operators arrange itineraries featuring accommodations in castles or historic inns; see your travel agent for current offerings.

## Castle touring in Britain & Ireland

It's easy to return to the days of chivalry in Britain and Ireland. Historic strongholds there are marvelous settings for imaginary medieval living. You may pass a knight's armor in the hall on your way to your canopied bed.

**Britain.** Accommodations in castle hotels and stately homes range from Spartan simplicity to regal elegance and luxury. Some of the country's castles are more than 700 years old.

If you'd like to spend a weekend as a guest at a country estate with the marquess or duke as your host, it can be arranged discreetly and courteously by a London agency—for a hefty price. You'll get acquainted with your host over tea, take a tour of the house and grounds, dress for dinner and partake with the family and other guests, and spend the night in a room furnished with antiques.

For a different experience, consider the great Victorian and Edwardian hotels built in the mid-19th century. Spacious and uncrowded, British Railway Hotels echo with memories of a more leisurely age.

If you believe that small is beautiful, you'll find many independent hotels, including those of the Prestige Hotels consortium, that strive to provide personal service and luxury to guests.

For information on castle hotels, overnight visits to stately homes, and other hotels with special appeal, write to the British Tourist Authority.

**Ireland.** Castles were built for strength rather than beauty in Ireland. Mellowed by time, they evoke memories of the country's colorful families and tempestuous history.

Twelve Irish castles are now hotels; three of them date from the 12th century. All offer not only history but warm hospitality amid luxurious furnishings. Guests spend days exploring the countryside, fishing, riding, playing golf, or enjoying other outdoor activities. For a descriptive leaflet on the castle hotels—or castles that you can rent—write to the Irish Tourist board.

## France's châteaux & country hotels

Travelers who relish the luxurious life enjoy France's châteaux hotels. These renowned establishments can be found in all parts of the country—perched atop cliffs, commanding valleys and rivers, surrounded by manicured fields. Each has its own personality, history, and décor. Other elegant country hotels occupy former abbeys, coaching inns, mills, and manor houses.

Many of France's outstanding country hotels and restaurants belong to an association—Relais de Campagne, Châteaux-Hôtels, and Relais Gourmands. A current directory of member hostelries can be purchased in travel bookstores or through the organization's representative (see page 41). The French Government can also provide information on country hotels.

## Historic hotels in the Netherlands

If you enjoy hotels with special atmosphere, you'll find several dozen possibilities in the Netherlands.

You can sleep under the gabled roof of a stately country castle, stroll through its gardens or wooded park, and dine by candlelight amid antiques. Write to the Netherlands Board of Tourism for a list of castles and country estates that are now hotels.

## Ancient castles of Central Europe

Many of the fine old castles of Austria, Germany, and Switzerland date from the Middle Ages, when they were built as defensive fortresses crowning wooded hills and commanding river valleys. Feudal rulers often collected tolls from passing travelers. Other castles were built as country residences or retreats.

These noble shelters differ extensively in size, age, original purpose, and state of repair. Properly, a fortified castle built as a defensive stronghold is called a *Burg;* often it is enclosed or flanked by mossy ruined walls and ancient towers. A residential castle or manor house is a *Schloss;* many have been owned by the same families for generations and continuously occupied for centuries.

**Austria.** You can stay in more than two dozen castle hotels and elegant mansions in Austria—above the Danube or beside a lake, near health resorts, high in the mountains, or in former hunting lodges in the forest.

They reflect the luxurious style and comfort enjoyed by generations of royalty who passed the time in pleasant diversions on their private reserves. You'll find forest paths for walking, trails for riding, hunting and trout fishing on the castle preserve, and other outdoor attractions. Lakeside castles have private beaches. Many hotels pride themselves on their cuisine and wine cellars.

For descriptive information, write to the Austrian National Tourist Office for "Castle Hotels and Mansions in Austria."

**Germany.** About 50 German castle hotels belong to an association called Gast im Schloss (Guest in a Castle). An illustrated directory describing the member hotels is available from the German National Tourist Office.

You can sleep in a four-poster bed in a medieval castle that crowns a wooded hill or sample wine made from a castle's own vineyards. Though dungeon towers have been converted into honeymoon suites and ancient moats replaced by tennis courts, the charming castles cling to an aura of mystery and romance.

**Switzerland.** For information on historic castle hotels, write to the Swiss National Tourist Office. Some castles are

situated in parklike grounds encircled by trees or a moat; others enjoy a dramatic site edging a lake or dominating a town from a wooded slope.

## Elegance prevails at Italy's historic hotels

Many of Italy's medieval and Renaissance castles and patrician villas have been converted into elegant hotels and restaurants. Located in all parts of the country, these venerable structures now house hotels and pensions in a broad range of price categories. You can also stay in former palaces; in convents, cloisters, and monasteries; and in historic townhouses and country villas once owned by Italian aristocrats. For a copy of the booklet "Hotels & Restaurants in Italy of Special Interest," write to the Italian Government Travel Office.

## Finding your castles in Spain & Portugal

Many former castles, palaces, convents, and monasteries in Spain and Portugal have been transformed into government-operated hotels of exceptional ambience. In settings of regal splendor or intimate charm, the *paradores* of Spain (see page 117) and *pousadas* of Portugal (see page 125) are enjoying renewed activity and international renown. Other historic buildings have been converted into luxury hotels.

Some of the historic buildings have only a few rooms which are reserved far in advance by knowledgeable travelers.

# Wine Tasting in the Mosel Valley

Stop in pleasant riverside towns to savor Mosel wines and explore hilltop castles overlooking vast vineyards

Navigable for nearly 170 miles/270 km, the Mosel is a watery highway busy with barges transporting freight. From mid-May through October, day excursion boats cruise the river between Trier and Koblenz, with stops at Bernkastel-Kues, Traben-Trarbach, Beilstein, and Cochem. Trains zip though the valley, stopping at the riverside towns of Bullay and Cochem. Local buses serve smaller towns along the Mosel.

The heart of the Mosel wine country begins near Trier and continues intermittently all the way to Cochem. Paved two-lane roads closely parallel the winding river, and you'll occasionally cross from one bank to the other. Steeply terraced vineyards face south to catch the full warmth of the sun. Almost every town is a winemaking center; many have autumn wine festivals.

German wineries seldom invite the public to visit and sample the wares. If you make your own private arrangements in advance, you may gain entrance. Best place to sample and savor the region's wines is in a friendly *Weinstube* (wine tavern) or in one of the local hotels.

## Trier flourished under the Romans

Trier is one of Germany's oldest cities. Though it was officially founded by the Romans in the century before Christ, legend says the town originated before 2000 B.C. as an Assyrian settlement. Trier's heyday extended from the end of the 3rd to the 5th century, when the city was the capital of Gaul, northern gateway to the Roman Empire and one of the imperial residences. Ramparts were built, as were impressive civic and religious structures.

Trier's landmark is the magnificent Porta Nigra. The splendid fortified gate was assembled from large mortarless limestone blocks held together only by a few iron crampons. Over the centuries, a dark patina formed on the limestone, giving the monument its name. Arcades, guarded by outside towers, lead to an exposed inner court where aggressors could be attacked on all sides by defenders. From the upper floors, you'll have good views over the town.

After a stop at the nearby tourist office, walk up the main shopping street to the Hauptmarkt, where open-air markets have been held for more than 1,000 years. On all sides, buildings reflect Trier's history—the Porta Nigra representing the Roman era, churches dating from the Middle Ages, baroque and half-timbered burghers' houses echoing more recent prosperity. Today Trier is the commercial center for wine made from vineyards in the Mosel-Saar-Ruwer region.

In another few minutes you can walk from the Hauptmarkt to the formal Palace Gardens and to the Landesmuseum, where Roman antiquities are displayed. Nearby you can see remnants of the city wall and the imperial baths.

Wine fanciers will have good reason to smile contentedly during the autumn grape harvest in Germany's wine country. There's special pleasure in sampling the local wines while workers gather the current year's grapes in nearby vineyards. Wine towns are most festive at harvest time, but you'll enjoy this peaceful region in other seasons as well.

The winding Mosel (called the Moselle in France, where it originates) cuts between the mountains of the Eifel on the northwest and the Hunsrück on the southeast. Life along the river moves at a relaxed pace, and your journey through the region might as well, too. Diversions are simple—inviting old riverside towns, towering castles atop promontories, terraced vineyards climbing the hills, marvelous delicate wines.

Several castle hotels near the Mosel accommodate overnight guests, or a local inn may be more to your liking. During summer and fall you'll probably need reservations, particularly on weekends.

## Down the winding Mosel valley

In the heart of the valley, castles and ruined fortresses tower over riverside villages. Terraced vineyards climb slopes above the Mosel, their grapevines trained upright on tall poles. On the steepest hillsides, equipment is winched up by rope and pulley, and workers climb slate steps cut into the slopes.

The most scenic stretch extends from Bernkastel to Cochem. Here the valley walls become steeper, the foliage more abundant, the river more twisting in exaggerated bends.

Attractive towns and villages in the valley are hard to pass up. Roads and footpaths lead up to castle ruins and into the hills. On weekends you'll see anglers and picnicking families along the river.

Below the 11th century ruins of Burg Landshut, Bernkastel faces its twin town of Kues across the river. Narrow cobbled lanes wind between timber and stone buildings to Bernkastel's delightful little market square, where an angel tops the 17th century fountain. Wrought iron signs and lanterns add charming touches.

Downstream, on the west bank, Ürzig's timbered houses are topped by tall gables. Handsome 17th and 18th century houses face the Mosel at Kröv.

A maiden carrying grapes stands atop Traben's fountain. Across the river, the ruins of Grevenburg Castle tower above Trarbach, the wine center of the central Mosel. North of Trarbach, detour into quiet Enkirch, where whimsical carved and painted signs identify streets near the Marktplatz.

Guarded by old fortifications, Zell stretches out along the east bank of the Mosel; for the best views, cross to the highway which climbs through vineyards along the opposite bank. Alf lies at the foot of Marienburg and Arras castles.

Wearying of vineyards? Seek out one of the small spas in the side valleys, such as Bad Wildstein east of Bernkastel or Bad Bertrich west of Alf.

A small car ferry makes frequent trips across the Mosel at Beilstein, a tiny market town tucked below the ruins of Burg Metternich. Walk up through terraced vineyards to the castle for a good view over the valley.

Cochem is a popular riverside resort on the Mosel's west bank. You can wander along the riverside promenade or follow the path from the Markt up to the ruins of Burg Cochem.

It takes extra effort to reach Burg Eltz, in the hills above Moselkern at the end of the wild Eltz valley. From the parking area it's a 45-minute walk through woods to the castle, one of the finest in Germany. Bristling with towers, the fortress looms through the trees. (Printed English translations of the guide's comments about the castle are available if you request them before the tour begins.)

East of Brodenbach are the ruins of once-powerful Ehrenburg, built on the remains of a Roman fortress.

Small riverside villages border the lower river. The ruins of two castles overlook Kobern, and vast vineyards surround Winningen.

The Mosel flows into the Rhine at Koblenz, a busy tourist center. Boat excursions on both the Mosel and the Rhine depart from Koblenz, and railways branch in all directions. If you're here overnight, stop at the Weindorf, along the Rhine just upriver from the main bridge, to enjoy music and open-air wine gardens.

**Burg Cochem commands Mosel valley above Cochem. From Markt square, footpath leads up through vineyards to castle.**

**Whimsical carved and painted signs add a charming note to main streets in village of Enkirch, north of Trarbach.**

# Graphic Road Signs Direct Motorists

**Closed to all vehicles** — **No entry** — **No parking** — **No stopping** — **No entry for automobiles**

**Stop at intersection** — **No left turn** — **Yield to approaching traffic** — **Passing prohibited** — **Speed limit (KPH)**

**Speed limit ends** — **Minimum speed limit** — **Parking card required** — **Priority road** — **Priority road ends**

**Customs stop** — **Road intersection** — **Right curve** — **Side road ahead** — **Yield right of way**

**Traffic light ahead** — **Caution** — **Road narrows** — **Dangerous curves** — **Rail crossing (no gates)**

**Rail crossing (with gates)** — **Quay or river bank** — **Children crossing** — **Road work in progress** — **Rough road**

**Slippery road** — **Animal crossing** — **Parking** — **Parking allowed on sidewalk** — **Mechanical help**

**Camping site** — **Telephone** — **Motorway** — **Dead end road** — **First aid station**

If you plan to drive during part of your European visit, never fear: you can understand the traffic signs even if you don't understand the language. Graphic symbols on international road signs minimize the confusion of Europe's differing languages.

Most American drivers have little trouble making the changeover to the symbolic signs. Since embarrassing complications can result if a foreign visitor violates prohibitive signs, it's wise to study them in advance so you can recognize them quickly on the road.

International road signs are simple in design and based on geometric shapes: triangles, circles, and rectangles. The colors are bold—red, white, blue, yellow, and black. Most countries use the same symbols, though there may be variations in color combinations and arrangements. The most common signs are shown at left.

**Circular signs.** Red circles convey definite driving instructions, usually prohibitions. A red circle with a white center means "road closed to vehicles." A circle with a white bar means "no entry in this direction"; it's probably a one-way street. A black symbol on white background inside the circle shows what is prohibited; signs may give speed limits, prohibit passing, show compulsory right of way. A similar road sign cut by a diagonal line means the prohibition has ended.

The stop sign is a red circle enclosing a red triangle with "STOP" in black on a white background. The familiar octagonal red-and-white stop sign is also widely used.

A blue circle with a white symbol indicates compulsory instructions—the route to follow, the direction to proceed around a traffic circle, minimum speed, pedestrian or cycle routes.

**Triangular signs.** Red triangular signs call attention to dangers ahead. The danger is illustrated by a black symbol on a white background. These signs may announce curves, steep slopes, slippery or rough roads, rights of way, pedestrian or animal crossings, traffic lights, falling rocks, road repair, or railroad crossings.

**Rectangular signs.** These signs give information. Blue signs with the symbol in white, or against a white background, indicate such conveniences as parking, gas stations, telephones, and first-aid stations.

Distances, road numbers, and directional information appear on rectangular signs. Schematic maps provide advance directions for crossroads or complex junctions.

In cities, motorists can park in certain areas only with a parking card (check the glove compartment of your rental car). Other signs specify parking on alternate sides of the street on alternate days (odd or even-numbered days), with the parking times given in the 24-hour clock.

# special interests

# In Germany

## TRAINS TO AIRPORTS

Travelers arriving at or departing from Frankfurt or Düsseldorf airports find direct rail links connecting the airport and the city's central railway station. Rail service also operates from the Frankfurt airport to Mainz and Wiesbaden.

Airport train passengers must obtain tickets before boarding; no tickets can be purchased on board. Inspectors check the trains, and passengers apprehended without valid tickets must pay sizable fines.

## CALENDAR OF EVENTS

A "Calendar of Events" is published twice a year, in April and October, by the German National Tourist Office. The free booklet lists dates of folk festivals, theater and opera performances, sports events, trade fairs, and other activities being held in the Federal Republic of Germany and in West Berlin.

## LIFT A GLASS

Germany's delicate white wines and sturdy beers are world famous. To visit a German winery or brewery during your visit, check with local tourist offices or with the German National Tourist Office.

Wine fanciers can sample local vintages in congenial surroundings in towns along the Mosel (see page 62), the Rhine (such as Rudesheim or the "Weindorf" in Koblenz), and in other vineyard districts. In late summer and autumn, every wine area celebrates the vintage with festivals.

*Apfelwein* (apple wine, or dry cider) is Frankfurt's local specialty; you'll enjoy it in wine taverns in the Sachsenhausen "old town" district just south of the Main River.

Many beer enthusiasts plan their holidays around Munich's annual Oktoberfest, a 2-week celebration beginning in mid-September. You can sample the *gemütlich* atmosphere the year around at Munich's Hofbrauhaus or other beer halls.

## HOBBY VACATIONS

If you'd like to pursue a favorite sport or hobby during your visit to Germany, consult your travel agent or write to the German National Tourist Office for specific information on such topics as arts and crafts instruction, camping, horseback riding, mountain climbing, sailing, spa holidays, wine tasting, and winter sports.

## CASTLE HOTELS

If you yearn for accommodations with an air of romance and mystery, plan to stay in one or more of Germany's castle hotels. Ask the German National Tourist Office for a brochure describing the various castles, their history, and facilities. About 50 castles belong to the Gast im Schloss (Guest in a Castle) organization.

## MOUNTAIN HUTS

The German Alpine Association (Deutscher Alpen Verein, Prater Insel 5, D-8000 Munich 22) maintains mountain trails throughout Germany. The association's mountain huts in the Alps and central uplands may also be used by nonmembers.

## RAIL TRAVEL BARGAINS

Holders of a Germanrail Tourist Card can travel wherever they wish on West Germany's extensive rail network. The unlimited-mileage ticket can be purchased for first or second-class rail travel for 9 or 16 days. It includes free or reduced-rate travel by bus or boat on selected routes and a reduced-rate round-trip rail ticket to West Berlin.

Senior travelers (women 60 years of age, men 65 and older) and young people aged 12 to 23 can purchase special passes entitling them to reduced fares.

Germanrail offers numerous short, non-escorted tours to more than 50 cities and some 60 resort and health spas. Packages include transportation, overnight accommodations with breakfast, and sightseeing. For information, see your travel agent, or write to an office of the German Federal Railroad or the German National Tourist Office.

## THEATER AND OPERA

In most German cities, the theater and opera season begins in mid-September and runs to the beginning of June. Except for special music festivals, schedules are printed only two months in advance. You can make reservations through the local ticket or tourist office or through your hotel.

## BOAT TRIPS

During the tourist season, excursion boats operate on many German lakes and rivers and along the North Sea coast. Regularly scheduled river boats cruise the Danube, Elbe, Main, Mosel, Necker, Rhine, and Weser rivers. Other boats operate on the Bodensee (Lake Constance) and the Bavarian lakes, and link North Sea ports with the East and North Frisian islands.

## VISITING BERLIN

You can reach West Berlin by plane, train, bus, or car from major cities in West Germany. Visitors traveling by surface transport need a valid passport to enter the German Democratic Republic (East Germany). Transit visas are issued at border checkpoints and on all transit trains. For more information, write to the German National Tourist Office.

Travelers wishing to enter East Berlin can obtain information at the Berlin Tourist Office near the Zoo Railroad Station or at Tegel Airport.

**For information on travel in Germany, write to the German National Tourist Office (addresses on page 7).**

# Pastoral Loop South from Bern

Explore country towns, hike in the mountains, or watch cheesemakers at work in this rural district

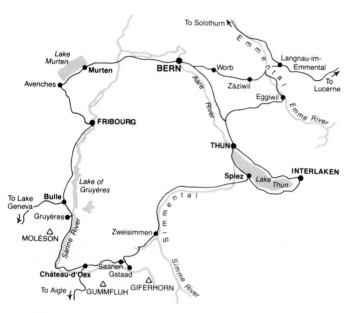

One of Switzerland's most enjoyable regions lies south of Bern, linking the country's French and German-speaking districts. In this pastoral countryside, deeply rooted traditions still survive. Trains link the region's towns; a favorite of rail fans is the MOB narrow-gauge railway between Zweisimmen and Montreux on Lake Geneva.

Country roads and railways traverse pastoral valleys where black-and-white cows graze placidly and family cheesemakers ply their trade. As in other rural regions, the ascent of the cows to the mountain pastures in spring is a cause for festivity, and their return in early autumn is also a joyous occasion. Their horns adorned with ribbons and flowers, the cows stop traffic as they plod through village streets.

Many regional holidays revolve around religious celebrations, both Catholic and Protestant. In the autumn, harvest *bénichon* festivals take place in many towns in the Fribourg countryside, marked by plentiful food, dancing, fairs, and traveling shows. Livestock markets are held regularly in towns throughout the region.

Boxes of gaudy geraniums brighten houses and village fountains. You can stop in walled towns or alpine resorts, view Roman ruins or ride mountain funiculars, seek out country inns or stay in modern hotels. When you're ready for a brisk walk, look for a yellow *wanderweg* sign; it indicates both trail destination and approximate hiking time.

## Ancient towns recall past glories

Encircled by ramparts and towers and guarded by its castle, medieval Murten (also called Morat in this bilingual region) overlooks a lake that bears its name. In a battle on

---

**Thun's red roofs and white buildings gleam in sunlight, though clouds hide high peaks of the Bernese Oberland.**

this site in 1476, the Swiss defeated Charles the Bold, Duke of Burgundy.

You enter this charming town through fortified gates. Shopping arcades line its attractive main street. A walk atop the city walls offers fascinating views down into the town's streets and gardens. In summer, passenger boats cruise the lake.

About 5 miles/9 km southwest is the small town of Avenches, once the administrative and cultural capital of Roman Switzerland. Julius Caesar and his legions took this area from the Celts nearly 2,000 years ago. The Romans founded the town of Aventicum, which at its peak in the 2nd century housed approximately 50,000 people.

Fortified walls over 20 feet high ringed the Roman city, and the amphitheater erected here could seat up to 15,000. Remnants of that era remain, and a museum (closed Tuesdays in winter) displays Roman artifacts discovered during excavations.

## The lush Fribourg countryside

The Sarine River cuts through the green pastures of the Fribourg countryside, marking the region's bilingual border. Hamlets on the left bank have French names; those on the right bank, to the east, bear German names.

Capital of the canton (state) is the city of Fribourg, perched dramatically above a deep bend in the river. Several impressive bridges span the deep, V-shaped gorge.

Rising from the Sarine to the Upper Town, the old section of the city bristles with church towers. Numerous old buildings mingle with modern ones, for Fribourg is an international business center and university town. On Wednesday and Saturday mornings, market stalls sprout like mushrooms after a rain.

Bulle is the gateway to the Gruyère region. Fire leveled the medieval town in 1805, so most buildings present a solid 19th century façade. You can learn about the district in the local museum, which features regional costumes and furniture among its exhibits.

A short distance south, delightful Gruyères sits on a rocky spur above the Sarine valley, its ramparts and castle etched against the sky. An arched gate frames the town's wide cobbled street and facing rows of Renaissance houses. As you make your way up the street toward the castle, you'll pass hollowed-out stone basins that served as grain and corn measures in earlier days.

Once the home of the counts of Gruyères, the 15th century castle is now owned by the canton of Fribourg. Inside, you'll see a simple kitchen of feudal times and the comforts and touches added several centuries later. Outside, a small chapel on the terrace overlooks the Sarine valley and the lake of Gruyères, formed by a dam downstream.

Below the town, you can tour a model cheese factory to see how Gruyère cheese is made.

## Mountain valleys & Alpine resorts

As you follow the Sarine upriver, it curves east into a broad, high mountain valley called the Pays d'Enhaut.

Hub of this splendidly scenic region is Château-d'Oex (pronounced "day"), a summer and winter family resort in the Vaudois Alps. An excellent regional history museum includes furnished interiors of old mountain houses and, in a separate building, a traditional cheesemaking center with giant copper cauldron.

Wooden houses decorated in Bernese Oberland style (a huge roof, almost touching the ground, that covers both house and barn) line the main road of Saanen, a quiet, old-fashioned valley town that contrasts markedly with its more famous neighbor, Gstaad.

Unexpectedly, however, this fashionable ski center is small and unpretentious. Winter is the social season in Gstaad, but even then a pleasant informality prevails in the village. Cable cars climb the slopes, carrying skiers in winter and hikers and sightseers in summer.

At Zweisimmen you meet the Simme River and follow it down through the Simmental to Lake Thun.

## Along Lake Thun

Attractive lakeside towns and resorts share the beauty of deep blue Lake Thun, nestled at the base of the Bernese Alps. Lake steamers ply its waters from early April to late October.

Built on a steep slope overlooking the water, the town of Spiez looks toward the impressive medieval castle that guards its sheltered harbor. Moored pleasure boats add bright spots of color. You can tour parts of the castle and climb to the top of its main tower for a splendid view of the lake and mountains.

Straddling the Aare River where it flows from the lake, Thun is a lively town midway between Bern and Interlaken. Along its hilly main street, the Hauptgasse, you'll notice that stores in the ground-level arcades are topped by houses, so pedestrians on the upper level walk on the roofs of the shops. Arcaded buildings also edge the attractive Rathausplatz. Near the lake's outlet, a weathered old covered bridge spans the foaming river. Vendors set up market stalls in the central district on Wednesday and Saturday mornings.

At the upper end of the Hauptgasse, a covered stairway leads to the parish church and the castle of Kyburg, a massive fortress rising majestically above the city. Dating from 1186, it contains an excellent historical museum (open April through October). Magnificent medieval tapestries hang in the castle's spacious Knights' Hall. From the top floor, you can climb the turrets for views across Thun and the lake to the Bernese Alps.

## Cheesemaking in the Emmental

A northeastern loop offers a look at Switzerland's most famous cheese valley, the tranquil Emmental. Flowering geraniums brighten immense wooden farmhouses, whose steeply pitched shingled roofs almost touch the ground.

Cheesemaking dominates valley life, for this is the home of Emmental cheese—the one with holes that many Americans call "Swiss cheese." You can arrange to visit a local *kaserei* to see how the cheese is churned, seeped, and put aside to cure with the fermenting bubbles that leave the characteristic holes.

# Markets Teem with Produce & Flowers

Awnings shade stalls where vendors display a colorful array of vegetables, fruits, cheese, fish, and flowers

One of the liveliest and most colorful parts of a European city or town is the marketplace. You'll find at least one market in nearly every sizable town. It's the social center for greeting friends, exchanging gossip, and complaining about the weather or government.

Most markets are held near the heart of town, often in a large square near the town hall or main church. Bright awnings and umbrellas shade stalls where sellers spread their offerings. Local or regional tourist offices can tell you exact sites, days, and hours.

### Fish is king in Scandinavia

Lively fish markets are one of Scandinavia's attractions, but you'll also find markets selling produce, flowers, and second-hand merchandise.

**Norway.** Housewives arrive early on weekday mornings at Bergen's busy fish market, located beside the harbor.

Oslo's outdoor flower market faces the cathedral; nearby, an indoor bazaar of arts and crafts workshops attracts shoppers seeking handmade articles.

**Sweden.** In front of Stockholm's Concert Hall, you'll find colorful stalls of produce and flowers, Lapp handicrafts, ceramics, and other crafts.

The fish auction starts at 7 A.M. in Gothenburg's harborside Fish Church, an immense fish market where you'll see varieties of fresh seafood from all over Scandinavia.

**Denmark.** One of the largest Scandinavian flea markets takes place in Copenhagen's Israel Place on Saturdays from 8 A.M. to 2 P.M. from April to October.

In Esbjerg, early risers enjoy the action at the morning fish auction on weekdays beginning at 7.

**Finland.** On weekday mornings, fishing boats arrive in Helsinki's harbor with cargoes of fresh and pickled herring, which are sold outdoors in Kauppatori Square.

In Turku, you'll find the market in the city's old market hall. Country markets take place in many Finnish towns.

### Street markets brighten Britain & Ireland

Country markets in Britain and Ireland sell local produce, baked goods, homemade preserves, and country crafts.

**Britain.** London has numerous street markets, where hoarse-voiced Cockney vendors cheerfully call out their wares. Antique hunters visit the Friday Caledonian Market. On Saturdays, Portobello Road in Notting Hill Gate features minor antiques and curios. Petticoat Lane (actually Middlesex Street) in London's East End draws Sunday bargain hunters.

London's famous Billingsgate fish market in Lower Thames Street opens at 6 A.M.; porters balance boxes of fish on their heads, braced by flat-topped leather hats.

In Aberdeen, headquarters of Scotland's fishing industry, the catch is unloaded from trawlers in early morning and auctioned in the covered fish market nearby.

**Ireland.** Dublin's colorful Moore Street Market is lined with portable stalls where competitive vendors sing out their wares and prices.

### Markets abound in the Low Countries

You can buy everything from wooden shoes and vegetables to attic discards and garden plants at these markets.

**Netherlands.** Amsterdammers buy food and clothing outdoors at lively Albert Cuypstraat market. You'll find cut flowers and plants at the Singel Canal flower market near the Mint Tower. Flea market fans find a marvelous hodgepodge of curiosities on Valkenburgerstraat.

Many country towns have weekly markets.

**Belgium.** Plants and flowers brighten the Grand'Place in Brussels each morning. On weekends you can look over antiques and curios at the Place du Sablon Market or flea market merchandise at the Place du Jeu de Balle.

Children find new pets at Antwerp's Sunday morning bird market.

**Luxembourg.** Produce and flower markets are held each Wednesday and Saturday morning in Luxembourg-City on the Place Guillaume square.

On Easter Monday, the ancient Emais'chen market is held in the heart of the old city.

## Lively street fairs in France & Germany

Frequently, you'll find markets and street fairs in French and German country towns.

**France.** Paris has many street markets; among the best are those on Rue Mouffetard and Rue Lepic. Weekend browsers prowl flea market stalls near Porte de Clignancourt. You can also visit a weekday flower market and Sunday bird market on the Île de la Cité; the stamp market at Avenue Gabriel and Avenue Marigny on Thursday, Saturday, and Sunday; and fabric stores of Marché St-Pierre rimming the square below Sacré Coeur.

Stroll amid fragrant flower stalls in the old town of Nice; when selling begins, most of the flowers are bought by retailers within a few minutes.

Itinerant merchants *(forains)* travel from town to town in France, selling their wares at country markets.

**Germany.** You'll find fish markets in various North Sea ports; Hamburg's is held Sunday morning from 6 to 10.

Bavarian farm families sell produce in Munich's open-air Viktualienmarkt near the Peterskirche.

Largest of the autumn wine markets and festivals is the wine and sausage market in Bad Dürkheim.

## Market day in Switzerland & Austria

Market stalls offer a colorful array of produce and other merchandise in many Swiss and Austrian towns.

**Switzerland.** Wednesday and Saturday are market days in Lausanne, when narrow streets in the center of town teem with produce and flower stands.

In Lucerne, market stalls line the banks of the Reuss River on Tuesday and Saturday mornings.

On Geneva's Plaine de Plainpalais, you'll find produce stands on Tuesday and Friday, antiques and flea market merchandise on Wednesday and Saturday.

Berne's colorful market is held Tuesday and Saturday mornings, centered in the Barenplatz and Bundesplatz. A handicraft market is held on the first Saturday of the month in the Munsterplatz-Munstergasse. Berne's annual onion market is held on the fourth Monday in November.

**Austria.** Viennese housewives shop for produce at the Naschmarkt, near the city center.

On Saturday mornings, vendors offer antiques, paintings, and curios at Vienna's flea market, which begins at one end of the Naschmarkt.

## Shopping in southern Europe

Markets become even more colorful, noisy, and aromatic as you travel farther south.

**Italy.** Vendors compete in shouting matches in Rome's famous Campo dei Fiori market. Sunday shopping focuses on the Porta Portese flea market in the Trastevere section.

You can buy straw goods and inexpensive leather items at Florence's Mercato del Porcellino (Straw Market).

Saturday is market day in the Piedmontese town of Alba; during the October truffle fair, a separate courtyard is set aside for a truffle market.

**Greece.** Flea markets in Athens and Salonika (Thessalonica) are open daily, but Sunday is the best day for shopping. Expect to bargain for items.

**Yugoslavia.** In the center of Zagreb, the Tržnica-Dolac market contains not only produce, flowers, and fish, but also folk artifacts and clothing.

The Baš-Caršija market in the center of Sarajevo is open daily. You can find copperwork, rugs, embroidery, wood carvings, folk artifacts, and jewelry.

## Street markets in Spain & Portugal

Open-air markets are favorite Iberian places for strolling, shopping, and socializing. At country fairs, you'll see everything from meat and produce to handwoven rugs and pottery.

**Spain.** In the heart of old Madrid is El Rastro. On Sunday morning you can buy everything from Gothic carvings to bullfighters' suits. Collectors visit the Sunday stamp and coin market in Plaza Mayor.

Barcelona shoppers head for trade stalls along Las Ramblas, the tree-lined market thoroughfare.

**Portugal.** Lisbon's ancient Feira da Ladra, held on Tuesday and Saturday behind the church of São Vicente, offers flea market variety beneath canvas-roofed booths and stalls.

# Exploring Northeast Switzerland

Follow country roads to quiet villages, journey along the Rhine, and enjoy Appenzell's rolling green hills

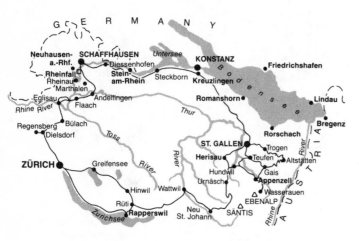

Pastoral traditions still thrive in the gentle green hills of northeast Switzerland. Farmhouses dot the slopes on which dairy cows graze placidly. Country roads lead to tiny villages (each grouped around a small church) and medieval towns with frescoed houses and flower-decked fountains. Charming country hotels and cozy inns offer good value in meals and accommodations.

On holidays and other ceremonial occasions, women of the Appenzell district don traditional dress and beribboned headdresses with immense tulle wings. To be festive also, Appenzell men wear bright red embroidered vests and flat hats adorned with flowers. Cause for local celebration is the annual trek of cows to the Alpine pastures and their triumphal return in the fall, cowbells tolling and horns entwined with flowers and ribbons.

Motorists travel the country roads leisurely, but many visitors prefer to use the efficient Swiss transportation system. Trains, supplemented by postal buses and river steamers, give an intimate look at the countryside.

## North to the Rhine

From Zürich, roads head north toward the Rhine. About 10 miles/16 km northwest of the city, a short detour from Dielsdorf leads to captivating Regensberg, which rises above vineyards and farm lands along the crest of a hill. Follow its one long street through an archway into the tree-shaded main square, where small gardens front many of the steeply roofed houses. For views over the countryside, climb to the top of the round tower.

You travel on country roads northeast from Dielsdorf through Bülach to Eglisau. Upriver, trees and shrubs grow in lush profusion along this little-known stretch of the Rhine.

Continue on through Flaach, a May destination for asparagus lovers, to see Andelfingen's half-timbered houses and wooden bridge. In these rural villages, barns adjoin the houses with the barnyard facing the road. Northwest of Marthalen at Rheinau, boats head upriver toward the Rheinfall.

## Europe's most powerful waterfall

Since the Middle Ages, the Rhine has been an important river highway. Steamers and barges ferry passengers and freight along more than 250 miles/400 km of navigable waterway, from the North Sea through Holland and Germany and along Switzerland's northern border. In medieval days, Schaffhausen grew as a depot for river cargoes, which had to be unloaded and portaged around river rapids and the powerful Rheinfall.

Above the falls, the river is nearly 500 feet/175 meters wide. Rounding a deep curve, it suddenly narrows, surging in thundering, foamy cascades around a pair of shrubbery-covered rocks to plunge some 70 feet/22 meters into a wide river basin.

You can view the river from either bank, but you get the closest look directly below Schloss Laufen on the left bank. Stairs lead from the castle courtyard down to a viewing platform suspended over the water. Spray is heavy in spring and early summer, so bring a protective raincoat. Adventurous visitors can take a wet boat ride to the main rock in midriver.

Schaffhausen and its industrial suburb, Neuhausen, lie north of the river. Frescoed houses face Schaffhausen streets in the old quarter, giving the town a pleasant medieval air. Stroll down the Vordergasse to see paintings on the façade of the "Haus zum Ritter." Dominating town and river from atop a hill is the massive 16th century Munot Castle, linked with the old quarter by a covered passageway.

## River route along the Rhine

Steamers ply the Rhine from Schaffhausen upriver to Kreuzlingen on the Bodensee (Lake Constance), a splendidly scenic half-day trip along reed-bordered banks. Road and railway closely parallel the river route. Scenery changes constantly as you pass wooded hills and vineyards, small tidy villages, and ancient hilltop castles.

Pause awhile at charming Stein-am-Rhein, one of Switzerland's prettiest medieval towns. Lining the streets are frescoed houses ornamented with oriel windows (called *Erker*) and flower-filled window boxes; you'll find the best paintings on buildings facing the town hall square. After you've enjoyed the painted houses and wrought iron signs, wander along the Rhine promenade or stop at a riverside cafe.

Upstream the Rhine widens into the Untersee. Castles crown the hills, and attractive villages border the river. At Kreuzlingen you meet the Bodensee and turn south toward St. Gallen and the Appenzell district.

## St. Gallen's priceless library

St. Gallen's early fame rested on its abbey, founded in 612 and recognized throughout Europe during the Middle Ages as a center of religious teaching. Scholars still use the abbey library with its priceless collection of 100,000 volumes dating from the 8th century.

The library's main hall is a Swiss rococo gem—a light and airy room, all white and gold and pastel, with a dazzling display of painted ceilings and rich woodwork. Visitors exchange shoes for felt slippers to walk on the beautiful parquet floors.

Symbol of St. Gallen is the 18th century cathedral, its elegant twin towers topped by bulbous belfries. The church's sober exterior doesn't prepare you for its joyful interior, created by the same architects who designed the library.

Proceed north of the cathedral through the old town streets to see centuries-old houses adorned with carved and painted wooden oriel windows, painted façades, and wrought iron trim.

Fine embroidery has been a regional industry since the Middle Ages. Locally made lace and embroidery from different periods are exhibited in St. Gallen's Gewerbemuseum in Vadianstrasse.

Painted façades, oriel windows, and scarlet geraniums adorn buildings along main street in Stein-am-Rhein.

## Exploring pastoral Appenzell

Paths wind across grassy slopes in northeast Switzerland. Small towns and scattered houses dot the countryside.

From St. Gallen you set off by road or rail for the prosperous Appenzell countryside. Narrow-gauge trains, sometimes only two or three cars long, climb into the heartland to link the few settlements. Marking the rolling green hills are farmhouses built in traditional style: barn and gabled house combined in a single building facing the valley.

Gais is worth a stop to see the market town's main square, faced by rows of adjoining gabled houses adorned with carved woodwork. Pedestrian arcades give Altstätten's main street a medieval mood; above, its houses with pointed gables present a jagged skyline. Rustic Urnäsch is one of the canton's oldest communities.

Tucked in a valley below the Alpstein Massif, the town of Appenzell is relatively busy and just the right size to explore on foot. Shops along the Hauptgasse display not only the expected embroidery and cowbells but also cheesemaking implements and the traditional Appenzell honey cakes (Biber). Whimsical painted or carved designs decorate many buildings. There's a folklore museum in the old town hall.

Above Appenzell, craggy mountains jut skyward. You can ascend both the Ebenalp and towering, 8,209-foot/2,502-meter Säntis, renowned for its panoramic views over eastern Switzerland. Marked footpaths traverse the slopes of the lower Alps, opening the woods and sunny, flower-strewn hills to walkers and hikers.

# Relaxing in the Engadine

This mountain vacationland offers marvelous hiking trails, alpine sports, and tradition-steeped villages

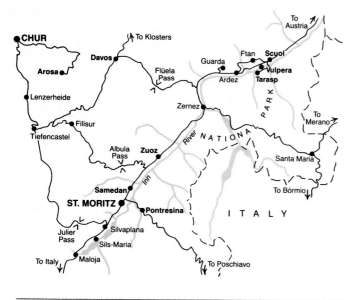

**Well-sited bench above Ftan tempts walkers to pause and enjoy expansive view of rugged, snow-dusted Grisons.**

Nestling between Alpine ranges in southeastern Switzerland, the sunny valley of the Inn River cuts for some 60 miles/95 km through the vast mountain canton of the Grisons. Many knowledgeable Europeans spend their holidays here in the Engadine region, drawn by the sparkling climate and excellent sports facilities.

Hub of the region is St. Moritz, a fashionable, international winter playground. In summer you can choose from an array of sports or resort activities, or limit yourself to nothing more strenuous than rambling along mountain paths and exploring pleasant villages. Smaller Engadine towns offer vacation retreats in working farm communities, where you stay in family-run inns and enjoy country cooking. Early-summer and autumn visitors often enjoy off-season prices.

Once somewhat isolated, the Engadine is now accessible the year round by road and rail. Bright yellow postal buses and the red and green cars of the narrow-gauge Rhaetian Railway probe the mountains and valleys, allowing you to devote full attention to the scenery. Motorists who prefer to minimize their mountain driving can transport cars by rail through the major tunnels.

## Life in the Engadine

Engadine villagers speak their own language—Ladin, a branch of Romansch. Traditional dwellings are built in a broad-gabled style, their white-plastered stone façades decorated with *sgraffiti* (designs in plaster) in geometric, floral, or heraldic patterns. The Engadine Museum in St. Moritz, built in local style, provides an introduction to Engadine home life. You'll find the work of local weavers and woodcarvers in *Heimatwerk* shops.

Most charming of the upper Engadine villages is Zuoz. Guarda typifies lower Engadine towns with its fountains, decorated houses, and steep streets paved in cobblestones. Ardez, dominated by castle ruins, contains more painted houses. From its mountain terrace, Ftan commands a broad view of the lower Engadine valley.

Chair lifts, cable cars, and mountain railways yo-yo up the slopes to mountain restaurants with sunny south-facing terraces. Skiing lasts well into summer on the high slopes. Down in the valley, ice rinks attract skaters. Golf, tennis, fishing, riding, mountaineering, swimming, and mineral baths are available in upper Engadine resorts and the lower Engadine spa of Scuol-Tarasp-Vulpera.

Marked paths follow the shores of the upper Engadine lakes, cut through fragrant larch and cembra-pine woods, and traverse wildflower meadows to view points. Local tourist offices can provide maps showing walking routes. Southeast of Zernez, nature lovers in search of solitude enjoy the trails of the vast Swiss National Park. Here Alpine flowers bloom in profusion (usually at their best in late June), and wild animals roam the mountains and forests. In summer you can join guided nature walks.

# special interests

# In Switzerland

## SPORT AND HOBBY VACATIONS

Switzerland offers many holiday programs featuring sports and hobbies. Write to the Swiss National Tourist Office for vacation ideas on your favorite activity: hiking, mountaineering, camping, angling, tennis, golf, skiing, horseback riding, cycling, canoeing, sailing, and other sports.

You can also enjoy various hobbies including art museum touring, botanical walks, photography, and painting. If you'd like to learn a new skill, you can join a class in rustic painting, woodcarving, puppetry, alphorn playing, or other subjects.

## SWISS HANDICRAFTS

Families in many mountain valleys continue traditional crafts, which shoppers find in *Heimatwerk* shops in major Swiss cities.

Many handcrafted objects, such as woven textiles and lace, painted pottery, and toys, come from the Bernese Oberland; look for woodcarvings and Christmas ornaments in Brienz. The Appenzell district is renowned for folk art and embroidery.

## SWISS TRAVEL BARGAINS

In Switzerland it's easy to travel independently by public transportation. Trains, postal buses, and lake steamers travel to nearly every Swiss town and village.

Nonresidents can purchase a Swiss Holiday Card—good for unlimited travel by train, boat, and postal bus—for periods of 4 days, 8 days, 15 days, or 1 month.

A new Half Fare Travel Card, available to travelers of all ages, may be purchased for one or 12 months. It allows the holder to purchase tickets for first or second-class rail travel at half price.

Regional Holiday Season Tickets, good for discounted travel excursions within a single region, are available for varying periods in the following areas: Montreux/Vevey; Bernese Oberland; Lake Lucerne; Grisons, Locarno/Ascona; and Lugano.

For more information on various transportation tickets, write to the Swiss National Tourist Office.

Official timetables covering train, bus, and lake steamer schedules can be purchased in main rail stations and Swiss National Tourist Offices. Previously printed in summer and winter editions, the timetable will be published annually beginning June 1987.

## STEAM ACROSS SWITZERLAND

More than 20 steam railways still operate in Switzerland. In summer a rack-and-pinion mountain railway climbs from Brienz (on Lake Brienz in the Bernese Oberland) up the Rothorn slopes, where you'll enjoy a magnificent panorama of high peaks. Other steam railways operate only on weekends or on specific dates.

Paddle steamers cruise four Swiss lakes—Brienz, Zürich, Lucerne, and Geneva—on scheduled summer trips.

For information on steam railway and paddle steamer service, write to the Swiss National Tourist Office.

## TRAFFIC-FREE TOWNS

Many Swiss mountain resorts and country villages boast an absence of automobiles. Some towns are accessible by road to the village entrances; others can be reached only by mountain railroad, aerial cable car, or chair lift. Towns range from well-known resorts to hamlets with only one hotel.

For a list of traffic-free towns and directions for getting there, write to the Swiss National Tourist Office.

## MOUNTAIN RAMBLES

Footpaths wander across the Swiss countryside—outside villages, across gentle slopes, into the high hills. Stop at the local tourist information office for route suggestions. Yellow signs point the way to destinations and indicate approximate hiking time.

You'll find easy walks just a few minutes from town, or you can board a bus and take a 10-minute ride into the hills, returning to town on foot.

Cable cars provide easy access to alpine pastures where wildflowers bloom in late spring and summer. You'll follow cowpaths through mountain meadows, and in summer perhaps come upon dairy herdsmen at work in an Alpine cheesemaking hut.

## WINTER SPORTS

Renowned for its outstanding winter sports activities, Switzerland offers many programs for both skiers and nonskiers. In addition to skiing, you can enjoy ice skating, curling, sledding, riding, sleigh rides, and winter walks through the snow. For information on winter activities, write to the Swiss National Tourist Office.

## HOTEL VALUES FOR SENIORS

Senior travelers (men over 65 years, women over 62) are eligible for special rates (including room, breakfast, service charges, and taxes) at many Swiss hotels. For a list of participating hotels, write to the Swiss National Tourist Office.

## CALENDAR OF EVENTS

To help you plan your visit, the Swiss National Tourist Office publishes a general calendar of events annually. In addition, a calendar of music and theater events is available covering attractions from July to the following June.

## EQUESTRIAN HOLIDAYS

If you're happiest astride a horse, consider a Swiss riding holiday. In many parts of the country, special programs offer horseback riding and instruction.

You can also hire horse-drawn caravans in the Jura and in central Switzerland or join a mule safari through the Valais Alps. For information on various riding courses and holidays, write to the Swiss National Tourist Office.

**For information on travel in Switzerland, write to the Swiss National Tourist Office (addresses on page 7).**

# Austria's Enchanting Lakes

Southeast of Salzburg, unwind in lakeside towns, go deep into salt mines, and enjoy the mountains

**Excursion boat pulls near shore at Hallstatt. Balconied houses climb steep slopes above shimmering Hallstättersee.**

**Dressed in coveralls, couple descends steep wooden slides through dark mountain tunnels on salt mine tour.**

Cozy towns and villages snuggle along curving lake shores and mountain valleys in Austria's enchanting Salzkammergut. You can follow trails winding across mountain slopes, or explore subterranean pathways that penetrate ancient salt mines and ice caves. Cable cars and cog railways climb to mountaintop lookouts. Some 40 lakes nestle amid the green valleys, wooded hills, and towering peaks.

Since prehistoric days, salt mining has played an important role in the Salzburg region. The syllable *salz* or *hall* (both meaning "salt") is part of many place names. Mines are still worked, and adventurous travelers can tour several of them.

In Salzburg you can board a postal bus for St. Gilgen, St. Wolfgang, Bad Ischl, and other Salzkammergut towns. From Bad Ischl, trains depart for Obertraun/Hallstatt. In summer, motorcoach excursions operate from Salzburg.

Be forewarned: During warm weather it rains often in the lake district. In sunny autumn, there's a nip in the air; many rural towns mark the harvest season with noisy, joyous festivals.

## Sampling the Salzkammergut

From the mid-19th century to the outbreak of World War I, the lake-dotted Salzkammergut was the fashionable summer retreat of Europe's royal families and leading personalities in the theater, music, and art worlds. Emperor Franz Josef presided over the light-hearted group as they waltzed to Johann Strauss melodies and hummed songs from Franz Lehár operettas.

One of the Salzkammergut's gems is the lake of St. Wolfgang. Sailboats flit across the water between St. Gilgen at one end, Strobl at the other, and St. Wolfgang on the northern shore. In keeping with the holiday atmosphere, you can travel by boat from the southern shore to St. Wolfgang.

Sitting on a rocky spur, St. Wolfgang's church is known for its artistic altar, but don't miss the arcaded cloisters high above the water and the glimpses of the lake they offer you. You'll also want to stroll along the shore to the Weisses Rössl, the famed White Horse Inn that once inspired an operetta. From mid-May through September, an old-fashioned cogwheel train leaves St. Wolfgang to chug up the slopes of the Schafberg. On a clear day you can see more than a dozen of the Salzkammergut lakes from the summit.

Franz Josef made the spa of Bad Ischl his summer residence. From May through September, you can visit the Hapsburg imperial villa in the landscaped Kaiserpark north of town. A photography museum is housed in the Marmorschlossl, Empress Elisabeth's tea house. You can also visit the villa of composer Franz Lehár, whose operettas are performed here in summer.

Surrounded by wooded hills, the resort clusters within a river bend at the confluence of the Traun and Ischl streams. You'll enjoy Bad Ischl's relaxed 19th century ambience on a stroll along the shop-lined Pfarrgasse or upstream from Elisabeth Bridge along the Traun River.

## Austria's oldest settlement

Hallstatt's scenic setting gives few clues to its remarkable past. Balconied houses cling precariously to a wooded slope above the deep-blue waters of Lake Hallstatt. Narrow, curving streets follow the contours of the steep hillside, into which Celtic tribesmen dug for salt a thousand years before Christ. Above the town rise the sheer granite walls of the Dachstein.

Archeologists have discovered more than a thousand graves of these prehistoric lake dwellers, who built their homes on pilings above the water. Because of these important discoveries, the early part of the Iron Age was named the "Hallstatt Period." Objects discovered during the excavations, including primitive miners' clothing and tools from 2,500 years ago, are displayed in a museum.

Climb the steep covered stairway to the large parish church for a look at its handsome carved altar, then walk through Hallstatt's small cemetery. Due to lack of space, bones are dug up periodically and neatly labeled skulls are placed in the small chapel at the rear of the graveyard.

If the water looks inviting, rent a rowboat or arrange for a ride in one of Hallstatt's long, flat-bottomed gondolalike boats with an up-curving prow. Each spring, Hallstatters celebrate the Corpus Christi holiday with a lake procession of decorated boats.

Swimmers find pleasant beaches on the lake's eastern shore near Obertraun. Summer evenings are usually warm enough for diners to linger over dinner in outdoor lakeside restaurants.

## Salt mines & an ice cave

Salt is still being mined in the Salzburg region. You can tour mines (Salzbergwerk) near Hallstatt, Bad Ischl, Altaussee, and Hallein. Hours are May through September from 9 A.M. to 4:30 P.M.; April and October from 9 to 2:30.

Across the lake from Hallstatt at Obertraun, cable cars take visitors up to the famous Dachstein ice cave, continuing on to the summit of the Krippenstein, an impressive view point overlooking the Dachstein plateau. Allow at least half a day for the full trip and tour of the caves (open May to mid-October). In summer, an early start will help avoid midday crowds. Don't forget a warm wrap, for the temperature inside the caves stays near freezing even in midsummer.

Lights illuminate the subterranean caverns of the ice caves, where hanging icicles and ice draperies create a fairy-tale scene. In the Mammoth's Cave, you follow the guide through a labyrinth of passages into a majestic cavern over 130 feet/40 meters high.

## Down the Salzach valley

Motorists can return to Salzburg by another scenic route—across the Gschütt Pass and down the gentle Salzach River valley.

From Lake Hallstatt, drive west to the village of Gosau, then take a side road south to unspoiled Lake Gosau. Mirrorlike waters of this alpine lake offer a breathtaking view, reflecting the high, rugged peaks and icy glacier of the Dachstein. Views are especially memorable in early morning or late afternoon, when light bathes the peaks and glaciers while the valley floor is in shadow. Footpaths curve around the lake and up the valley.

West of the Gschütt Pass, you'll descend through the pastoral Abtenau basin and follow the Lammer River. Tiny belfries cap the chalet farmhouses, and field fences of interwoven laths border the roads. Summer and fall travelers see hay drying on long racks.

At Golling you meet the Salzach River. From the village, a short detour leads to the Gollinger Waterfall. Cross the Salzach bridge and follow *Wasserfall* signs posted along country roads. From Golling you'll follow the river north across the wooded slopes edging the Tennengau basin.

Ancient Hallein grew up around its salt mining and refining industry. Reached by cable car, the Dürrnberg mines are a favorite day excursion for Salzburg visitors.

# Train Travel: Fast, Convenient, Fun

Europe's economical and efficient railways speed travelers from Scandinavia to southern Europe

Travel by rail can be a memorable—and practical—part of your European vacation. Modern electric and turbo-powered trains can't match the nostalgic mystique of old-timers like the Orient Express. But they are clean, efficient, frequent, and fast (some travel over 100 mph/160 kph).

Europeans ride the rails everywhere. When you join them, you watch the countryside unfold. You glide past lush farm lands and majestic castles, peer intimately into home gardens, and marvel at snowy mountain panoramas. At the same time, you can rest, read up on the next destination, or converse with fellow passengers.

To use trains to best advantage, plan your progress from country to country to avoid unnecessary backtracking. You can also use the train for short day excursions from cities to countryside destinations.

For detailed planning, obtain condensed national or regional timetables from your travel agent or U.S. offices of various European railroads. Even more helpful is a copy of the Thomas Cook *International Timetable*. In the United States you can obtain this comprehensive timetable from a few metropolitan bookstores specializing in travel books or by mail from Forsyth Travel Library, P.O. Box 2975, Shawnee Mission, KS 66201 (send a large, stamped, self-addressed envelope for a price list and order form).

## Kinds of trains and classes

More than 100,000 miles/160,000 km of track crisscross Western Europe. Long-distance and main-line equipment range from fairly modern to the latest in luxury.

The crack trains are those of the TEE (Trans-Europ-Express), linking 130 cities and vying with each other in speed and service. Most have names and are known for the routes they run. The TEE trains are all first-class, reserved seat only, and they cost a few dollars more than other first-class trains. Next best, and often just as comfortable, are the fast, long distance, InterCity (IC) express trains. Other categories are intermediate fast trains (international and domestic), and short-haul locals.

You'll find two classes of service: first and second. Second-class seats cost about two-thirds of first-class fare. You meet people more easily in second class, but accommodations are more austere and usually much more crowded.

## Saving money with rail passes

If you plan extensive travel over long distances, the Eurailpass can be a remarkable bargain. It is valid for unlimited first-class rail travel—and some ferry, steamer, and bus transportation—in 16 countries: Austria, Belgium, Denmark, Finland, France, Germany, Greece, Holland, Ireland, Italy, Luxembourg, Norway, Portugal, Spain, Sweden, and Switzerland. You need a separate BritRail Pass for British trains (see page 21).

You can buy a Eurailpass for periods of 15 or 21 days, or 1, 2, or 3 months; travelers under 26 years may purchase a Eurail Youthpass, good for 2 months of second-class rail travel. Your pass lets you avoid standing in ticket lines; just show it to the conductor along with your passport. You still must stand in line for seat reservations and TEE reservations. The Eurailpass eliminates the TEE surcharge but not the seat booking charge.

If you plan to visit just one or two countries, a national or regional transportation pass may be economical for you. For information, consult your travel agent, the government tourist offices, or national railways.

## Finding your way around the rail station

Trains depart and arrive in the heart of the city, convenient to public transportation, hotels, and the business district. Many services are available in the typical European city rail station: baggage checking, lockers, currency exchange, post office, newsstand, public telephones, restaurant or snack bar, washroom facilities, bicycle rentals. Often there's a tourist information booth where you can book local lodgings for a small fee. Pictograms direct travelers to various services.

When you arrive, it's a good idea to check the schedule of departing trains and make your seat reservation (if desired) before leaving the station.

**Timetables.** You'll find timetables (the route and times of each train) and schedules (all arriving and departing trains) posted inside the station. Trains operate on the 24-hour clock.

Schedules of departing trains are usually printed on yellow paper, arrivals on white paper. Red ink entries show express trains, black ink identifies local trains.

Note pertinent information including train number, track and platform numbers, time of departure, and important routing points. Symbols denote meal, bar, and sleeper service. Many cities have more than one station, so make sure you know the right one.

Trains begin summer service the last week in May and shift to winter service the final week of September.

**Seat reservations.** Even a first-class ticket doesn't guarantee you a seat. In busy seasons and on long trips, a seat reservation is a wise investment to make sure you won't have to stand all the way. (On local and many middle-distance routes, all seats are unreserved.)

To obtain a seat reservation, you must stand in line at

the station and pay a modest charge to request a specific seat (window or aisle, smoking or nonsmoking compartment). Usually you can get immediate confirmation of a reservation on a train leaving from your station.

The reservation form indicates the car and seat numbers. To board the train, look for car numbers on the outside. Seat numbers are posted outside individual compartments; a tag in the panel indicates a reserved seat, and you find the seat that matches your number.

**Luggage handling.** Your agility and freedom en route will be directly related to your restraint in packing. At most stations, porters are rare or nonexistent; some stations have self-service pushcarts. It's quickest and simplest to carry luggage aboard the train with you. On most trains, you'll have to heave carry-on bags into an overhead rack. You can usually check bulky luggage in the baggage car.

All major stations have coin-operated lockers where you can store suitcases and packages between trains or while you look for a hotel. Oversize bags and backpacks can be checked at the baggage storage area.

## You're on your way

For a worry-free departure, arrive at the station in plenty of time, and find the correct track and platform. Signs on some station platforms have diagrams showing the makeup of the train; this helps you position yourself to get on the right car during the train's brief stop.

Train cars are marked with car number, class of service (I or II), smoking or nonsmoking compartments, and other functions (sleeper, diner, baggage). An identification panel lists the originating city (on top), the destination city (on the bottom), and important stops along the way.

It's up to you to determine the schedule before you board. Carry a map and timetable, and note the stations as you pass through. A few minutes before you expect to arrive, post yourself and your luggage near the exit. Conductors neither announce stations nor open the doors, and most stops are brief. Keep your ticket in case you need to show it when you leave the train at your destination.

**Food and beverages.** Dining can involve a sumptuous—and expensive—meal on a luxury train or just a snack from a cart. It's common practice for travelers to bring along food—hearty sandwiches and a bottle of wine, perhaps—for a picnic aboard the train. You can buy cold food at the departure station, but for a more appetizing selection, find a good delicatessen near the station.

Almost all TEE and many intercity runs have white tablecloth dining. Many trains—but not all—have aisle beverage and snack service. Trains seldom have drinking water, so bring bottled water or other beverages. Have local currency to pay for food and beverages.

**Border and customs control.** When the train approaches the border, immigration officials will inspect your passport or other required documents right in the compartment. You'll be asked if you have anything to declare. Occasionally the customs officer may ask to inspect your luggage.

**Sleeping arrangements.** If you'll be covering long distances while you sleep, you can reserve and pay a surcharge for sleeping accommodations.

Couchettes are communal quarters which offer little privacy, four or six bunks to a compartment; sexes may be mixed. Wear something that's comfortable to sleep in. An attendant provides sheetbags and blankets; washing facilities are at the end of the car.

At greater cost you can have a larger and more private compartment that converts into a two or three-bed unit. Each compartment has a washbasin, soap, and towels. Men and women are usually segregated, though persons traveling together can book a single compartment.

# Villages along the Danube

Visit charming riverside villages of the Wachau district, then return to the capital through the Vienna Woods

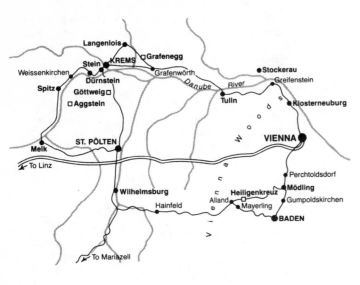

On pleasant weekends Viennese families often head up the Danube valley or into the Vienna Woods. Ancient castles and imposing abbeys tower above attractive riverside towns. In the thickly wooded hills of the *Wienerwald,* you can join walkers striding energetically along forest paths. Wine gardens in vineyard villages near Vienna offer residents and visitors alike a pleasant opportunity to savor the local wine.

You'll discover plenty of picnic sites, or you may prefer to stop for lunch in a rustic country *Gasthaus* (inn). Spring-blossoming fruit trees and summer wildflowers add attractive accents to the countryside. In September and October, clusters of grapes hang heavy on the vines, and vintners' villages celebrate the harvest with lively festivities.

Country back roads are best explored by car, but Danube steamers offer a pleasant option for enjoying the river scenery. From May to September, passenger boats cruise the Danube between Passau (in Germany) and Vienna, continuing downstream to the Black Sea. Day excursions travel from Vienna upstream through the Wachau section of the river valley to Linz, docking briefly at small riverside towns.

Trains run west from Vienna to St. Pölten and Melk, and south to Baden. Tram cars and buses link Vienna with many suburban areas.

You can vary the loop trip suggested here in several ways, or if you prefer, break it into several separate excursions.

## Up the historic Danube

Europe's longest river, the Danube, either crosses or borders 8 countries on its 1,754-mile/2,826-km course from the Black Forest region of Germany to the Black Sea.

Through the centuries, the Danube valley has been a strategic route—or barrier—between Europe and the East. Romans, Huns, and Crusaders followed this gray-brown river highway; later came the Turks, followed by the Swedes during the Thirty Years' War; after them came Napoleon. Local rulers built castles on crags high above the river. Along its banks, they constructed fortified villages to collect taxes from passing ships carrying salt, iron, and wine.

From Vienna, follow the river north to 12th century Klosterneuburg Abbey, pass tiny Greifenstein and its medieval castle, and cut through the woods toward Tulln. Cross the river here and turn west toward Krems.

The road from Tulln through Neustift i. Felde and Grafenwörth passes a huge field of flowers, where you can buy bunches of freshly cut blooms at a roadside stall. Villages offer their backsides to the road, farmers preferring to decorate their inside courtyards in the East European manner. You can break the trip with a picnic or garden stroll at Schloss Grafenegg, a fascinating little castle enclosed by walls and a moat.

From Krems you can continue upriver to Dürnstein and Melk or cross the big bridge over the Danube and head south, past the Benedictine abbey of Göttweig, to St. Pölten and the forested hills and wine-making villages of the Vienna Woods.

## Through the Wachau

Krems marks the beginning of the Wachau, the scenic section of the Danube valley renowned for its riverside villages, vineyards, and impressive castle ruins.

Best way to enjoy the Wachau is to stay in a Danube-side village for several days and take your time getting acquainted with the area. Many of the riverside towns were founded in the 9th and 10th centuries. Almost every one has its quiet square and old houses, dominated by a lovely Gothic church. Many of the churches contain beautiful paintings or carved wooden statues.

A delightful old town at the foot of terraced, vine-covered hills, Krems has a number of historic buildings and a wine museum showing items connected with the vineyards of the Danube valley.

One of the prettiest Wachau towns is Dürnstein, with the ruins of Dürnstein Castle towering above it. Walls were built up from the river to surround the village. Inside the gate, medieval and Renaissance houses and inns line the narrow streets. Just off the main street is the vil-

Crenelated medieval wall still girdles Dürnstein, one of several charming Wachau towns bordering the Danube.

Bulbous-domed belfry rises above Schönbühel Castle, built on a rock above the Danube downstream from Melk.

lage church, known throughout Austria for its baroque tower and stucco ceiling. A rocky path leads to the castle ruins where, according to legend, King Richard the Lion-Hearted was imprisoned in 1193 while returning from the Crusades.

In the charming medieval market town of Weissen-kirchen, a covered wooden stairway leads up to the fortified parish church. In the 16th century, villagers surrounded the church with a wall to protect it from invading Turks. The Wachau Museum is located in the Teisenhofer-Hof, a fortified 16th century dwelling with an attractive arcaded courtyard.

Upstream is the fortified church of St. Michael, flanked by a round tower. Spitz lies off the road, hidden behind fruit trees at the foot of terraced vineyards; arcades and balconies enhance its old houses, and the 15th century parish church is worth a visit.

Across the river, the ruins of Aggstein mark the site of one of the most formidable medieval fortresses in the heart of the Wachau. A steep path climbs uphill from the village of Aggstein to the castle.

## Melk's magnificent abbey

Overlooking the Danube from a high bluff on the south bank is the magnificent Abbey of Melk, its domes and symmetrical towers standing out against the sky. One of Austria's most beautiful existing baroque churches, it also has a vivid history.

First built as a castle in the 10th century, the building was turned over to the Benedictine order and converted into a fortified abbey. During the Turkish invasion of 1683, the monastery was gutted by fire. Napoleon established his headquarters in the rebuilt abbey during his successful campaigns against Austria in 1805 and 1809.

Guided tours allow visitors to see many of the artistic treasures preserved within the immense complex of buildings. Dominating the monastery is the beautiful church, lavishly decorated in baroque style.

## Wooded hills & wine villages

From Melk, head east toward the old city of St. Pölten and follow country roads southeast through the densely forested hills of the Wienerwald. Footpaths crisscross the rolling countryside, and small towns and country inns may prompt you to stop.

East of Alland you pass the site of the Mayerling tragedy (the double suicide in 1889 of Archduke Rudolf and his young mistress). A side road leads to the Abbey of Heiligenkreuz, founded here in the 12th century. Surrounded by forested hills and vineyards, the famous old spa of Baden has been a favorite of generations of Viennese; in summer, concerts and operettas are performed in the Kurpark.

You return to Vienna along the Weinstrasse through a series of charming wine villages—Gumpoldskirchen, Mödling, and Perchtoldsdorf—which produce white wines enjoyed in the local *Heurigen* (wine gardens). Look for a branch of greenery hanging over the door, then enter the vine-draped courtyard to enjoy a mug of chilled white wine. Frequently a musician or two will add to the festivity.

# Busy Town on the Bodensee

Lively Bregenz offers lake sports, a summer music festival, and nearby mountain trails

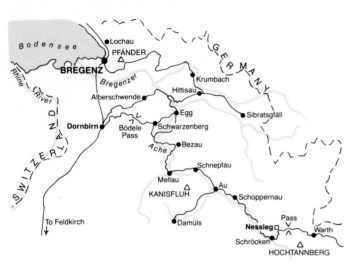

**Bright flags add festive air to traditional buildings in busy town of Bregenz at edge of Bodensee.**

Climbing the wooded slopes at the east end of the Bodensee (Lake Constance), Bregenz overlooks a panorama spanning three countries. Administrative capital of Austria's Vorarlberg province, it lies within minutes of the German and Swiss borders.

The site of present-day Bregenz was colonized by the Celts about 400 B.C., and the Romans established a lakeside trading camp here about 15 B.C. The fortified medieval town, built on high ground overlooking the lake, took shape during the reign of the counts of Bregenz and Montfort, who ruled until the 15th century.

A landscaped 5-mile/8-km promenade rims the lake shore, providing a place for strollers to watch water sports and harbor activity. Boat trips to lakeside towns depart from spring to early autumn. During the month-long Bregenz Festival in July and August, operas are presented outdoors on a stage built over the water.

The city's shopping district clusters below the old town. Regional handicrafts are available at Heimatwerk-Vorarlberger, Montfortstrasse 4. You can learn about regional history and culture at the Vorarlberger Landesmuseum (closed Mondays) on the Kornmarktplatz.

An impressive gateway marks the entrance to the old town, where quiet streets and weathered buildings lend a storybook air. In the ancient Martinsturm, chapel frescoes date from the 14th century and attic skylights offer glimpses of the lake and the old town.

From town, the Pfänderbahn cable car climbs in 6 minutes to a superb view point overlooking parts of three countries and the entire length of the shimmering lake. A network of mountain trails traverse the Pfänder; hikers can follow paths downhill to Bregenz.

## Through the Bregenzerwald

From Bregenz a scenic road cuts southeast for 48 miles/77 km, climbing through gentle foothills to end dramatically at Warth in the high Alpine regions of the Hochtannberg. The Bregenzerwald covers a wide area of densely wooded highlands, green valleys, and lush meadows set against the majestic Alps. It is a favorite destination for a day excursion or a mountain holiday. The narrow-gauge Bregenz Forest Railway links villages between Bregenz and Bezau.

If your visit coincides with a holiday or other festive event, you'll see Bregenzerwald women and members of local men's brass bands in regional dress.

Near the village of Egg the valley branches. A country road leads north to the lower Bregenzerwald and villages such as Krumbach, Hittisau, and Sibratsgfäll.

The highway continues up the main valley to Bezau, a village set amid fruit trees. From Mellau you climb still higher, through Schnepfau to Au, where a side road leads to Damüls, highest village of the Bregenzerwald.

Above Schröcken, clustered around its church, the steep road winds up through woods to Nessleg, a view point for enjoying the upper gorge and high peaks. You cross 5,495-foot/1,675-meter Hochtannberg Pass and continue through pasture lands to Warth.

# special interests

# In Austria

## MUSIC IN THE AIR

If any country can claim to be the capital of music, it's Austria. Many renowned composers have lived and worked there.

Most of the country's major music festivals take place in summer. From autumn to spring, the spotlight focuses on Vienna.

Productions of the Vienna State Opera draw international acclaim, and notable conductors lead the Vienna Philharmonic Orchestra. Musicals are performed in the Theater an der Wien. More opera is presented at the Volksoper, and small chamber orchestras and choirs perform in the city's concert halls.

Write to the Austrian National Tourist Office for information on major musical events and to learn how overseas visitors can obtain tickets.

## SUMMER IN THE ALPS

Do your spirits soar at high altitudes? In the Austrian Alps from June through October, novice mountaineers learn basic climbing techniques at mountaineering schools, and experts scale the high peaks. Guides can be hired at all centers.

Hikers and walkers follow footpaths threading Alpine peaks and valleys. Trails lead from one mountain hut to another. Overseas visitors can join the Austrian Alpine Club (Österreichischer Alpenverein) to obtain special rates for overnight accommodation in mountain huts and reduced fares on some lifts and trains. Write to the Austrian National Tourist Office for more information on mountain holidays.

## WINTER SPORTS

Skiing is a way of life in Austria. Both experts and casual skiers enjoy wide-open slopes and well-marked trails linked by lifts. About 50 resorts draw international skiers, though some 800 towns and villages have ski facilities.

At winter resorts you can rent skis, poles, and boots for both alpine (downhill) and cross-country skiing; instruction is available. Nonskiers enjoy tobogganing or "mini-bob" sledding, ice skating, and *Eisschiessen* (a team sport reminiscent of curling). In many resorts you can ride horseback through the snow or enjoy a sleigh ride through the winter forest.

For more information on winter sports resorts and activities, write to the Austrian National Tourist Office.

## ART AND ANTIQUES

Vienna's galleries and antique shops delight art lovers and collectors. In second-hand bookshops and city art galleries, you can purchase intriguing old books, engravings and etchings, oils and water colors.

Unique in Europe is the state Dorotheum, located at Dorotheergasse 17 in Vienna (near the Hofburg), and in other Austrian cities. Established about 270 years ago by order of Emperor Josef I, "Aunt Dorothy" organizes auctions of art works, household furnishings, silver, and other articles for private dealers.

The Dorotheum is open weekdays from 10 to 6 and Saturdays from 8:30 a.m. to noon. You can browse through the rooms to inspect items before the auction; each article is marked with the calling price and date of auction.

## TRANSPORTATION BARGAINS

Travelers who purchase an Austrian Network Pass enjoy unlimited travel on all trains and other transport operated by the Austrian Federal Railways. The tickets can be obtained for first or second-class travel for 9 or 16 days or 1 month. They include free travel on many lake steamers, cogwheel railways, and cable cars, and on some buses. Young people between 6 and 26 years of age can purchase the Austria Ticket (youth pass), good for 9 or 16 days of second-class rail travel. Both can be obtained at all Austrian rail stations.

Senior travelers (women 60 years and older, men over 65) qualify for half-fare passes valid on Austrian Federal Railways and the bus system of the Federal Railways and Postal Service; the passes must be obtained in Europe. Seniors need a special identification card, which can be obtained by mail.

For information on all rail passes, contact the Austrian National Tourist Office.

## VIENNA'S COFFEE HOUSES

A Viennese and his coffee house are inseparable. You'll see habitués settling in for hours—reading the newspapers, meeting friends, enjoying coffee and pastries, watching passers-by. The coffee house becomes a peaceful refuge, an office, a drawing room. Some people even have mail sent to their coffee houses and take their telephone calls there!

When you visit a *Konditorei* (confectioner's shop), you'll face a mouth-watering array of tortes, strudels, and other delectable pastries. Ordering coffee is a science in itself. Viennese traditionally enjoy a hearty afternoon *Jause* (tea) with coffee and cakes before attending the opera or theater, then have supper afterward.

## HOLIDAYS IN THE SADDLE

In Austria, an interest in horses can be pursued in a variety of ways. You can take lessons at one of many riding schools (most operate the year around), join a trekking party, or participate in jumping or dressage competitions.

Spectators can enjoy classical riding at the Spanish Riding School in Vienna, attend racing or trotting events, or visit any of the many country horse shows. For information on equestrian sports activities, write to the Austrian National Tourist Office.

## TOURING VIENNA BY FIACRE

The clip-clop of horses' hooves still echoes through Vienna's historic central district. Passengers can climb aboard a *Fiacre* (horse-drawn cab) for sightseeing around the Hofburg, favorite residence of the Hapsburg monarchs; along the "Ring" boulevard curving around the heart of this baroque city; or to other parts of the old town.

Buggies can carry four passengers. Agree on a fare with the driver before starting out; rates vary according to the cab, the route taken, and time of day.

**For information on travel in Austria, write to the Austrian National Tourist Office (address on page 7).**

# Tuscany's Hill Towns & Chianti Wine

In the earthy heart of central Italy, tour medieval art cities and visit wineries in the Chianti vineyards

Probably no other region in Italy contains such a wealth of art as Tuscany, despite damage wrought by time and man. Here in central Italy, the mysterious ancient race of Etruscans left their Greek-influenced art and fortified ruins scattered across the fertile valleys and hills. Many towns contain art treasures, ranging from Etruscan urns to medieval frescoes and Renaissance paintings.

Adorned in a palette of earthy colors, the landscape is a delight of changing patterns—verdant fields, silvery gray groves of rounded olive trees, leafy vineyards alternating with great rectangles of ripening corn, tawny haystacks drying in the sun, dark green cypress trees etched against a pale blue sky.

Fortified towns crown the strategic hills, remnants of medieval conflicts between Florence and Siena. Tucked back in valleys or perched atop hills are towns and villages little changed in appearance since the Middle Ages. In Tuscany's Chianti Classico region, you visit wineries that have been producing for centuries.

You'll find the hill towns most pleasant to visit in spring and autumn, for temperatures soar in central Italy during the midsummer months.

From Florence you can travel by train to Arezzo, Poggibonsi, or Siena in 1 to 2 hours. CIAT buses (a national line) and various tours also serve the historic towns.

## Above the Arno valley

From Florence, drive along the Arno River to Pontassieve and begin to climb into the hills and valleys of the Prato-

**Square stone towers form skyline of ancient San Gimignano, an inhabited town preserved as a national monument.**

magno Massif. You'll find splendid views at Vallombrosa and at nearby Saltino, overlooking Florence, the Arno valley, and the Chianti vineyards.

In the hilltop fortress town of Poppi, the palace (now the town hall) shows visitors its shaded esplanade and a court decorated with coats of arms.

Impressive monasteries are isolated in the mountains north and east of Poppi. Founded in the 11th century, Camaldoli is reached by a narrow road climbing through rugged country above the Arno. La Verna Monastery, founded by St. Francis of Assisi in 1216, became a place of pilgrimage during the Middle Ages.

## Tuscan art cities

In the beautiful Etruscan hill town of Arezzo, travelers converge on the Church of San Francesco to view the magnificent frescoes painted by Piero della Francesca during the mid-15th century. In understated tones of blue, gray, and reddish brown, the frescoes depict the story of the Holy Cross. Their unusual visual quality, facial expressiveness, and subdued use of light marks a departure from the work of earlier artists. Don't miss the splendid stained glass window of St. Francis offering roses to the Pope; it was created by master French glass-stainer Guillaume de Marcillat, who settled in Arezzo after working at the Vatican with painters Raphael and Michelangelo.

Medieval houses and palaces surround Arezzo's Piazza Grande. To get the flavor of the town, explore the narrow side streets south and east of the great square lined with old houses, small churches, and palaces.

About 20 miles/30 km south, Cortona clings to a steep slope above the broad plain. This silent town has changed little since the Renaissance. For its size, Cortona boasts the work of a remarkable number of Italy's great artists.

Best preserved of the art cities is Siena, an enchanting treasure of medieval art and architecture. In the Middle Ages, Siena was Italy's financial capital, rivaling Florence in wealth and importance before finally bowing to the powerful Medicis.

Eleven streets lead into the striking, fan-shaped Piazza del Campo, where the famous Palio festival is held each July 2 and August 16. Patrician houses built by the town's wealthy merchants line the lively streets just above the piazza. In late afternoon, pause at an outdoor cafe at the edge of Il Campo and enjoy the animated scene while sipping a *campari* or *espresso.*

You'll find many of Siena's art treasures near the Piazza del Duomo. Inside the cathedral, notice the unique mosaic paving that depicts allegories and scenes from the Bible. Nearby is the Piccolomini Library with its famed Pinturicchio frescoes. The city's art gallery is one of Italy's finest, highlighted by an extensive collection of paintings of the 13th to 16 centuries.

## Ancient villages crown the hilltops

North of Siena, detour to the medieval village of Monteriggioni, mentioned by Dante in his *Inferno* and a bastion in Siena's continuing battles with Florence. You'll find the town's walls and towers intact. A single street skirts the thick 13th century walls, offering glimpses of home gardens. Farm families still use the 12th century church and the cistern in the piazza.

Colle di Val d'Elsa appears suddenly, sitting high on a ridge above the Volterra road. You enter its massive fortified gate through a stone arch wide enough for only a single car. Handsome old medieval houses and *palazzi* line the town's long single street; narrow alleys occasionally angle off. Once a Renaissance palace, the town hall bears a Medici insignia over its door. An Etruscan archeological museum contains exhibits dating from the 4th century B.C.

Ancient, gray Volterra commands an austere countryside, many of its buildings dating from the 13th century. You can see works of Tuscan painters in the art gallery and Etruscan funeral urns in the local museum. From the Porta all'Arco, the town's only remaining Etruscan gate, walk uphill and left along the Via Fornelli. Through open doorways you'll see men and boys working in the alabaster workshops.

In the 13th century, dozens of square stone towers jutted above the walled town of San Gimignano; today 14 remain, mellowed by the centuries.

Popular San Gimignano is best seen on a weekday out of season. Hours pass quickly as you amble along the narrow streets of this beautiful little national monument. At noontime the sound of bells fills the town, reverberating from the tower walls.

One pleasant spot is the Piazza Cisterna, characterized by a patterned brick pavement and 13th century octagonal well faced with travertine (a type of limestone) panels; towers and patrician homes face the piazza. From the rooms and terraces of the Albergo Cisterna, you see laundry hanging in the sun and garden patios where children and their teacher-nuns study in the open air.

## A taste of Chianti country

Vineyards frequently cover the rolling hills between Florence and Siena. This is Chianti Classico country, a lovely historic region where Chianti wine has been produced since the 13th century. Hundreds of vintners are located here, and many wineries are housed in medieval castles, villas, and monasteries.

Wines produced in this area that meet government standards are labeled Chianti Classico and wear the famous *gallo nero* (black rooster) trademark.

Tuscany's traditional wine road is the Chiantigiana, winding south from Florence through the towns of Greve and Castellina in Chianti amid the heart of the vineyards. If you'd like information about touring the area and perhaps visiting a winery or two, write or visit the Chianti Classico Wine Consortium, Via dei Serragli 146, Florence.

Black rooster signs mark the Chianti country roads. Wineries off the main routes are signposted with an arrow, the name of the winery, and the rooster. Many wineries are closed on Sundays. You can taste wine at some of the larger wineries, but don't count on a tour unless you've made an appointment through the Chianti Classico office or the tourist office in Greve. Some winery tour leaders speak English, but most wine workers do not.

# Food—a Favorite Travel Discovery

Snack on street food...shop for a picnic...discover new treats in restaurants, pubs, and pastry shops

Any traveler who ventures beyond Europe's major cities quickly learns of the interesting variety in foods and preparation methods. These change not only from country to country but also within different regions of a nation.

To penetrate a region's culinary mysteries, you must look at its geographical location and the cultural origins of its people. Each country traditionally borrows ideas and methods from neighboring countries, from other nations who governed it, or from its colonies.

Regional dishes primarily reflect the products of the land. In one region you'll find an abundance of cream and butter; in another, an emphasis on hearty servings of meat and game; in a third, a spareness in cooking typical of the land itself. Seasonal foods and local wines add flair to regional menus.

## Where shall we eat?

If you want to make a self-guided food tour—or at least locate some excellent restaurants where you'll enjoy both the food and atmosphere—jot down appealing ones you discover in your reading. You'll find restaurant suggestions in all price categories listed in travel guidebooks and other publications. Ask well-traveled friends with similar tastes for recommendations.

On the scene, you can ask tourist officials or your hotel concierge for suggestions. Be as specific as possible about the type of restaurant you want—price range, location, lively or quiet ambience, type of cuisine.

## What shall we have for dinner?

Do a little homework to minimize the trauma when you first confront a handwritten menu in a foreign language without English subtitles. Read about a country's cuisine and regional food specialties.

Unless you're exceptionally fluent in the language of the country, you'll find no substitute for a good pocket-size menu translator. It can ease the problem of deciphering menus, and it will give you confidence to try new dishes. A good menu translator provides detailed definitions of dishes, along with information on types of restaurants, meal hours, kinds of beverages available, dining and drinking customs, and tipping.

Most European restaurants post the menu outside, so you can figure out the daily specials before you even open the door. Regional wines frequently go best with the food.

If you're looking for a good value, consider the menu of the day (also called the *Tagesmenu, menu du jour, menu del giorno,* or tourist menu). It is usually a 3-course meal that you can order at a clearly stated price with no extra costs except beverage. If a hearty single portion is ample for you, look for the words *Tellerservice* or *plat du jour* on the menu in modest restaurants.

## Snacking on street food

Europeans believe food and the outdoors go together—in open-air markets, picnicking and other *al fresco* dining, and in food stalls located on many city street corners.

Your food sampling need not be confined to restaurants. Sidewalk snacks are popular with locals-on-the-run, and offer more new food experiences for you. Food stalls can also be found at festivals and street fairs.

Sausages are a favorite snack in countries with a Germanic heritage. No morning visit to Munich's outdoor Viktualienmarkt is complete without a *Weisswurst* or two, eaten with fingers at a stand-up sausage stand. Viennese often stop at a *Wurstelstand* before an evening at the opera. In Scandinavian cities, you can buy hot tasty sausages at sidewalk *Polser* stands.

Want a quick sandwich? In the Netherlands, find the nearest *broodjeswinkel,* where the soft roll of your *broodje* is heaped with your choice of meat, fish, or salad fillings. In Germany, ask for a *Wurstsemmel* (sausage on a roll) or a *Schinkensemmel* (sliced ham on a roll); *Fischsemmel* is a favorite snack at the Viktualienmarkt.

The British snack on fish and chips. Belgians enjoy their *frites,* deep-fried potatoes wrapped in paper that are sold at strategic street corners. The Dutch like raw herring, popped into the mouth whole (minus the head), and eaten with chopped raw onions.

Another Belgian favorite is *gaufres* (waffles), baked in cast-iron molds and eaten warm. Ice cream lovers find interesting flavors but varying quality.

Autumn is ushered in by the sidewalk chestnut vendors, who tempt passers-by with hot sweet chestnuts freshly roasted on small portable stoves.

## Plan a picnic

Europeans are nature lovers, and they enjoy picnicking at every opportunity. You'll see them having lunch outdoors along country roads, beside streams in the forest, or on mountain benches with a view of snowy peaks.

For travelers, a picnic provides a delightful break. Pause in your journey or sightseeing and relax outdoors in the fresh air. Picnics can save time if you're driving and allow you to avoid a large midday meal.

Selecting a spot for your picnic can be as simple as pulling off the road beneath a tree or spreading your meal on a handy bench. Memorable picnics result when a dramatic setting enhances good food and good company.

**Shopping for your picnic.** Buying the makings of your lunch can be part of your eating adventure. Food shopping in foreign countries is intriguing.

Often you'll go from shop to shop, buying crusty rolls or a long thin *baguette* of French bread at the bakery, meats and cheese at another store, fruit in an outdoor market, cookies or tarts in a pastry shop, a bottle of wine in a wine store. Add a bit of elegance with slices of pâté, or individual quiches or pastries. European shopkeepers are accustomed to selling foods in small portions, even single pieces or slices. You pick and choose and point, dealing with friendly clerks who are anxious to help.

In cities, most large department stores have a food market and delicatessen section offering a cosmopolitan selection of hot dishes and cold foods that you can purchase in single-serving containers. They also carry an ample selection of cheese, bread, fruit, wine, and sweets.

**Your picnic kit.** If you plan to picnic often, bring along minimum picnic supplies from home: corkscrew, a small serrated knife, plastic glasses, foil-packed towelettes.

You may want to include a small cutting board, miniature salt and pepper shakers, paper plates and napkins, plastic forks and spoons. In Europe you can purchase tubes of mayonnaise, mustard, and catsup that need no refrigeration. A net or string bag is handy for carrying small purchases.

## Traditions linger on

Allow time in your travels to pause and join residents in enjoying some of these long-standing traditions.

**Coffeehouses.** A Viennese coffeehouse is a haven of peace where you're welcome to relax as long as you like—catching up with newspapers, conversing with friends, writing letters (see page 81).

**Lunch in a pub.** Some of the jolliest places in Britain are the pubs, which provide food, refreshment, and sometimes shelter for travelers. Most pubs serve simple lunches

at the bar or in a separate room. Try the ploughman's lunch—a plate of hearty bread, Cheddar cheese, sliced tomatoes, and a couple of pickled onions—washed down with a pint of "bitter" beer or local ale.

Hours are strictly controlled by law. Generally, pubs are open between 11 A.M. and 10:30 P.M., but they close for 2½ or 3 hours in the afternoon (shorter hours on Sundays). Women and couples normally use the "saloon" or "lounge bar" rather than the "public bar."

**Teatime.** The British take great pleasure in their tea, which is accompanied with marvelous breads, scones, crumpets, cakes, and dainty sandwiches. "Cream teas," with clotted cream and jam spread atop scones, are popular in Devon and Cornwall. Viennese enjoy *Jause,* when they pause for coffee and plenty of pastry.

**Cafe sitting.** When the first sunny days of spring arrive, Europeans move outside. Sidewalk cafes provide one of the best places for Europe's favorite spectator sport: people-watching. Late afternoon is a pleasant time, when you can relax after the day's activities before dinner.

**New wine.** The first new wine of the season is cause for celebration in *Heurigen* (wine gardens) in the vineyard suburbs around Vienna (see page 79). Arrival of the year's new Beaujolais wine in mid-November is likewise a cause for festivity in Paris and in good restaurants throughout France.

**Sweet tooth specials.** If dessert is your favorite part of the meal, you'll find a grand array of pastries, cakes, fruit tarts, and other confections. Window-shop the bakeries and pastry shops.

Chocolate candy reaches heavenly heights in Belgium, Holland, and Switzerland. In Swiss candy stores, take a basket from the stack by the door and select your choice from half-barrels of individually wrapped chocolates filled with fruits, nuts, creamy or chewy centers, or fruit-flavored liqueurs.

# Rediscover the Riches of Southern Italy

Explore excavated Roman towns along the Bay of Naples, then relax along the fabled Amalfi Coast

Many travelers prefer to bypass well-known destinations, yet in doing so they may miss some of the world's most satisfying travel experiences.

One of the richest of these regions lies south of Naples. You can explore excavated Roman towns buried 1,900 years ago by the volcanic rubble of Mount Vesuvius or idle away sunny days along an enchanting seacoast. Most of the buildings damaged in southern Italy's severe 1980 earthquake have been reopened to the public.

It's possible to make day trips south from Naples, but many travelers prefer to establish a suburban base at Sorrento or one of the towns along the Amalfi Coast.

You can reach Pompeii and Salerno by train from Naples (Central Station); trains for Sorrento depart from Circumvesuviana Station. Herculaneum lies just off the autostrada between Naples and Pompeii. Local buses travel the twisting coastal roads of the Sorrentine Peninsula, allowing passengers to enjoy the magnificient views between Sorrento and the towns along the Amalfi Coast. Steamers and hydrofoils provide year-round service from Naples and Sorrento to the isle of Capri. Small boats also serve peninsula ports.

The main tourist season extends from June to mid-October, but many British and northern European visitors come here in winter seeking Italy's warm sunshine.

## Buried by a volcano's fury

Mount Vesuvius suddenly looms up southeast of Naples, a beautiful yet menacing vision dominating the countryside. On an August day in A.D. 79, Vesuvius erupted spectacularly, spewing superheated mud, lava, and hot cinders over Roman towns and luxurious villas facing the Bay of Naples. Among the towns buried were Herculaneum and Pompeii, both rediscovered and excavated in recent centuries.

Pompeii usually receives top billing for its varied and striking ruins. Herculaneum, northwest of its more famous neighbor, is noted for the outstanding preservation of its private homes. Silent streets offer glimpses of both the simple and grand ways of Roman life, catastrophically preserved for later discovery. Many valuable relics have been moved to the National Museum in Naples.

At both sites you can hire an English-speaking guide and perhaps team up with a few other visitors. If you prefer to tour the ruins independently, purchase a well-illustrated, English-language guidebook. Many interesting buildings are protected behind locked gates; you can usually find a courteous guard who will unlock the door.

If the excavated Roman cities of Herculaneum and Pompeii whet your interest in antiquity, consider a visit to the ancient Greek colony of Paestum, 25 miles/41 km southeast of Salerno. Founded in the 6th century B.C., it was rediscovered in the 18th century. The massive Temple of Neptune is among the best preserved in Europe.

**Herculaneum.** Until its destruction, Herculaneum was a popular country resort on the Bay of Naples. Buried by mud and lava, it was better preserved and more carefully excavated than Pompeii, and offers a fascinating look at life in a 1st century Roman provincial town.

You explore along three main streets, each lined by houses up to three stories high. Furniture is often intact. A bakery contains an oven, flour mills, and even jars for storing grain. A wooden clothespress stands in a dyer's shop. Frescoes and other works of art ornament the House of the Stags, a mansion featuring a central garden and a sun porch overlooking the sea.

**Pompeii.** When Vesuvius erupted, this town of 20,000 people was literally interred in more than 20 feet/7 meters of cinders and ashes. Though only 2 miles/3 km in circumference, Pompeii has too many attractions to see thoroughly in a single day. At the museum, castings, models, and excavated objects introduce you to Pompeii's daily life and grim fate.

As you explore Pompeii's cobbled streets, you'll see ruts etched by the wheels of Roman chariots. Highlights include the Forum, center of Pompeii's political, social, and religious life; the public bathhouses; and the open-air theaters and stadium where actors, musicians, dancers, and athletes entertained the citizens. Large patrician villas such as the House of the Vettii provide a look at the sybaritic life of wealthy Romans.

## To Sorrento and Capri

Praised by poets and musicians, Sorrento overlooks the Bay of Naples from cliffs that drop straight to the clear blue sea. Off season, the town has an almost quiet air.

You can use Sorrento as headquarters for sightseeing, craft shopping, or sunbathing. Life centers around several small *piazze* (squares) each with its statue surrounded by flowers and greenery. Numerous short piers—used solely by sunbathers—extend from shore. At night, fishermen sail out in their small boats, lighted lanterns gleaming like stars in the darkness to attract the fish.

Across a 10-mile/16-km channel from Sorrento is Capri, an island jewel in the crown of Neapolitan attractions. Granite cliffs honeycombed with grottoes shoot up from the deep-blue sea to a pair of suspended, flower-decked towns. Numerous villas peek out from subtropical greenery.

Buses and taxis link the small island's two harbors with the towns of Capri and Anacapri, but the most charming way to get around is by horse-drawn *carrozzelle*. Capri is a town of small squares and rustic alleyways. Pedestrians follow narrow, stone walks that wind among shops, houses, and walled gardens.

A road carved in the cliff provides breathtaking views as you climb to delightful Anacapri. A chair lift transports you even higher to the summit of Monte Solaro, 951 feet/290 meters above the sea.

From Marina Grande, motorboats take visitors to the entrance to the Blue Grotto, where you transfer to a small rowboat to enter the cave. Inside, you are suddenly floating on a shimmering blue sea as refracted sunlight illuminates the large cavern to dazzling brightness.

## Along the Amalfi Coast

Few mountain routes offer the exhilarating beauty of the Amalfi Drive, the corniche road linking Sorrento and Salerno. Dipping and climbing along steep cliffs above the sea, the twisting route passes terraced vineyards and vegetable gardens, small cliffside resorts, and fishing villages nestling beside curving bays. Belvederes offer magnificent vistas. Pine trees, citrus blossoms, and flowers perfume the sea air.

Driving the narrow coastal road can be difficult, and trucks and buses can bring traffic to a halt. Take a bus and enjoy the ride. Comfortable hotels and inns serve guests at Positano, Amalfi, Ravello, and smaller towns along the coast.

From Sorrento the road climbs through citrus orchards, then descends steeply toward the peninsula's south coast. Through the trees you glimpse the sea far below.

Sheltered on each side by hills, the fishing village of Positano spills down the mountainside. Small shops tucked in narrow lanes offer an array of merchandise ranging from local crafts to chic Italian wares. Living like cliff dwellers, Positano's residents descend steep stone stairways to reach the pebbly beach.

The twisting road climbs around Cape Sottile and passes through the small resort and fishing village of Praiano. You reach the Emerald Grotto by elevator from the road.

Amalfi's site is spectacular—tall, white houses rising from rocky slopes overlooking a blue bay. It prospered as a 9th century trading town, and by the 11th century it

Houses and shops of Positano spill down terraced slope above blue sea. You descend stairs to reach small beach.

In excavated Roman resort of Herculaneum, south of Naples, you stroll streets where Roman chariots once traveled.

regulated all Mediterranean navigation under the world's oldest maritime code. The cathedral, begun in the 11th century, blends Oriental splendor and Romanesque austerity. Walkers join the promenade along the oleander-lined Corso Flavio Gioia or take the path up the Mulini valley.

East of Amalfi, a winding mountain road climbs through vineyards to Ravello, which hangs like a balcony suspended between sky and sea. Cool and peaceful, Ravello is a town of small squares, covered passageways, and gardened stairways. Everything is within strolling distance of the central piazza. Dating from the 11th century are the cathedral, with Byzantine mosaics in its nave, and the Villa Rufolo, residence of several popes and other illustrious guests. Gardens of the Villa Cimbrone extend to a view point overlooking the sea.

# Exploring the Trulli District

Fantasy villages of whitewashed huts are sprinkled across the Apulian hills deep in southern Italy

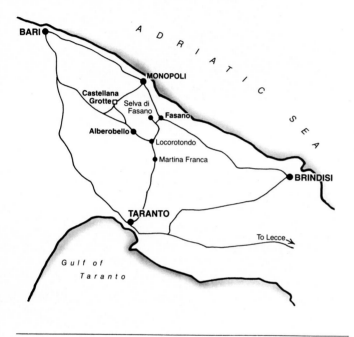

**Gleaming white buildings topped by conical, dry stone roofs line streets in Alberobello, heart of the trulli district.**

Few travelers venture deep into the Apulia region, which stretches along southern Italy's Adriatic shore between the ports of Bari and Brindisi. In the heel of Italy's boot, you'll discover fantasy villages where each whitewashed house is topped by a conical dome and hex signs are often painted on the stone roof tiles.

From the rounded hills above the Itria valley, groups of the white, cone-topped *trulli* enliven the ocher and green landscape. The district extends from Monopoli south to Martina Franca. The best display is found in Alberobello, where more than a thousand of the unusual buildings climb the side of a wooded hill.

A strange, white, dry-stone structure with a domed tile roof, a *trullo* is the typical peasant house of the region. Each house is built on a square plan. The loose-laid walls have no mortar and are plastered a dazzling white. Crowning each building is a pointed dome, covered with concentric slabs of smooth gray stone and closed by a slender finial. Astrological and religious symbols deco-

rate some houses. Origin of the primitive dwellings is somewhat obscure, but they show traces of the prehistoric Saracens and early Christian civilizations.

Rental cars are available in both Bari and Brindisi, and you can stay in Alberobello and other nearby towns. The region is most pleasant in the spring, when everything is in bloom, or during the mild fall months. Weather extremes make summer and winter travel uncomfortable.

## Driving in the *trulli* district

You'll have good views from the hills of the trulli-dotted landscape, particularly near Selva di Fasano and from the Locorotondo - Martina Franca road. Vineyards and olive orchards grow in the umber-colored soil, and each plot of farm land has its white house, topped by the distinctive cone roofs marked with hex signs to ward off evil spirits.

Center of the trulli district is the hilly town of Alberobello, about 35 miles/56 km south of Bari. Virtually the entire town is composed of the unusual white buildings, their stone-tiled domes pointing skyward like a fanciful garden city.

Alberobello's most characteristic quarter lies on a wooded slope to the south, beyond a mall. As you walk along the town's narrow, flagstone streets, you'll pass dark-garbed women sitting in front of their houses, weaving mats and shawls from threads hung on nails. In the upper part of the quarter, you'll see the trullo-shaped Church of Sant'Antonio.

North of Alberobello are the caverns of Castellana, the largest and most noted caves in Italy.

# Cliffside Path Links Five Coast Towns

Along the Italian Riviera, you walk from village to village on a scenic footpath above the sea

**Vernazza's promontory commands broad seascape. Distant Montorosso al Mare is reached by rocky coastal path.**

A world apart from the crowded resorts of the Riviera, five unspoiled Ligurian fishing villages of the Cinque Terre (Five Lands) cling to a steep section of the Mediterranean coast north of La Spezia. Terraced vineyards climb the ridges above the rugged shore.

You catch glimpses of the villages—Riomaggiore, Manarola, Corniglia, Vernazza, and Monterosso al Mare—on a train ride between La Spezia and Genoa. But for a memorable interlude to your trip, leave the train and walk the footpaths that lead the short distance from one village to another. A seaside pathway cuts across cliffs above the Mediterranean, and an upper pathway threads among the vineyards and wooded areas. During the grape harvest, the upper path is crowded with vineyard workers carrying great baskets of grapes to the villages below. Hillside erosion may make passage difficult on some parts of the paths.

Until recent years these cliffside villages were isolated, accessible only by rail and water and linked only by paths. However, the days of isolation are limited. A new corniche highway being built high above the sea between La Spezia and Levanto will have spur roads descending to the settlements.

All five villages can be reached by train. Local Genoa to La Spezia trains stop in each village; some direct trains stop at Monterosso. In summer, excursion boats cruise to the Cinque Terre from Portofino, Levanto, and other ports.

## Along the seaside path

One good way to sample this steep, dramatic stretch of coast is to leave the train at Riomaggiore at the southern end of the string. Crowded into a narrow valley, its old houses climb slopes on either side. It's less than 1 mile/1½ km—about a 20-minute walk—north to Manarola along a section of path known as the *Via dell'Amore* (Lovers' Walk). A guard rail bounds the seaward side of the level flagstone path.

Most rugged of the five villages, Manarola perches precariously just out of reach of the crashing waves, its colorful houses clinging to the slope above the dock. You can decide whether to continue your walk or wait for the next train. If you walk farther, you'll find the trail to Corniglia unpaved, slightly more rugged, and often littered with fallen rocks; it takes about an hour.

Corniglia has tall houses carved from the rock along very narrow streets. Its Romanesque church has an elegant rose window. Steepest part of the trail is between Corniglia and Vernazza; allow 1½ hours for this section.

High on a rocky promontory, Vernazza has a breathtaking view of the sea. Narrow streets lined with colorful old houses radiate from a small square, and a fort—built to repel invading Saracens—overlooks the village. Fishing boats bob in the tiny harbor cove. It's a steep 4-mile/6-km descent from Vernazza to Monterosso; walkers enjoy sweeping views during the 1½-hour jaunt.

Monterosso al Mare, largest of the towns, has a long swimming beach and good resort hotels.

# Alpine Loop through the Dolomites

East of Bolzano, historic routes wind through the rugged mountains to spectacular alpine valleys

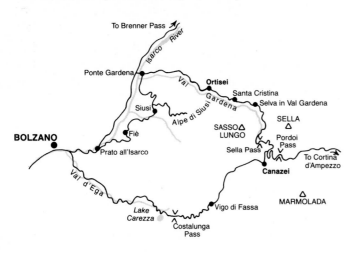

Many fast-moving travelers speed south from Austria straight to the cities of central Italy, bypassing a spectacular mountain region just a few miles east of the Brenner Highway. Here the craggy peaks of the Dolomites jut skyward behind sun-bathed valleys and flowery meadows.

Though best known for their excellent winter sports facilities, the rugged Dolomites and the beautiful Val Gardena make a delightful detour in any season. When skiers and skaters depart, the climbers arrive. Mountaineers come to the Dolomites for some of the best climbing on the Continent. Hikers enjoy country walks through valleys and across slopes; paths are well marked, and rest huts are spaced conveniently along many routes.

During the spring you'll enjoy green hillsides and valley fruit trees in full bloom. In early summer, dwarf pink rhododendrons, blue gentians, and other wildflowers brighten the high alpine meadows; jagged peaks form a rocky backdrop. Late-season travelers appreciate the cool clean mountain air, unspoiled villages, and many opportunities for outdoor excursions. From Bolzano, capital of the district, there is daily bus service to the Val Gardena and across the Dolomite Road to Cortina d'Ampezzo.

## A blending of cultures

Originally part of Austria, the South Tyrol was annexed to Italy after World War I, its autonomy guaranteed in language and education. Like everything else in this region, the food combines Italian and Austrian influences. Signs identify streets in both German and Italian. Most

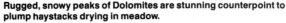

**Rugged, snowy peaks of Dolomites are stunning counterpoint to plump haystacks drying in meadow.**

houses are constructed in Tyrolean style (chalets with broad, low-pitched roofs and long balconies).

Geographically, the region lies between the Germanic and Mediterranean worlds. Its valleys are protected by high mountains from the fierce northern winds, while receiving the southern sun.

Bolzano, the previously mentioned capital of the mountainous Alto Adige district, is an old commercial city that manages to retain much of its medieval charm. It borders the Brenner Pass route, the main traffic artery linking the German North with the Latin South for more than 2,000 years.

You'll see this blend of cultures in Bolzano's old district where high-gabled houses line narrow streets. Stroll down the Via dei Portici, the arcaded main commercial street, to the Piazza delle Erbe where a weekday fruit market takes place. Center of town is the Piazza Walther; facing it is the cathedral, built in Romanesque Gothic style with a tall, open belfry.

## Scenic route across the Dolomites

Cutting a spectacular route through these mountains, the great Dolomite Road is a superb example of engineering. It twists through high mountains for a thrilling 68 miles/ 110 km, linking Bolzano and Cortina d'Ampezzo. Much of the way, it follows a historic route once used by Renaissance merchants traveling from Venice to Germany.

You can drive the complete distance in about 3 hours, but you may prefer to travel by bus or chauffeured car so you can give full attention to the landscape. Scenery along the way is dramatic, dominated by rugged limestone rocks that are pinkish in color but change with the light. Wind and rain have eroded the high peaks into ragged towers and rough domes, too steep for glaciers to form. At their bases lie gentler slopes, covered with alpine pastures, evergreen forests, or cultivated land.

Southeast of Bolzano, the Dolomite Road angles between high cliffs into the narrow Ega Valley gorge. High above on a cliff, Cornedo Castle guards the gorge and its turbulent little river. You climb slowly past small villages to tiny Lake Carezza. A small blue jewel edged by dark green conifers, it reflects the jagged peaks of the Catinaccio and Latemar massifs.

Here you begin to feel the Alpine grandeur of the Dolomites. Long ago these coral-tinted rocks thrust above an ancient sea. Glaciers covered them during the Ice Age. Later, wind and rain eroded them into weird towers and spires and sculptured the wall faces.

Cross the Costalunga Pass, then descend the winding road to Canazei, a busy summer and winter sports resort deep in the mountains. Climbers use the town as a base for summer mountaineering excursions into the Marmolada range to the south.

If you continue east on the Dolomite Road, you'll cross the high and desolate Pordoi and Falzarego passes. Pause and absorb the view before making the awe-inspiring descent to the elegant mountain resort of Cortina d'Ampezzo, site of the 1956 Winter Olympics.

To loop back toward the Brenner Highway, turn north off the Dolomite Road above Canazei toward the Sella Pass. Its extensive panorama encompasses the mountain massifs of Sasso Lungo to the west, Marmolada to the south, and Sella to the east.

## Slow-paced life in the Val Gardena

From the Sella Pass you descend into the Val Gardena. One of the most typical valleys in the Dolomites, it offers incomparable views of the mountains, an abundance of woods and open meadows, and a wide choice of excursions, walks, and climbs. The verdant valley widens and narrows by turns, its slopes covered with forests, cascading streams, and mountain dwellings.

Isolated high in the mountains, the valley opened to visitors only a century ago. It is the home of the Ladini, descendants of Roman soldiers sent here centuries ago to conquer the area. Traditional customs and skills have been retained.

Three Ladin communities—Selva, Santa Cristina, and Ortisei—sit astride the road that winds through the valley; all have an Alpine flavor. Life moves at a relaxed pace, particularly in the spur valleys. The people speak the Ladin-Romansch dialect. Some occasionally wear regional costumes to church and at weddings and other special celebrations.

This region is one of the major European centers of woodcarving, a family industry going back to the 17th century. Nearly every family has at least one skilled member carving traditional toys and statuettes. You can arrange to see woodcarvers at work in their shops and homes.

One of Europe's fashionable Alpine ski resorts, the Val Gardena hosted the World Alpine Ski Championships in 1970. Numerous lifts and cableways transport skiers to the slopes, where powdery snow lasts until spring. The three towns are also summer resorts; Ortisei is the valley's main town.

A cableway links Ortisei with the snowfields—or summer flowers—on the Alpe di Siusi. You'll see Alpine flowers here not found at lower elevations. From this high point, you'll have superb vistas over valley and peaks.

## An idyllic Alpine meadow

If you're driving this Alpine loop, you can follow mountain roads to the Alpe di Siusi high above the Val Gardena.

To reach this beautiful Alpine meadow, take the scenic road heading southeast from Ponte Gardena; about 1 mile/1½ km north of Siusi, take the side road veering eastward and uphill. It will lead you to the center of the lovely Siusi Alp.

This great open Alpine pasture is an enchanting place—an idyllic sea of wildflowers in late spring and early summer, a vast snowfield with splendid ski slopes in winter. From the high plateau, you have breathtaking views of the Dolomite peaks and the Val Gardena. If you like, you can use Siusi as a base for wonderful alpine walks or climbing excursions.

To return to Bolzano, go south from Siusi on the panoramic road winding high above the Isarco River valley. At Prato all'Isarco you meet the Brenner Highway and continue west to Bolzano.

# Seeking Family Ties in "The Old Country"

Learn more about your origins or meet distant cousins when you visit the land of your ancestors

Many travelers combine European travel with a bit of amateur genealogy when they visit the land from which their ancestors emigrated. Searching for family ties in "the old country" can be personally fulfilling and add pleasure to your holiday, as you learn more about your family origins and gain a new sense of identity.

Even if you don't add a new limb to your family tree, the effort provides a chance to meet people. You'll make new friends who will try to help you find your cousins or trace your ancestors.

Your search may lead to out-of-the-way hamlets, into dusty old church records, even to a court or a jail. Perhaps you'll walk the same narrow old streets to the house where your great-great-grandparents lived a century or more ago. In the parish cemetery, weathered tombstones may provide a tangible link with the past.

### What facts will you need?

Before you fly off on a roots-finding trip, write to the appropriate tourist information office to learn exactly what facts and records will be most helpful in your search. Britain,

Ireland, and some of the Scandinavian countries have leaflets suggesting ways to proceed. Other countries also can offer ideas on sources of family information.

Try to learn in advance the town or region of your family's origin; their birth dates; name of their parish church; what they did for a living (tenant farmer, laborer, servant, fisherman); and when the family migrated to the New World and where they settled. The precise spelling of the family name before they emigrated can be important because original versions sometimes suggest areas of birth or residence (many names were shortened or misspelled by immigration clerks at Ellis Island or other entry ports).

### How to find information at home

Talk to members of your family, keeping a separate record of pertinent dates and facts for each ancestor you learn about. Ask older relatives and long-time family friends for information about deceased family members and precise information on names, birth and death dates, home towns, and marriages.

Examine written family records including Bibles, birth and marriage certificates, correspondence, documents, diaries, photograph albums, and scrapbooks.

Your local library or historical society can direct you to a variety of sources of genealogical information and give you suggestions on how to proceed in your genealogical research.

You can trace your ancestors in America back through state archives, census records, and the National Archives in Washington, D.C. (which has such documents as passenger lists for arriving ships, homestead applications, and naturalization records). The Church of Jesus Christ of Latter-day Saints maintains a vast repository of family genealogical information in Salt Lake City, open to persons of all faiths.

### Tracking down new family ties abroad

Armed with curiosity and a few clues about your ancestors, you're ready to learn more about your family's origins. Pack some chocolate bars and an orange in your pocket and set off on your quest.

The search can be a diverting challenge, leading to interesting places you'd otherwise have missed. When you know your family's home town or region of origin, check with the local tourist office or town authorities to find where records are kept. Registrars in vital statistics offices maintain records of births, marriages, and deaths. In some countries, church registers go back for centuries and are a vital source of family information.

On-the-spot research is far from dull. Discovering an original handwritten record penned by a contemporary of your great-grandfather may give you a special thrill. And each time you discover a new clue in your quest, your sense of excitement grows into a renewed urge for further research.

# special interests

# In Italy

## OPERA & MUSIC FESTIVALS

Opera began in Italy in the 16th century, and it has flourished in succeeding centuries. The Grand Opera season opens late in the year in Italy, usually in November or December, and runs through May or June.

Most famous of Italy's opera houses are La Scala in Milan, Teatro dell'Opera in Rome, La Fenice in Venice, Massimo in Palermo, and San Carlo in Naples, but many other Italian towns also have performances during the season. In summer, operas are performed outdoors in a number of cities, including Naples, Rome, and Verona.

Florence's outstanding festival of the performing arts, "Maggio Musicale Fiorentino," takes place in May and June.

For more information on Italian musical events, write to the Italian Government Travel Office.

## GASOLINE DISCOUNT COUPONS

Foreign motorists traveling to Italy can purchase a Carta Carburante Turistica offering special benefits, including gasoline coupons sold at a reduced rate, free motorway toll vouchers, and free breakdown service. Purchased abroad or at Italian border stations, four types are available for motoring in various regions of Italy. For more information, write to the Italian Government Tourist Office.

## ITALY'S ARTISTIC LEGACY

For the art lover, Italy is one vast museum whose rich artistic history dates back to the Etruscans in the 9th century B.C. Its heritage includes a considerable amount of Greek art, as well as architecture and early Christian art from the Roman era, Gothic churches, and sculpture and painting from the medieval period.

Nearly every town in Italy carries the imprint of the Renaissance. Later, during the baroque period, Italy again brought new inspiration to European culture.

For more information on Italy's artistic heritage, museums, and art cities, write to the Italian Government Travel Office.

## BRENTA CANAL BY BOAT

During the 17th and 18th centuries, wealthy Venetians retreated in summer to their villas along the quiet Brenta Canal. Evening gatherings were lighted by flickering lanterns as hidden orchestras played softly.

You can enjoy a link with the past aboard a modern canal boat that makes summer excursions along the tree-lined canal linking Venice and Padua. The motorized Il Burchiello leaves three times weekly from Easter through mid-October. Each boat trip lasts all day; you return to your starting point by bus.

The boat crosses the Venetian lagoon and cruises up the calm canal past elegant villas. You stop at Stra for a visit to the Villa Pisani and its park, and at Oriago for lunch in a canalside restaurant.

## BOATS TO ISLANDS

Steamers and hydrofoils transport travelers from Italy's mainland ports to Capri, Elba, Ischia, Procida, Sardinia, Sicily, and many small islands along the Italian coast.

Steamers, car ferries, and hydrofoils also operate on lakes Como, Garda, and Maggiore.

For information on steamer, car ferry, and hydrofoil services, write to the Italian Government Travel Office.

## TRAIN TRAVEL TICKETS

The Italian State Railway (FS) offers train travelers a BTLC Italian Tourist Ticket, which can be purchased for first or second-class travel for periods of 8, 15, 21, or 30 days. The ticket features unlimited travel on the entire system.

Ticket holders pay no supplement to ride Rapido trains (express and fast trains), and owners of first-class passes do not have to pay a surcharge to travel on TEE
(Trans-Europ-Express) and other top trains. The BTLC Ticket also allows free seat reservations, obtained at rail stations in Italy.

The Italian Kilometric Ticket can be purchased for first or second-class travel. Good for 2 months on regular trains of the Italian State Railway system, the ticket is good for 20 trips totalling 3,000 kilometers (1,875 miles). It can be used by as many as five people at a time, related or unrelated; each trip is calculated by multiplying the distance traveled by the number using the card. Children aged 4 through 11 are charged half-distance.

Both tickets can be purchased at offices of the Italian State Railway (in New York, Chicago, Los Angeles, and Dayton, Ohio) and in Italy at the central railway station in principal cities.

## SKI HOLIDAYS

Italy's major ski resorts are scattered across the northern part of the country, where the Italian Alps arc from France east to Yugoslavia. Within this sea of white peaks lie some of the world's finest winter playgrounds. Skiing continues through the summer at some high resorts.

Among Italy's leading winter sports areas are well-known names like Courmayeur, Breuil-Cervinia, and Cortina d'Ampezzo. Some of Italy's best kept secrets are resorts such as Piancavallo, Bormio, and Madesimo—friendly informal villages where skiing is a way of life.

Many ski packages are available combining accommodations and lift passes with instruction, meals, or car rental. See your travel agent or an international airline for more information.

## SKIN DIVING

The clear Mediterranean waters along Italy's rocky coasts offer excellent skin and scuba diving and spear fishing. Diving is allowed everywhere except in harbors; no license is required for spear fishing. Check regulations on use of equipment.

Best diving months are March through May and September-October. Best times of day are from 6 to 8 A.M. and 5 to 8 P.M. Equipment is available for rent or purchase at main seaside resorts.

**For information on travel in Italy, write to the Italian Government Travel Office (addresses on page 7).**

# Cruising in the Cyclades

Island-hopping in the central Aegean, you visit dazzling-white port towns, hillside chapels, ancient ruins

You could spend a lifetime traveling in the Greek islands and never visit them all. About 1,400 islands, each with its distinct identity, are scattered over a large area of the eastern Mediterranean. Some are lush and green, others arid and rocky. Some have resort hotels and lively nightlife; many remain relatively untouched by modern influences.

Typifying this variety is the Cyclades group, a few dozen islands in the central Aegean encircling the holy island of Delos. Here you'll find whitewashed fishing villages rimming a deep-blue sea, small chapels tucked in folds of the hills, ancient monuments, and a history stretching back 5,000 years.

## Getting around in the Cyclades

You can explore the Cyclades in four ways: by air, cruise ship, chartered yacht, or ferry.

In summer, daily flights leave Athens for Mykonos, Milos, and Thera (Santorini).

**Cruise ships.** From the end of March to late October, cruise ships depart from Piraeus, the large harbor southwest of Athens, on cruises varying from 3 to 14 days. The ship becomes a floating hotel where passengers sleep and eat most of their meals. It sails during the night, and each day passengers go ashore at a new port. Only a few islands can accommodate the crowds of visitors who flock ashore from cruise ships.

**Independent touring.** If you have the time and want to plan your own tour of the Cyclades, you and your group can charter a yacht, or you can sail aboard the public ferries to visit islands off the routes of the cruise ships.

Most ferries depart from Piraeus. Major islands—Mykonos, Naxos, Paros, Siros, Thera, and Tinos—usually have daily service in summer; ferries call less frequently (two or three times a week) at other populated islands. Ferries for some northern Cyclades islands sail from Rafina, northeast of Athens.

In the office of a Greek shipping line, you can book space aboard one of the ferries that ploughs through the Aegean and stops occasionally to pick up and deposit passengers, cars, and cargo. Budget travelers usually book deck space, but on longer trips you may prefer to go second-class, which entitles you to seats in a salon.

It is relatively easy to stop at several islands along the same route, but arrangements can get complicated if you want to cross between shipping lines.

The strong north wind called the *meltémi* blows from about mid-July to mid-September in the Cyclades, when rough seas can make sea travel unpleasant. Three to 6 days of wind are followed by a similar period of calm seas. Winds are strongest from sunrise to noon; their force abates in afternoon and air is still at night.

## Which island for you?

Today's island-hopping travelers continue a long tradition. The waters of the Aegean have been well traveled since the Greeks fought the Trojans. Phoenicians, Carthaginians, Romans, and Crusaders sailed these seas, stopping at islands along the way.

The Greek islands offer different things to different people. Each island has its special attractions and atmosphere, but they share sunshine, beaches, hospitable residents—and multitudes of summer visitors.

In the Cyclades, travelers who enjoy activity and nightlife head for Mykonos. The sacred isle of Delos draws those interested in the monuments of antiquity. Paros and Naxos offer attractive towns, modern accommodations, good beaches, and island excursions without the crowds of Mykonos. On Thera, cruise ship passengers climb the side of a volcanic crater by donkey to reach the clifftop town.

Travelers find varied accommodations on Andros, Mykonos, Naxos, Paros, Siros, Thera, and Tinos. Smaller islands offer less selection. Most of the better hotels and restaurants, which primarily serve vacationers, close during the winter.

**Delos.** Renowned for its archeological wealth, Delos is a strange, haunting place. Long ago it was the religious center of the Aegean.

Most important of the remaining monuments is the Terrace of the Lions, where five stone beasts still stand as symbolic guardians of the sanctuary. A narrow street climbs toward the remains of a Hellenistic city and theater. A museum houses some archeological finds, but the best are now in the National Museum in Athens.

**Mykonos.** An international playground, Mykonos is favored for its dazzling-white town, active nightlife, and sandy swimming beaches (including some coves for topless bathers). Brightly colored flowers spill over balconies and staircases. Round, thatch-topped windmills with small canvas sails are a special attraction.

Boutiques, tavernas, jewelry shops, restaurants, and discothèques line streets near the waterfront. If you enjoy people-watching, sit in one of the harborside cafes. Behind the waterfront, you'll enjoy wandering through the maze of narrow twisting lanes.

**Paros.** Undulating hills greet your approach to the island's capital, Parikia. Ruins of a Venetian castle overlook the whitewashed town.

In Parikia's narrow streets, elderly Greek women dressed in black mingle with backpackers. The town's windmill serves as information office, bus stop, and local gathering place. Parikia's treasure is its 6th century Church of the Hundred Gates (Ekatontapyliani), one of the loveliest in the Aegean.

Best beaches are at the north end of the island, about a half-hour by bus from Parikia, around the bay from the fishing village of Naoussa. You can visit the quarries that produced the famous white Parian marble favored by classical sculptors or enjoy the quiet Garden of the Butterflies. Boats take passengers to the large satellite island of Antiparos for cave exploring.

**Naxos.** Largest and greenest of the Cyclades islands, Naxos has a spacious harbor and attractive main town. You'll enjoy strolling through the narrow covered streets and stairways of this old Venetian settlement.

Agriculture has made Naxos more self-sufficient than most islands, so its tourist development has been slower. Travelers stop here to enjoy the beaches, explore the island's charming villages and fertile interior, and see its relics. Ancient ruins dot the island.

**Thera** (Santorini). About 1,500 B.C., this was a thriving outpost of the Minoan empire. When the island's volcano erupted, it created a deep volcanic bowl and began the legend of Atlantis.

Cruise ships anchor in the broad, sea-filled crater while passengers go ashore, climb aboard donkeys, and climb the zigzag path up the steep crater wall. The white terraced town called Thera gleams along the cliff rim high above the sea. Shops line the narrow cobbled streets.

The island has dozens of churches. Most notable is the monastery Church of Profitis Ilias and its priceless collection of icons.

On the south coast, archeologists are excavating the Minoan village of Akrotiri, long buried under pumice and ash. In the seafarers' village of Ia at the north end of the island, guest houses have been opened in traditional Greek houses. Black sand beaches edge the greenish sea at Kamari and Perissa. Small boats transport visitors to the Burnt Islands in the middle of the crater.

Dazzling white buildings, accented by colorful awnings and shutters, rim water at Greek fishing port of Naxos.

Fishermen spread out saffron-colored nets on island docks preparing for next day's excursion into the Aegean.

**Other islands.** Less well-known islands offer small waterside villages, chapels and monasteries, quiet beaches, and a leisurely atmosphere. Distinctive windmills can be found on Serifos, Kea, and Sifnos.

Many wealthy shipowners live on the wooded island of Andros. Its attractions include good swimming beaches and ruins of an ancient city at Palaiopolis.

Mountainous Tinos contains traces of Venetian architecture and the enormous church of the Blessed Virgin, crowded with pilgrims on March 25 and August 15. Towered dovecotes and numerous chapels add charm.

Shipyards and associated industries give Siros a different atmosphere from the fishing and agriculture-based settlements on most other islands. The low-lying island has charming bays and good beaches.

A beautiful bay cuts into the olive-clad hills of Ios, a favorite island of backpackers. The white cubist architecture of the Cyclades is seen at its best on the beautiful and remote islands of Sifnos and Folegandros.

Great orange limestone cliffs rim Amorgos's eastern coast, where the small white Monastery of the Virgin (Hozoviotissa) overlooks the sea. Volcanic Milos has three excavated prehistoric towns and ancient catacombs.

# Through the Ruins of Delphi

On Mount Parnassus, follow the Sacred Way up through classical ruins to the Temple of Apollo

**Sun's rays highlight 4th century B.C. rotunda at Temple of Athena, part of sanctuary ruins on slope of Parnassus.**

April to mid-October, gates to the sacred city are open weekdays from 7:30 A.M. to 7:30 P.M., Sundays and holidays from 10 to 6. Hours are shortened in winter.

Greeks consider May and September their land's best months. In midsummer the country is crowded, and searing sun beats down on the old ruins.

## Seeking the spirit of Delphi

If you're touring independently, take along an illustrated English-language guidebook as you set out in search of the spirit of Delphi, a site entwined in Greek legends.

Begin your walk at the sanctuary of Athena Pronaia, below the road on a narrow terrace surrounded by olive trees. Known as Marmaria (The Marbles), it includes the 4th century B.C. Tholos, or rotunda, one of Delphi's finest Doric monuments. Beyond are the gymnasium and other facilities where athletes trained.

Along the roadside, a sign indicates the Castalian Spring where priests and pilgrims cleansed themselves before presenting their questions for the oracle.

Ruins of ancient treasuries (small temples containing offerings) and monuments commemorating great military victories flank the Sacred Way, the route followed by pilgrims nearly 3,000 years ago.

From the southeastern side, a flagstone path winds uphill to the Temple of Apollo, a large Doric temple dominating the site. Ancient philosophers once inscribed maxims—such as "Know thyself" and "Avoid excess"—on these walls. Here the oracle Pythia pronounced her prophecies, which were interpreted and written down by priests and presented to visitors as advice from the gods.

At the end of the Sacred Way is the open-air theater, built of white marble with space for 5,000 spectators. It overlooks the Temple of Apollo and a spectacular panorama. Higher on the slope, rimmed by pine trees, is the 7,000-seat stadium, once the site of musical and athletic competitions.

Statues, friezes, altars, and other treasures from ancient Delphi can be seen in the modern museum.

To the ancient Greeks, Delphi was the center of the world, the point where earth touched heaven. Pilgrims journeyed to the Delphic oracle to learn of the future. Today travelers visit these famous ruins in search of the past.

Delphi is about 110 miles/180 km northwest of Athens, through Thebes and Levadia. It's a 3 to 4-hour trip by car or bus from Athens; you can travel independently or join a group.

Beyond the rug-making town of Arachova, the winding road descends through vineyards, almond and olive groves, and wheat fields until a sharp curve brings you suddenly to Delphi.

On the tree-covered southern slope of Mount Parnassus, the land forms an isolated, natural amphitheater facing the Gulf of Corinth. Sheltered at its base is the sanctuary of Apollo, antiquity's leading pilgrimage destination for many centuries. Visitors climbed difficult mountain paths to reach the shrine and seek the oracle's advice. Delphi lay buried for 15 centuries, until French archeologists began excavations at the end of the 19th century.

Delphi is most spellbinding during the serene hours of early morning or early evening, when low rays of sunlight illuminate temple fragments on the slope. From

# Ancient Refuges of Metéora

Perched precariously on rocky pillars, these medieval monasteries once sheltered hermits and monks

Ravine bridge and rocky stairs are sole terrestrial access to fortresslike Varlaam Monastery at remote Metéora.

Looming above the fertile plain of Thessaly in central Greece is an awesome sight: a strange forest of gigantic rock pillars rising up to 1,800 feet/550 meters in height. Topping some of the pinnacles are the medieval monasteries of Metéora, their balconies and red tile roofs projecting precariously into space. These ancient refuges symbolize a way of life that is almost extinct: religious fervor inspiring infinite labor, discomfort, and self-denial.

Guided bus tours depart from Athens for Metéora, or you can hire a car with a driver-guide. If you drive, you'll find the road good, but narrow and winding the last few miles. Many road signs are in English as well as Greek, but be sure to get detailed directions before you start out. Spring is the best season for traveling in this part of Greece, before summer's heat arrives.

## Refuge from medieval warfare

Ancient hermits sought solitude in the rifts and caves of these rock pillars, but the first monasteries were not built until the 14th century. While Serbians and Byzantines bat-tled for control of the Thessalian plain, the hermits could meditate, undisturbed by the warfare below.

After the first monastery was founded on the Great Meteoron, other hermitages evolved into monasteries. By the late 16th century, 24 rose atop the black pillars. Women were excluded, and inhabitants lived an austere life. Today only a few of the monasteries survive.

For centuries the sole access was by rope ladder or by net basket which the monks hoisted by windlass. Nets are still used to haul up provisions.

## Visiting the monasteries

The monasteries of Metéora are located about 6 miles/9 km northwest of Kalambaka. A road winds near the base of the cliffs, and visitors climb steps cut in the rock to reach the buildings. You must descend from one pinnacle and then climb another to reach the next monastery. Though some of the stone stairways are long and steep, they're not dangerous to climb.

Some of the monasteries are historical monuments; only four are still inhabited. Women visitors are expected to wear skirts, and sleeves should cover their shoulders.

Oldest and most important of the monasteries is the Great Meteoron, built about 1350. Perched atop an almost perpendicular cliff, it is reached by a strenuous climb. Its massive gate opens on a large courtyard. The monastery chapel at Metamorphosis contains an unusual 12-sided dome and beautiful frescoes.

A drawbridge connects Ayios Stefanos to the main cliff. Old treasured wood carvings and icons have been preserved here, and you have a magnificent panorama from the windows. Ayias Trias tops a particularly forbidding pinnacle; to reach it you climb a steep flight of steps cut into the rocky face.

Largest of the retreats is fortresslike Varlaam, notable for its restored frescoes in the chapel and a small museum containing ecclesiastical treasures. Ayias Roussani, now a convent, is located on the lowest rock and is less difficult to reach than most of the monasteries.

# Lush Oasis in the Ionian Sea

On the wooded island of Corfu, you enjoy a cosmopolitan blend of Greek and Western cultures

**Left. Stairways replace sidewalks between tile-roofed houses on slopes near Corfu's coast. Right. From Kanoni view point, you look down on Vlaherna Monastery and wooded Mouse Isle.**

few Americans find their way to Corfu, though it has been a favorite destination of Europeans for decades.

You can fly to Corfu (called Kerkira by the Greeks) from Athens or travel by ferry from the Greek towns of Igoumenitsa or Patras or the Italian port of Brindisi.

## Island life moves at a relaxed pace

Corfu is small enough to be friendly, large enough to provide a variety of destinations and activities. Life proceeds in a leisurely fashion, and you seldom see Corfiates engaging in strenuous activities.

Men gather before sunup at waterfront cafes to breakfast on strong coffee and crusty bread. Early-rising shopkeepers open their doors, ready to entice the passerby. About 11 A.M., tourists swamp the narrow streets and shops in a flurry of activity before the entire island shuts down for a 3-hour midday meal and siesta. You'll find the cooler early-evening hours (between 5 and 8) best for unhurried shopping. Townspeople spend evenings outdoors in a nightly promenade.

Village life follows nature's rhythms. Up in the hills you see shepherds minding their flocks and kerchief-topped women dressed in black working in olive groves or scrubbing laundry beside the road. Donkeys transport everything—including their owners, who customarily ride sidesaddle. Talkative patrons gather in local *tavernas*, spending hours exchanging tales over endless cups of strong coffee or *ouzo*, an anise-flavored liqueur.

Travelers accustomed to the austere barrenness of the Aegean islands delight in the lush greenery and mild climate of Corfu, a verdant oasis in the Ionian Sea. Terraced groves of silvery gray olive trees, many of them planted hundreds of years ago, mingle with orange and lemon orchards, pine, cypress, and aromatic shrubs to cover the island's rolling hills.

Corfu has a cosmopolitan legacy. Protected by the Venetians for more than 400 years, it retains an Italian touch in the narrow lanes of the old town and a pair of ancient fortresses guarding the harbor. French troops occupied Corfu during the Napoleonic era, followed by British rule until 1864.

Greek legends claim Jason and Medea were among the island's earliest tourists, and Homer's *Odyssey* recounts how Ulysses was shipwrecked here. Relatively

## Corfu Town—a blend of cultures

Situated on the island's east coast, the town of Corfu harmoniously blends varied traditions and architectural styles left by the Venetians, French, and British. Broad, tree-lined avenues sweep through the modern sector, but the old town is a labyrinth of pedestrian lanes.

Two medieval citadels—called the "old" and "new" fortresses—loom above the town and harbor. "Sound and Light" performances are presented in the twin-towered old fortress from mid-May through September. From atop the fortifications, you're afforded spectacular vistas of town, wooded island, and sea.

Getting around the old town is best done on foot, but you may enjoy riding through city streets in a horse-drawn carriage. Buses departing from Neo Frourio Square and San Rocco Square serve the town and other parts of the island. You can also arrange to tour the island's roads by rental car, motor bike, or taxi.

**Spianada.** Largest and most attractive of the town's squares is the Spianada, or esplanade, a favorite place for people-watching. Chess players ponder strategy in the warm sun, young mothers exchange news, and small boys kick balls on the cricket green where summer matches are still held in a surviving link with British tradition.

Along one side of the square, you can relax at cafe tables in the shade of the elegant Liston arcades, a reminder of the French era. In the evenings you can watch as townspeople promenade, men bowing formally to acquaintances and young men strutting to attract feminine attention. Occasional parades and religious processions wend through the grounds, and local bands present summer open-air concerts here.

At the north end of the Spianada is the Saints Michael and George Palace, built in 1823 as a residence for British high commissioners of the Ionian Islands. It now houses the Museum of Asiatic Art.

**The old town.** West of the Spianada, you'll discover the old Venetian section, a maze of narrow cobbled alleys called *cantounia*. Lining the passageways are multistoried houses, their vertical windows framed by ironwork balconies and tall shutters that close out the intense midday sun. Drying laundry hangs above the lanes on lines strung between upper windows.

You can purchase fleecy *flokati* rugs, worry beads, jewelry, colorful apparel, and other souvenirs along Spiridon Street or nearby Dousmani Street. The latter is a virtual supermarket of small stores where housewives shop for meats, produce, and household necessities.

Standing in the middle of the market place is Corfu's proudest monument, the Church of St. Spiridon. It contains relics of the town's patron saint which are paraded through town four times a year.

The town hall, built in 1663 as a club for Venetian nobility, is a splendid example of Venetian architecture. Other buildings reflect the French influence in arches and colonnades or the Georgian style popular in 19th century England.

Local archeological discoveries, including finds from the Roman period, are housed in the Archaeological Museum, 5 Vraila Street.

## Short excursions from town

Swimmers find a good public beach just south of town at Mon Repos, near the former royal villa. Continue on to the spectacular Kanoni view point about 2 miles/4 km south of Corfu, where you look down on a pair of lovely island monasteries. Walk across a narrow causeway to reach Vlaherna Monastery; from there you can board a motorboat to wooded Pondikonissi (Mouse Isle), site of a tiny 13th century chapel.

In the hills northwest of Corfu, you'll find the Village, a complex of buildings depicting the island's varied architectural styles. Visitors watch local artisans at work and enjoy taverna activity. Greek music and folk dancing are performed outdoors in the evenings.

If you want to explore the coastline or visit some of the smaller Ionian Islands, you can arrange motor launch trips in Corfu or smaller ports.

Golfers head for the island's 18-hole Ropa Valley course about a 20-minute drive west of town.

## Exploring the island

Roads spread over the island, following the coast through a succession of small fishing ports and climbing to neat whitewashed villages tucked into the green hills. Each village usually has at least one taverna where you can enjoy modest country lunches with local wine. Coastal restaurants frequently offer the catch of the day.

**North along the coast.** From Corfu, a coastal road follows the east shore north to bustling Dassia, then continues through a series of sprawling fishing villages, including Ipsos, Nissaki, and Kouloura. The road crosses the slope of Mount Pantokrator, then descends to Kassiopi on the north coast.

Farther west, Roda and Sidari have lovely beaches. Motorboats depart from these ports on day excursions to nearby islands.

**The west coast.** Weathered cliffs and white sand beaches rim secluded coves along the ruggest west coast. Most visitors head for Paleokastritsa, renowned for its clear waters, seafood restaurants, and good fishing. You can visit the 12th century monastery crowning the headland. Just north is the 13th century fort of Angelokastro and the Bella Vista view point, a natural balcony overlooking the coastal panorama.

If you prefer less crowded coves for swimming and sunning, try Glifada or Agios Gordis beaches farther south. At the end of the day, watch the sunset from the summit of Pélekas hill.

**South of town.** Gastouri is the site of Achilleion Palace, built in 1890 as a retreat for Empress Elisabeth of Austria and later owned by Kaiser Wilhelm II of Germany. Daytime visitors wander through terraced gardens overlooking the sea and tour a small museum. At night the building becomes a casino, where blackjack and roulette players gamble in royal chambers.

You follow the east coast to the colorful fishing village of Benitses, then continue through Lefkimi to Kavos near the island's southern tip. Small side roads lead from the main road to villages and beaches.

# On Sundays You See Europeans at Leisure

Visit the park or zoo, take a boat ride, visit a market, or join city families on a walk in the woods

On Sunday, a city shows a different face. Stores are closed, theaters and many restaurants are dark, traffic diminishes. For one day each week, the city pauses—and allows you to see its residents at play.

Earlier in the week, inquire at the local tourist office if any special weekend events are scheduled in the city or nearby areas. Perhaps you'll happen on a local wine festival, a folklore celebration, or a riverside band concert. If you enjoy sports events, you might attend a football match, bullfight, horse race, or sailing regatta.

Many persons enjoy visiting Europe's churches to admire the lofty architecture and stained glass windows. Sunday services add pageantry and music.

### Explore the city

With the aid of a good guidebook, plan your own walk through an interesting or historic section of the city. Or join an organized group walk; in London, these often start from Underground stations and encompass sights on a general theme, such as historic pubs.

Sunday is the week's busiest day at many museums, so plan to arrive early. In addition to superb exhibits of art, you'll discover many special interest museums.

**Visit the park.** Europe's city parks are a delight. Weekend afternoons, you'll see entire families relaxing—children sailing toy boats on ponds or watching Punch and Judy shows, young men in striped jerseys playing soccer, couples strolling along tidy gravel paths through beds of blooming flowers.

In Paris you can go cycling or rent a rowboat in the Bois de Boulogne; in Vienna, ride the giant *Reisenrad* wheel in the Prater; in London, go for a canal boat ride through Regent's Park or listen to impassioned speakers at Speakers' Corner in Hyde Park.

When you're tired, pause to enjoy a band concert, relax in an outdoor cafe, or just sit on a bench and watch life flow by.

**Go to the zoo.** Another great place for Sunday people-watching is the city zoo, where families are both entertained and educated by the world's animals and birds.

Children can ride gentle elephants at Zurich's zoo, watch pandas at London Zoo in Regent's Park, or observe reindeer at the zoo on Helsinki's Korkeasaari Island. In Germany you'll find excellent zoos in Berlin, Frankfurt, Hamburg, Munich, and other cities. You can also visit zoos in Amsterdam, Basel, Copenhagen, Dublin, Lisbon, Vienna, and many other large and small European cities.

**Prowl in the market.** Sunday shoppers head for city flea markets, where they browse amid colorful stalls of antiques and other used merchandise. Hucksters shout their wares over the noisy throngs.

Among the best flea markets are those in Athens (Monastriraki), Brussels (Marché aux Puces), London (Petticoat Lane), Madrid (El Rastro), Paris (Marché aux Puces), and Rome (Porta Portese).

Stamp collectors head for Madrid's Plaza Mayor on Sunday mornings. In London, artists, crafts people, and sidewalk entrepreneurs transform Bayswater Road into an outdoor art gallery.

### Take an excursion

No visit to a large city is complete without a look at nearby attractions. The city tourist information office can provide destination suggestions and advice on how to get there using public transportation.

**Walk in the woods.** Join city families for a Sunday walk in the forest. Plan ahead and purchase picnic supplies. Often you'll find wooded areas within the city itself, or you can head for the suburbs—such as the Vienna Woods or Epping Forest northeast of London.

**Board a boat.** Most large European cities are built along the coast or bordering a major inland waterway. For fresh perspectives of the city, take a sightseeing cruise—on the harbor, lake, river, fiord, or canal. On some trips you can disembark at a destination and return on a later boat.

# special interests

# In Greece

### GREEK TAVERNAS

Where is the best place to discover authentic Greek cooking in a hospitable atmosphere? The *taverna,* an institution as old as Greece itself.

Often the melancholy music of the *bouzouki* (a lutelike stringed instrument) guides you to the simple building where diners sit at hand-hewn wooden tables. Usually there is no menu; you walk into the kitchen, peer into pots simmering on the stove and into baskets of fresh fish and vegetables, then order your meal by pointing at the container whose contents most appeal to you.

Each taverna has its regular customers, who sip piquant, anise-flavored *ouzo* or the pungent, resinated Greek wine called *retsina* while enjoying music and companionship. Often the music ignites spontaneous singing and dancing.

### THE ULTIMATE MARATHON

Twice each year, runners from many nations gather in the fresh morning air at the little town of Marathon northeast of Athens. Their goal: the finish line of the Olympic Stadium in Athens, about 26 miles/50 km distant.

SEGAS, the Hellenic amateur athletic association (3 Georgiou Gennadiou, Athens 142) organizes two marathons each year: a national championship race in April and a popular marathon in October. The Greek National Tourist Organization can provide information on marathon dates and entrance requirements.

The marathon race commemorates the legendary messenger who in 490 B.C. sped from the battlefield at Marathon to Athens carrying word of the Athenian victory over Persian invaders. A sandy burial mound on the crescent-shaped Marathon plain covers the 192 Greek warriors who were slain; no tomb commemorates the 6,400 Persian dead.

### GREECE THROUGH THE AGES

No country is richer in historic monuments than Greece: its anthropologic remains date back to the Paleolithic Age. Your visit will be richer and more meaningful if you do a bit of homework so you can sort out the various civilizations and their contributions to Greek culture.

A visit to your local library or bookstore will provide books summarizing the highlights of ancient Greece, the Byzantine era, and the medieval period. You may also want to briefly review the background of major monuments you plan to visit in various regions of the country.

### CHARTER A YACHT

Round up a few friends, choose your islands, charter a yacht, and set sail on an exciting and memorable Greek holiday.

On your own chartered yacht, you can forget about hotels and restaurants, transportation schedules, and constant repacking; you sleep on board, with meals provided (or you can picnic or enjoy dinner ashore). You'll enjoy sightseeing on small islands off the cruise ship route; if you prefer, anchor for a leisurely swim in a rockbound cove.

For more information on chartering a yacht and a list of rental firms, write to the Greek National Tourist Organization.

### HIKING CRETE'S SAMARIA GORGE

Largest of the Greek islands, Crete was the birthplace of Europe's oldest civilization, the Minoans. A remarkable geographical feature of this ancient island is the Samaria Gorge, where hikers enjoy a majestic 12-mile/19-km nature walk through wild landscape.

From Hania, on the northwest coast, you travel south to the Omalos plateau. A steep zigzag path descends about 2,500 feet/800 meters into the tremendous gorge, which splits the cliffs for about 8 miles/12 km down to the sea.

Awesome in its grandeur and wild beauty, the gorge sometimes narrows to less than 15 feet/5 meters. Sheer walls rise high to hide the sunlight. A clear mountain stream rushes past. Trees cling to the rocks, birds swoop overhead, seasonal wildflowers abound.

Tourist offices organize guided trips which include transportation from Hania to the gorge entrance. From there, it takes 4 to 5 hours for casual hikers to reach the sea at the small port of Aghia Rouméli in early afternoon. After a drink or lunch at the cafe or snack bar, there's time to relax on the beach or go for a swim. In late afternoon, a boat arrives to take hikers to Chora Sfakion, where they board a waiting bus to return to Hania.

### LIVE IN A GREEK VILLAGE

If you'd like to live in a Greek village for a few days or weeks, write to the Greek National Tourist Organization. The government has restored several deserted villages into tourist complexes, providing visitors with glimpses of Greek rural life and expanding tourism to scenic areas and islands not generally visited. Settlements offer little formal entertainment.

Restored villages are Vathia, in the southern part of the Peloponnese called Mani; Makrinitsa, in the east central Pelion area near Volos; and in the northwest mountains near the city of Ioannina. Island villages have been restored at Ia on Thera (Santorini), at the fishing village of Fiscardo on unspoiled Cephalonia, and at Mesta on the island of Chios.

### POPULAR ART & HANDICRAFTS

Greek popular art reflects themes from the past—influences from the Byzantine, Hellenic, and even the prehistoric era. You'll admire these decorative motifs in hand-woven textiles, embroidery, lace, carpets and rugs, wall hangings, pottery and ceramics, metalwork and jewelry, woodworking, and painting.

You'll see handicrafts as you travel throughout the country. The National Organization of Hellenic Handicrafts sponsors a permanent show room in Athens (at 9 Mitropoleas Street, near Snytagma Square). Several nonprofit welfare and women's organizations also operate craft shops.

**For information on travel in Greece, write to the Greek National Tourist Organization (addresses on page 7).**

# Yugoslavia's Northwest Corner

Alpine lakes, winter sports, and resorts beside the Adriatic draw visitors to this diverse region

Yugoslavia's northwestern corner contains attractions to entice nearly any traveler: forest-rimmed lakes, alpine resorts, and relaxing towns beside the sea. For variety you can retreat to an Adriatic island, explore an awesome cave, or visit the original Lipizzaner horse breeding farm.

Trains link Ljubljana with the main tourist centers, where you board buses to reach smaller towns and coastal villages. Steamers, ferries, hydrofoils and launches operate from Rijeka and other coastal ports to Adriatic islands. Coach excursions depart from Opatija, Portorož, and Pula for regional points of interest.

## Alpine resorts

Austrians ruled Slovenia for more than a thousand years until 1918, and both the countryside and way of life in this Alpine region share similarities with Yugoslavia's northern neighbor. Here you'll discover a pair of lovely tree-rimmed lakes, Bled and Bohinj, tucked into the foothills of the Julian Alps.

Popular as both a summer and winter destination, the Julian Alps region has attracted generations of European vacationers. Only in recent years, however, has it been discovered by American visitors.

Climbers and mountaineers come here in summer, and hikers find challenging trails in a nearby wilderness area. You can also enjoy boating, fishing, and lake swimming. Yugoslavia's only golf course is located just east of Bled, above the Sava River gorge.

Winter visitors enjoy cross-country trails near Bled and Bohinj, and downhill skiing at Kranjska Gora. Other winter activites include skating and curling on frozen lakes, sledding and horse-drawn sleigh rides over the snow, and indoor swimming in Bled's thermally heated pool.

**Bled.** A favorite of 19th century Austro-Hungarian aristocrats, Bled retains the charm of an old-world spa. Wooded hills frame the lake, whose quiet waters reflect a small island in the middle and a castle looming on a high crag. Village shops and hotels border one shore. You can stroll along the paved lakeside promenade or climb aboard a horse-drawn carriage for a ride around the lake. On summer Sundays a local band often performs at the town bandstand.

You can hike a steep path or drive up to the 11th century castle topping a sheer bluff above the lake. From the terrace you'll gaze over a panorama of village, lake, and mountains. The castle also contains a small museum.

To explore the island, board one of the small gondolalike boats that transport visitors across Lake Bled. Rising above the foliage is an interesting 900-year-old church, built over a graveyard. Skeletons of early Slavs can be seen through a glass panel in the floor.

**Bohinj.** Beneath some of the country's highest peaks, the road to Lake Bohinj winds 17 miles/27 km west from Bled through the Sava Bohinjska River valley.

Less developed than Bled, Bohinj offers relaxation in a scenic setting. You can board a cable car that climbs to a view point high above the long, finger-shaped lake. A 20-minute trek along a wooded trail leads to the 195-foot/65-meter Savica waterfall.

**Kranjska Gora.** Slovenia's liveliest winter sports center is located just minutes from the Italian and Austrian borders. You'll find uncrowded skiing at Kranjska Gora; it's an international resort with challenging trails and lively après-ski activity.

## A vast cave and Lipizzaner horses

Between Ljubljana and the Istrian Peninsula you can detour to explore the Postojna Caves or visit the original Lipizzaner horse breeding farm.

Impressive illuminated limestone formations lie deep within a vast subterranean maze of caverns and passageways at Postojna Caves, located midway between Ljubljana and Opatija. You board an open, narrow-gauge electric train for a 10-minute ride into the caves, then take a guided group tour through the complex. It's chilly down there (42°F/6°C all year), but you can rent a warm cape.

During World War II, Nazi troops stored thousands of tons of aviation fuel in the caves. Yugoslav partisans sneaked in through a secret entrance, planted time bombs, and destroyed the fuel in a blaze that lasted for days. The tunnels are still smoke-blackened near the entrance.

Horse lovers head for Lipica, home of the world-famous Lipizzaner horses. Located 7 miles/11 km east of Trieste, the stud farm offers guided tours, lessons, performances, and other activities.

## Along the Istrian coast

Small tree-rimmed bays and attractive coastal towns mark the rocky coastline of the Istrian Peninsula. Subtropical plants and flowers flourish in the balmy climate. Resort activity centers around Portorož and Pula on the northern Adriatic coast and at Opatija facing Kvarner Bay.

**Down the west coast.** Historic villages mix with modern resorts on the peninsula's Adriatic shore.

Piran perches on a rocky headland above a sleepy fishing harbor. Narrow streets and Venetian-inspired buildings are part of the charm of the old town. Take a look at the remains of the town's medieval walls, climb the cathedral belfry for a sweeping view, then enjoy refreshment at an outdoor waterfront restaurant.

Fashionable Portorož (the Port of Roses) has broad seaside promenades bordered with palm trees and roses, luxury hillside hotels, and sophisticated after-dark entertainment.

Founded by the Romans, Poreč contains ruins of ancient temples and the city walls. However, its most important monument is the 6th century basilica, which boasts brilliantly colored mosaics.

The lovely old seaside town of Rovinj, a favorite of artists, is a maze of crooked streets and brightly painted houses overlooking a small harbor.

Near the peninsula's southern tip, the bustling city of Pula takes pride in its Roman arena. Today, the oval amphitheater is used for outdoor concerts, operatic performances, and an annual film festival. You'll also enjoy Pula's other Roman and medieval buildings, its archeological museum, and the busy and colorful harbor.

**Facing Kvarner Bay.** More flower-decked seaside resorts mark the Istrian Peninsula's southeast coast facing Kvarner Bay.

Main center for excursions along this coast is Opatija, a delightfully old-fashioned resort that was a turn-of-the-century playground for Hapsburg aristocrats. It has excellent beaches and evening entertainment. From the attractive village of Volosko, an Opatija suburb with 18th century houses, you can walk along the 3-mile/5-km coastal promenade to Lovran.

**Island hideaways.** The islands south of Opatija and Rijeka offer delightful possibilities for short excursions or prolonged relaxation. The port towns are popular with yachters, and many nudists come to these islands to soak up the sun.

From Rijeka, daily coastal steamers depart for the islands of Krk, Rab, Cres, and Lošinj. Hydrofoils also serve

Swimmers and sunbathers relax at Icici Beach, one of many inviting coves along Istrian Peninsula.

Bright rugs attract shoppers at open-air market in seaside resort of Rovinj on Istrian Peninsula.

the island ports. A car ferry connects Brestova, south of Opatija, with the island of Cres.

Island scenery is wild and majestic—luxuriant with subtropical plants and pine woods descending the western slopes, more arid and rocky bordering the eastern shores. Each island offers charming ports, swimming coves, and hideaway accommodations. The town of Krk has Roman monuments and mosaics as well as medieval fortifications. Baška, a charming seaside resort on Krk, attracts painters. The town of Rab, one of the country's most popular resorts, retains a medieval appearance.

# Plitvice's Lakes & Waterfalls

Shaded footpaths wind through a watery wonderland in Yugoslavia's scenic mountain park

Cascading waterfalls and tumbling streams link series of greenery-rimmed lakes at Plitvice Lakes National Park.

Plitvice is one of Europe's gems, a natural park cut into the mountains of northwest Yugoslavia some 50 miles/80 km inland from the sea. Thick forest rims a magnificent complex of 16 lakes, linked like a necklace of watery jewels by numerous waterfalls and cascades.

The country's best-known national park, Plitvice lies midway between Zagreb and Zadar, a 2 or 3-hour drive from the Adriatic coast. Asphalt roads connect the major towns. Coach excursions depart for the park from Zagreb and several Adriatic resorts.

Driving inland from the coastal town of Senj, you become aware of the mountains only after you climb high above the sea to a fertile plain.

Here you enjoy the peaceful scenes of the countryside—farmers plowing fields or pitching hay into bulbous stacks, village women wrapped in dark shawls exchanging the day's news, youngsters and their dogs

herding animals in from the fields. If you're driving, plan ahead; rural villages have few tourist services.

## Serene lakes & tumbling waterfalls

Many travelers regard the scenic, peaceful region around the Plitvice lakes as one of the most beautiful districts in Europe.

The park is lovely in any season. In spring, melting Balkan snows feed the lakes and thundering waterfalls. Lush greenery frames the blue-green lakes in summer. Autumn is a tranquil time, when still waters mirror their spectacular setting. Winter brings a white mantle of snow to the mountainous park.

From Lake Prošće, highest of the Plitvice lakes at some 2,000 feet/600 meters above sea level, water flows into a second lake, and from it spills over into a third. Filmy waterfalls and foaming cascades tumble over rocky ledges to connect the 16 lakes, which step down a total of several hundred feet.

Miles of paths wind through the park, edging some of the lakes and offering close views of certain waterfalls. Here and there, rough steps chiseled into the rock lead to a cave. From viewing terraces you can take in the broad scene of greenery-rimmed water, or you may prefer to find your own spot to linger, watching the play of light on water as sunbeams transform spray into a shimmering rainbow.

Water from the lowest lake flows northward as the Korana River. It offers excellent kayaking and fishing in lovely wooded country.

Several modern hotels serve park visitors. You can sample trout or salmon from local lakes and rivers, or fresh crayfish caught near the upper end of Lake Kozjak, largest of the lakes.

# Fortified Isle of Trogir

One of the Adriatic's medieval port towns, this tiny island has a cosmopolitan heritage

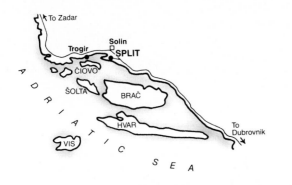

For decades Yugoslavia's sun-drenched Adriatic coast has been a favorite holiday destination, drawing European vacationers with its superb beaches and warm seas.

The Adriatic Highway winds like an asphalt ribbon above the water, climbing rugged promontories for lofty views and linking historic coastal towns and fashionable beach resorts. Off the jagged shoreline are nearly a thousand islands, varying in appearance, size, development, and accessibility.

From tourist centers you can board hydrofoils or ferryboats for excursions to the nearby islands. Bus service extends along the coast.

Spring is perhaps the prettiest time to visit. Knowledgeable travelers come before or after the summer crowds, who pack the beaches from mid-June to mid-September. (Many beaches are reserved for nude sunbathers and swimmers.) Warm sunny days linger into November, and even in midwinter you'll often enjoy brilliant sunshine.

## Trogir, a medieval masterpiece

Fortified medieval port towns stud the Adriatic coast and islands, recalling centuries of military conflict and foreign occupation. One of the most unspoiled is tiny Trogir, a 30-minute drive northwest of Split. Situated on a small island just offshore, the compact little town is connected to the mainland by a bridge.

Colonized by Greeks about 385 B.C., the settlement somehow escaped the raiding barbarians that sacked the nearby Roman city of Salona (Solin). Occupied in turn by Byzantines, Croats, Venetians, French, and Austrians, Trogir existed in relative isolation for centuries. An impressive number of medieval buildings mix the architectural styles of different cultures.

Passing through its narrow Renaissance gate and cramped streets, you'll feel transported to another era. Near the Porta Civitatis is the attractive little Renaissance loggia, once the civic center of Trogir. Just beyond, you enter the small town square, distinguished by its Venetian-inspired town hall and 15th century clock tower. The 9th century Church of St. Barbara is decorated in early Croatian style.

Trogir's most notable building—and one of Yugoslavia's best examples of medieval architecture—is the 13th century Cathedral of St. Lawrence, designed in the form of a Romanesque basilica. Opposite the cathedral is the 15th century Cipiko Palace, adorned with a decorative Venetian Gothic façade.

Other splendid medieval monuments in Trogir include churches and convents, palaces built by noble families during the Middle Ages, and the 15th century Kaštel-Kamerlengo fortress facing the nearby island of Čiovo. In times of war, heavy chains were stretched between Trogir and Čiovo to block the harbor entrance; today a bridge links the two islands.

**Many Europeans still use traditional skills in crafts. This Trogir cooper pounds pegs into barrel to tighten fit.**

# Inland to Mostar & Sarajevo

Domed mosques and slim minarets add an exotic air to these former outposts of the Ottoman Empire

**Humpbacked bridge arches across Neretva River at Mostar, framing stone buildings, domed mosque, and slender minarets.**

Slim minarets and rounded domes add an exotic oriental air to many towns in Bosnia-Herzegovina, a reminder that for more than four centuries much of Yugoslavia was ruled by the Ottoman Empire. Turkish forces occupied the region in 1463, and Eastern influences filtered into architecture, religion, foods, and other phases of local life. The mingling of cultures becomes increasingly evident as you venture from the coastal province of Bosnia inland to mountainous Herzegovina.

In the late 19th century, the Bosnians revolted and the Balkan Peninsula became a pawn among Europe's power-hungry countries. Franz Josef annexed the region as part of the Austro-Hungarian Empire despite determination on the part of southern Slavs to form a united and independent nation. Patriotic zeal culminated in the assassination of Archduke Franz Ferdinand, heir to the throne of Austria-Hungary, during a state visit to Sarajevo in June 1914.

## An unhurried style of living

Life proceeds at a leisurely pace in these inland provinces, so allow ample time if you plan to tour the area. In cafes and restaurants, men socialize over Turkish coffee or *šljivovica* (plum brandy), laughing, talking, and exchanging stories. Women take a less public role in this Moslem-influenced region.

The most pleasant time to visit is in spring or early autumn. Summer can be unpleasantly hot in some areas. Accommodations are limited outside the main cities and towns.

## Up the Neretva valley

From the Adriatic town of Ploče, road and railway head inland up the Neretva valley through Mostar, Jablanica, and Konjic to Sarajevo. The main rail line continues north through the Bosna valley to Vrpolje, where travelers change trains for Belgrade or Zagreb.

A network of buses also serves the region. Most main roads are adequate, except for the section between Sarajevo and Višegrad.

Marking your entry into this land of mosques and minarets is Počitelj, a centuries-old Turkish frontier post on the banks of the Neretva River about 20 miles/32 km south of Mostar. The charming little fortified village has been carefully restored. Almond and olive trees mingle with tobacco and cotton farms along the green valley floor.

Upriver from Počitelj, awesome cliffs flank both the road and railway. They rise more than 3,000 feet/1,000 meters above the Neretva valley.

## Enchanting Mostar

Even at first glimpse, Mostar has an exotic air. Thin minarets jut skyward against a backdrop of rugged purplish mountains.

The town's pride is its famous humpbacked stone bridge, built over the turquoise-colored Neretva by the Turks in 1556. Pedestrians stream across the bridge—housewives carrying wicker baskets of produce, farmers guiding mule carts, workers toting wine barrels. Local boys consider it a test of courage to dive from the arch 70 feet/21 meters into the chilly river. On the west side, a path winds down to a small sandy beach.

Stone houses and copper-domed mosques cluster upstream from the bridge. Along narrow lanes in the old section, sloping stone roofs overhang the houses; high-walled courtyards once shielded Moslem women from the outside world.

A village bazaar atmosphere prevails in the restored Kujundžiluk (Goldsmiths' Street), where metalsmiths and other crafts people work in the doorways of brightly painted shops facing a cobbled lane. You can visit the Karadžoz Beg mosque, notable for its graceful architecture and lavish interior decoration.

Mostar's rather stark business district dates from the Austrian occupation. On a slope above town is a memorial to World War II dead.

Yugoslavia's best white wine, made from Žilavka grapes, comes from the village of Blagaj southeast of Mostar.

Road and railway continue north, climbing the narrowing valley into the austere and mountainous Jablanica district. Konjic's old bridge near the fort dates from the 13th century. You descend Mount Ivan through the old Roman thermal spa of Ilidža to Sarajevo.

## Sarajevo, a meeting of East & West

Situated on the Miljačka River, Sarajevo has been inhabited since Neolithic times. Roman soliders built a military station here. In the 16th century, the settlement developed into an important caravansary on the ancient trade route through the Balkans to Central Europe. (A railway now follows the old caravan track about 190 miles/300 km north through the Bosna valley to Vrpolje.)

Capital of Bosnia-Herzegovina, Sarajevo is best known as the scene of the 1914 assassination of the Archduke Franz Ferdinand, an act that precipitated World War I. In recent decades this region has become one of Yugoslavia's leading timber-producing areas; green hills covered in spruce and pine ring the city. And you'll be hearing more about Sarajevo, selected to host the 1984 Olympic Winter Games.

An architectural blending of East and West, Sarajevo is an intriguing old oriental town sprinkled with impressive buildings left from the Hapsburg era. Many townspeople still wear regional dress to Sarajevo's Wednesday market.

To visit the fascinating quarter of *souks*, the ancient Turkish marketplace, walk from the old square (Baščaršija) through the maze of crowded narrow alleys. Crafts people sit at the entrances to their small shops, working in full view of passers-by.

Sarajevo has many superb mosques, the best of them built during the 16th century. Lovely in architecture, they contain handsome carpets, prayer rugs, and other valuable furnishings; you'll be expected to remove your shoes before entering. Among the most remarkable are the Baščaršija Mosque, just behind the souks; the Mosque of the Bey, containing an early copy of the Koran; the small but classic Ali Pasha Mosque; and the Emperor's Mosque, built by Sultan Suleiman.

You can visit several museums. In the Municipal Museum near the railway station, an excellent ethnographic collection includes reproductions of feudal Turkish dwellings and Bosnian peasant houses.

Opposite Princip Bridge, a plaque on the wall of the Young Bosnia Museum marks the spot where young student-patriot Gavrilo Princip fired the shots at the Austrian archduke.

Residential areas climb the slopes surrounding Sarajevo. You can ride a cable car to the summit of Mount Trebević or walk up to the ruins of the Benbasa fortress. Take time to enjoy the view from the terrace of a *kafana* (cafe).

Already a well known Yugoslavian winter sports center, Sarajevo is developing new Olympic facilities on the mountain slopes of Jahorina, Igman, Bjelašnica, and Trebević. Summer visitors also enjoy mountain sports—hiking through flower-filled meadows, mountaineering, horseback riding, and fishing in mountain streams.

## Thrilling ride by narrow-gauge railway

If you board the old narrow-gauge train in Sarajevo for the 80-mile/130-km trip to Višegrad, get ready for an exciting journey. (The route has been under repair and may be closed.)

On the half-day trip, the train climbs to awesome heights, cuts through dozens of tunnels, and crosses numerous bridges. You'll enjoy some of Yugoslavia's most beautiful mountain scenery—green forests, steep gorges, rushing streams and waterfalls.

## The Drina valley

Formerly a great Turkish stronghold, Višegrad is renowned for its great 11-arched stone bridge, built over the Drina River in the 16th century. Nobel Prize-winning author Ivo Andrić made the bridge famous as the locale of his novel, *The Bridge on the Drina*. The stone seats near the center of the bridge have become a local meeting spot for townspeople.

Marking the frontier between Bosnia and Serbia, the Drina River is a favorite of outdoors enthusiasts. Anglers come here for the superb trout and salmon in mountain streams. Kayakers and canoeists ride their craft downstream from Foča through moderately easy but exciting river rapids. In summer, visitors can float down the Drina on rafts made of large logs; two-day weekend rafting trips depart from Foča and travel downstream to Višegrad (see page 109).

# Discover Europe's Distinctive Crafts

Shop for handicrafts, visit a workshop or craft center, or combine travel with crafts instruction

During your European travels, you'll discover distinctive and imaginative handicrafts that can become useful and decorative souvenirs. You can choose objects for the home, jewelry or articles of apparel, handmade toys and dolls, or intricate Christmas ornaments and carvings.

Crafts vary from country to country, reflecting the practical needs of the people, available raw materials, and skills traditionally passed from parent to child for generations. Artistic designs often use cultural motifs. Rich craft regions developed where winter weather or isolation limited contact among people.

These are some of the crafts which flourish in Europe: pottery and ceramics, glassware, wood carving, lacemaking and embroidery, jewelry and filigree work, carpets and rugs, handwoven textiles, tapestries, metalwork, woven straw and wickerwork, basketry, and leatherwork.

## Beginning your search

If you want to learn more about a country's crafts, and possibly visit a workshop or two, where do you start?

Write to the government tourist offices (addresses on page 7) for information on regional crafts, craft centers or rural cooperatives, and perhaps instruction courses. In your travel reading, jot down regions noted for specific crafts. Ask your traveled friends about their discoveries.

Local tourist offices can direct you to sources of quality handicrafts and to crafts people who welcome visitors. Regional crafts are often displayed at markets and fairs.

Look for guidebooks listing regional workshops and retail outlets. In Britain, a booklet published by the Council for Small Industries in Rural Areas, "Craft Workshops in the English Countryside" (CoSIRA, 35 Camp Road, Wimbledon Common, London SW19 4UP), lists hundreds of places to investigate. Ask for publications on Scottish craft workshops at Tourist Information Centres in Scotland. Learn about Welsh crafts in "Crafts and Rural Industries," published by the Wales Tourist Board. At Irish tourist offices, ask for "The Craft Hunter's Pocket Guide."

## Design and craft centers

Several European nations have permanent juried exhibitions representing the best-designed current work by the country's artists and crafts people. Some centers have retail shops attached; others direct you to commercial outlets carrying the designer's work. For a look at new design trends, visit London's Design Centre and the permanent exhibitions in the Scandinavian capitals (see page 141).

In some countries, government-sponsored handicraft stores display regional work in provincial capitals and tourist centers. Look for *Heimatwerk* shops in Austria and Switzerland, *Artespaña* stores in Spain, *Narodna Radinost* shops in Yugoslavia.

Country crafts thrive in Britain, where many people work at home. You'll find quality crafts for sale at many shops such as Craftcentre Cymru, which has regional outlets throughout Wales. During your British travels, look over displays at National Trust shops (on the sites of many NT properties).

In Ireland, stop at the government-sponsored Kilkenny Design Workshops and local craft shops. In Amsterdam, watch artisans at the Dutch Art Centre (see page 53).

## Workshop visits

Some of the most satisfying—and economical—craft shopping is done on the scene, direct from the artist. Local tourist offices direct travelers to workshops that welcome visitors. Roadside signs also alert you to rural artisans and country craft shops.

Good cooks take special pleasure selecting French copper cookware in the Normandy town of Villedieu-les-Poëles, where it has been made for several hundred years. You can watch glass blowers work in tiny Wolfach, deep in Germany's Black Forest, or in modern factories in Sweden and Ireland. Wood furniture is still painted by hand in the Dutch village of Hindeloopen.

If you don't have luggage space for your purchases, inquire about shipping *before* you buy. Most small shops do not have packing and shipping facilities.

# special interests

# In Yugoslavia

## RAFTING ON THE DRINA

For a different holiday, float down the Drina River on a log raft. The long narrow rafts are made of large logs bound together as they were in ancient times. The beautiful Drina is a relatively calm river; rafters seeking white-water thrills head farther upstream to the Tara River, a tributary of the Drina. Experienced kayakers also ride down these rivers.

Two-day rafting trips depart once each week from late June to early September from Foča, southeast of Sarajevo. After a 5-hour trip, you arrive in Goražde, where you spend the night in a hotel. Next morning, you continue downstream, arriving in Višegrad in midafternoon.

Groups can organize 4-day raft trips on the Tara and Drina rivers, departing from Djurdevića Tara and ending in Foča. Each night, rafters camp out in tents beside the river.

For more information on river trips, write to the Yugoslav National Tourist Office.

## TOURIST GASOLINE DISCOUNTS

Foreign tourists can buy vouchers for discount-priced gasoline in Yugoslavia. The coupons are available at border crossings.

Vouchers are sold at 20 percent below the usual gasoline prices. Only U.S. dollars, other Western currencies, and Yugoslav National Bank checks can be used to purchase the coupons, which are valid for 1 year. Unused coupons can be returned for full refund at the place of purchase or mailed to the Auto-Motor Association of Yugoslavia (in which case a handling fee is deducted).

## WINTER SPORTS CENTERS

Winter sports enthusiasts find plenty of activity in Yugoslavia's mountain regions. Resorts are located in many parts of the country, with concentrations in the Julian Alps just south of the Austrian border and through the inland mountains from Sarajevo (host of the 1984 Olympic Winter Games) south and east into Macedonia in the southernmost part of the country. At Delnice near Rijeka, you can combine a skiing and seaside holiday.

For more information on skiing and other winter sports, write to the Yugoslav National Tourist Office.

## FERRIES & HYDROFOILS

Modern ferries link ports in neighboring Italy and Greece with harbors along Yugoslavia's Adriatic Coast. Ships also travel between major Yugoslav seaports such as Rijeka, Zadar, Split, and Dubrovnik. Travelers board ferries and hydrofoils in these coastal towns for trips to larger islands.

## MAP FOR MOTORISTS

For help in planning your trip to Yugoslavia, write to the Yugoslav National Tourist Office for a detailed map of the country. Illustrated in color, the map features eight motoring routes covering all regions of Yugoslavia. In addition, it summarizes border and customs formalities, currency exchange, motorists' information, and other topics.

## DANUBE TRIP

From April through September, hydrofoil excursion boats operate on the Danube from Belgrade downstream to Kladovo. Tickets for the trips can be obtained at any travel agency in Belgrade.

Below Belgrade, the Danube flows through the fertile Serbian plain, passes the famous Lepenski Vir archeological site (a Neolithic settlement was uncovered here), then enters the awesome Djerdap Gorge.

Commonly known as the Iron Gate, this stretch of river between Yugoslavia and Romania is one of the most famous in the world. For about 20 miles/32 km, the river is imprisoned between tall cliffs. On the right (Yugoslav) bank, you can see remains of a Roman road cut in the rock in the 1st century. At the east end of the gorge near Kladovo is the massive Djerdap Hydroelectric Dam.

## SHOPPING FOR ART & CRAFTS

Yugoslavia's handicrafts still bear the marks of the country's rich folklore.

In larger towns and resorts, *Narodna Radinost* (folk crafts) shops and other stores offer such items as hand-embroidered articles with regional motifs, lace, national costumes, leather articles, woodcarvings, cloth, handmade carpets, filigree jewelry, ceramics, tapestries, and paintings by Yugoslav artists.

## CRUISING THE ADRIATIC COAST

Marked by numerous islands, bays, and gulfs, Yugoslavia's jagged coastline is ideal for cruising. Yachts and other craft sail these warm waters, docking in island and mainland ports.

Sailors enjoy the coast's natural beauty, lively port towns, and many excellent beaches and swimming coves. You can spend a morning fishing or anchor near shore for a swim or picnic. Along the coast are numerous yacht harbors, equipped to furnish supplies and repair boats.

## RAIL TRAVEL

Yugoslavia does not recognize the Eurailpass, but you can travel to many Yugoslav cities by train. Railway lines link the country with many European cities. You can book space through any of the European national railway offices.

**For information on travel in Yugoslavia, write to the Yugoslav National Tourist Office (address on page 7).**

# Castile, Heart of Iberia

Discover Spain's cultural legacy—spanning Romans, Moors, and Iberian royalty—in three fascinating cities

You'll discover the heart of Iberia in Castile. Mountains rim the magnificently vast and stark countryside, providing a natural frontier around the tawny plain. Medieval cities and impressive castles dot the landscape.

The Kingdom of Castile was established in Christian Spain in 957, and it became the representative kingdom for the entire country. Its monarchs helped other Iberian rulers oust the Moors and led the way in developing the culture of modern Spain. Castilian royalty built lavish country palaces and gardens, such as Aranjuez and El Pardo, for their personal pleasure. Many Castilian showplaces can be reached easily from Madrid.

Three impressive cities—Toledo, Segovia, and Ávila—offer fascinating glimpses of Castile's past. Each is about 1½ to 2 hours from Madrid by car, bus, or train, or you can choose from a variety of escorted tours.

Spring and autumn are Castile's best seasons. Springtime visitors enjoy colorful fiestas and Easter celebrations, but travelers who arrive in autumn find better weather. Harsh sun bakes the land in summer, and biting cold winds sweep across the dry plateau in winter.

## Toledo, a living museum

From its hilly site overlooking the Tagus River, Toledo spreads like a vast and complex mosaic. Dominating the skyline is the Alcázar, now restored to its 16th century appearance. A national monument, Toledo is a treasure house of art and Mudéjar (Spanish-Moorish) architecture, reflecting the grandeur of Spanish civilization and the varied influences contributing to it.

Settled by the Romans, Toledo underwent long occupations by the Visigoths and Moors before Alfonso VI reconquered the city in 1085. For nearly 500 years it was the capital of the monarchy and the heart and soul of Spain. Toledo became a leading center of medieval learning and a rich commercial and industrial city. Art and architecture flourished.

Toledo's traditional market square is the Plaza Zocodover, once the site of public executions. Time has mellowed and softened buildings constructed centuries ago by proud artisans whose work reflects their skill and imagination. Talented crafts people still practice here; the most distinctive of regional handicrafts is damascene work (steel inlaid with gold).

Spanish influences enhance Toledo's magnificent 13th century Gothic cathedral. Richly ornamented both inside and out, the immense church contains many priceless works of art. Other churches also reflect the city's medieval wealth.

Painter Domenicos Theotokopoulos (El Greco) found inspiration in Toledo, where he lived for nearly 30 years until his death in 1614. His house is open to the public; from its garden you have a view of the city and the Tagus. Many of his paintings may be seen in a nearby museum and in the Church of San Tomé.

More of Toledo's artistic legacy can be seen in a pair of historic buildings that have been converted into museums. Exquisite paintings hang in the Palacio de Lerma (sometimes called de Taverna), a 15th century feudal mansion. The former Hospital de Santa Cruz is now the Municipal Museum of Toledo.

A maze of narrow, steep, cobbled alleys, Toledo contains more treasures than you can possibly absorb in a single day. You can hire open carriages and taxis, but many fascinating corners can be explored only on foot. Many houses are built Moorish style around attractive patios; windowless walls and barred gates screen household activity from passers-by. Toledo's daytime crowds depart around sunset, and the city reverts to the Toledaños and the mood of an earlier era.

To view Toledo's striking site from all sides, drive around the town on the Carretera de Circunvalación, a route that is especially enjoyable at dusk.

## Elegant Segovia

The atmosphere of medieval Spain pervades Segovia. Soft, clear light washes over the town's ocher-colored buildings and red tile roofs. Romanesque churches and small houses decorated with ironwork and flowers are scattered along the narrow streets and small squares.

You'll enjoy roaming around this relatively small and compact hill town. Many of its crooked, crowded streets are too narrow for cars. Facing the cathedral is the Plaza de Franco, Segovia's main square, with side streets radiating from it. Walk around the city ramparts for superb views of one of the world's loveliest old cities.

Three historic structures reflect aspects of Segovia's past: the aqueduct, the Alcázar, and the cathedral.

Built of huge, uncemented blocks of granite, the majestic arches of the Roman aqueduct have towered over Segovia for more than 2,000 years. In a graceful double tier, they rise about 90 feet/30 meters above the Plaza Azoguejo, supporting a conduit that still carries water to town from the distant mountains.

One of medieval Spain's great fortress-castles, the romantic Alcázar crowns a rocky spur above converging river valleys. Before you cross the drawbridge over the moat, walk along the curving terrace and gaze over the valley. Look up at the castle's pointed turrets with the battlemented central tower rising above. In 1474 Isabella was proclaimed Queen of Castile in the castle's throne room, and in 1505 Christopher Columbus made his will here with King Ferdinand acting as a witness.

Segovia has many beautiful churches, most built in Romanesque style during the 12th and 13th centuries. The elegant 16th century cathedral occupies a place of honor above the town. Splendid stained glass windows, carved choir stalls, wrought iron chapel gates, and tapestries distinguish the interior. Don't miss the Gothic cloisters and the museum.

## Thick walls encircle Ávila

Impressive walls completely enclose Ávila, renowned as one of Europe's most complete medieval fortifications. Begun about 1090, the fortress commands a high plateau between the Gredos and Guadarrama mountain ranges. The walls contain 9 arched gateways and 88 towers and extend more than 1½ miles/2½ km around the town.

Ávila is a monument to St. Teresa, founder of many of Spain's religious institutions, who was born here in 1515. The square-towered cathedral dominates the low skyline. The town has many handsome and historic churches, convents, and fortified palaces.

## Other nearby attractions

On a trip from Madrid to Segovia, you cross the pine-covered Guadarrama Mountains by one of two routes, over the Guadarrama Pass (or through the toll tunnel) or by way of the Navacerrada Pass and La Granja. Madrileños come to these mountains for climbing in summer and skiing in winter.

One of Spain's showplaces, the royal hunting lodge of La Granja was built by homesick Bourbon King Philip V to remind him of Versailles. Formal gardens with fountains surround the castle. The province of Segovia has many handsome castles and palaces, most reached by short detours from main roads.

Southwest of Ávila, the Sierra de Gredos range has much to offer sports enthusiasts: mountain climbing, horseback riding, fishing, and hunting.

El Escorial brings back the grim days of the Inquisition. Built by Philip II in the late 16th century as palace,

Balloon vendor adds splash of color to Plaza Zocodover, Toledo's traditional market square and meeting place.

Majestic Roman aqueduct, built more than 2,000 years ago, arches above Segovia's streets and squares.

monastery, and mausoleum, El Escorial was a bulwark against heresy, proclaiming the absolutism of the monarch and the Church.

Not far from El Escorial is the Valley of the Fallen, a monument to Spanish Civil War dead. A cathedral built inside the mountain houses the tomb of Francisco Franco.

# Legendary Montserrat

Enhanced by the grandeur of its mountain setting, this monastery is a magnet for religious pilgrims

For more than a thousand years, pilgrims have come to pay homage at the monastery of Montserrat, about 35 miles/56 km northwest of Barcelona. Standing on the edge of a deep ravine, the Benedictine monastery is dwarfed by the grandeur of its setting.

Strangely gnarled granite pillars loom above the huge mountain mass like sculptured stone figures, dominating the sawtoothed skyline as you approach from any direction.

You can reach Montserrat easily from Barcelona—by bus, rental car, or group excursion. Try to arrive early in the morning. Crowds peak about midday, but you can still find solitude away from the center of activity.

Tranquillity descends in the evening. If you stay overnight at one of the village's two central hotels, you can enjoy the choir at evening vespers and listen as church bells ring out each quarter hour.

## Legends surround Montserrat

One of Montserrat's legends inspired Richard Wagner's opera *Parsifal,* perpetuating the theme that Montserrat was the home of the Holy Grail.

Another legend recounts how shepherds found an image of a black Virgin—supposedly carved by St. Luke and brought to Spain by St. Peter—deep in a cave on the mountainside where it had been hidden during the Moorish occupation. You can see the ancient wooden statue encased in glass in a high niche behind the altar of the monastery cathedral. Miracles have been attributed to the statue.

For Catalan people, a visit to Montserrat is like a holiday. Families come here on feast days, anniversaries, and school holidays. Church services, conducted in the local Catalan language, are rich in pageantry. The famous boys' choir, founded in the 13th century, sings most of the year for morning Mass (at 7 weekdays and at 11 on Sundays and feast days) and again at evening vespers.

Footpaths wind across the slopes. On a quiet path near the monastery, you'll come upon a statue of cellist Pablo Casals, a Catalan who achieved worldwide fame.

Montserrat has several funiculars and *teleféricos* (a type of cable car) that transport visitors up the heights—more than 4,000 feet/1,300 meters above sea level—and down into the valleys. When the weather is favorable, views from the top are magnificent—extending to the eastern Pyrenees and the Balearic Islands.

## Driving Catalonian back roads

Motorists can take regional country roads for a look at inland Catalonia. Severe farmhouses built of pink or gray stone are scattered across green fields.

Small villages cluster around dignified churches. Each town has its central square or promenade, where villagers stroll each evening.

**Gnarled granite pillars rise behind Benedictine monastery of Montserrat, a destination of religious pilgrims.**

# Córdoba, City of the Caliphs

Whitewashed buildings, narrow alleys, and flower-filled courtyards recall the days of Islamic Spain

Córdoba's red tile roofs, white buildings, open patios, and patterned sidewalks spread in an intriguing mosaic.

A Moorish aura and spirit lingers in Córdoba, the ancient city of the caliphs in the heart of Andalusia. Between the 8th and 11th centuries, it flourished as the capital of Islamic Spain and a cultural center of science, philosophy, and the arts.

Three different races—the Romans, Visigoths, and Moors—and religions left early imprints on Córdoba. In 1236 during the Spanish Reconquest, Ferdinand III of Castile captured the city and added it to his kingdom.

In spring, Córdoba resembles one vast flower garden. Blooming plants cascade over balconies, climb trellises and walls, and brighten parks and courtyards. During May fiestas, flamenco singers, dancers, and guitar players add spirit to the merrymaking.

Autumn visitors enjoy soft, balmy weather, but in midsummer the torrid sun beats relentlessly on this inland city. Winters are relatively mild.

## Getting acquainted with Córdoba

One of Spain's oldest cities, Córdoba is built along the Guadalquivir River. Though its landmarks date from the Roman era, the city blossomed under Arab rule.

Most lasting monument of the Moorish dynasty is the Great Mosque, an 8th century masterpiece built on the foundation of a Visigoth church. The mosque was converted into a Christian cathedral in the 16th century. Its airy forest of 850 marble columns supports a double canopy of red-and-white striped stone arches. The Mihrab Chapel features a spectacular jewel-like inlaid dome and a rich array of mosaic work.

Motor traffic crosses the Guadalquivir on a Roman bridge built in the 2nd century. At one end is a triumphal arch, the Gate of El Puente; La Calahorra fortress guards the far side. Downstream from the bridge, you can see the remains of several Moorish windmills.

Near the mosque and bridge is the Alcázar, the 14th century palace-fortress of the Christian kings. Its gardens, pools, and fountains alone are worth a visit.

You'll discover the essence of old Córdoba as you stroll its *callejas*, narrow alleys lined with white-washed buildings. The lanes wind through some of the city's most characteristic quarters. Handsome black iron gates offer glimpses of flower-filled courtyards.

Most of Córdoba's beautiful old churches face onto charming plazas such as the Capuchinos, Los Dolores, Flores Square, and Plaza del Potro. Plaza de Colón and its old park face the old convent of La Merced. Spacious 17th century arcades surround the Corredera, queen of Córdoba's plazas, where you can observe lively bargaining at the open-air market. Modern Córdoba centers around the Plaza de Jose Antonio, rimmed with outdoor cafes. Statues in plazas celebrate local heroes.

Art lovers find two excellent collections—the Provincial Fine Arts Gallery and the Julio Romero de Torres Museum—housed in the old Hôpital de la Caridad on the Plaza del Potro. The Córdoban crafts of silverwork and embossed leatherwork are featured, along with bullfight memorabilia, in the Museum of Bullfighting, Córdoban Art, and Folk Craft near Plaza de las Bulas.

SPAIN

· Madrid

# Journey to Galicia

Follow the Cantabrian Coast or the old pilgrimage road to Santiago de Compostela and the rugged Atlantic shore

Interesting, historic, and relatively remote and unexplored, Galicia is Spain's green and mountainous northwest corner. Settled by the Celts and unconquered by the Moors, it has a rich and ancient folklore that retains many Celtic influences. The region's primary attraction is Santiago de Compostela, a pilgrimage destination since the Middle Ages.

Oxen still draw wooden-wheeled carts along rural roads, and you'll see farmers cutting hay with scythes and tilling fields with hoes. Small vineyards cover many hills, and elevated corncribs dot the countryside.

The gentle, rolling, green landscape of inland Galicia turns grander as you approach the sea. Narrow arms of the Atlantic (called *rías*) cut deep, fiord-like inlets in the coastline at La Coruña and Pontevedra.

Mist and fog frequently shroud the rocky shore, and rain showers roll in from the Atlantic, keeping the inland valleys sparkling green and streams filled with water. The marine climate—cool summers and mild winters—offers relief from the temperature extremes of interior Spain.

You can reach the region's main cities from Madrid by road, rail, or air. More interesting, however, are two other approaches: the scenic route along the Cantabrian Coast, and the historic pilgrimage road to Santiago de Compostela.

Trains and buses link Galicia's larger towns, but you'll see much more if you can explore the coast and interior valleys by car. Visitors without transportation will find Santiago and Vigo the best centers.

## Along the Cantabrian Coast

Donkeys and oxen still plod country roads near Spain's northern shore, in the lovely but often bypassed region known as the Cantabrian Coast. Local trains and buses and a coastal road connect the fishing villages and resorts where many Europeans spend their summer holidays. You'll find resort cities crowded during July and August, since the beaches are a refuge from inland heat.

Major cities along this coast are San Sebastián, Spain's cosmopolitan summer capital; industrial Bilbao; and the resort of Santander, bordering a beautiful bay.

Secondary roads veer from the main route to coastal headlands where red-roofed fishing villages hang above the sea, and up inland valleys to Basque settlements.

East of San Sebastián, Fuenterrabía is a colorful port at the mouth of the Bidasoa River. Between San Sebastián and Bilbao, detour to Guetaria, built on a rocky promontory; Zumaya, an attractive port with an art museum; Elanchove, a village clinging to the side of a cliff; and Motrico, a quiet town containing ancestral homes of some noble Basque families.

**Glimpses of the past.** Preserved on the walls and ceilings of more than a dozen caverns in Santander and Vizcaya provinces are paintings, drawings, and engravings created 12,000 to 20,000 years ago. Bison, deer, wild horses, and other animals emerge from the shadows as the guide plays his light across the cave walls.

Most famous of the prehistoric art caves are Altamira, west of Santillana, and El Castillo, south of Santander near Puente Viesgo. Altamira and some of the other

**Baroque towers of historic cathedral soar high above buildings of Santiago de Compostela.**

caves have been closed to visitors to protect the paintings; inquire locally to learn which are open to the public.

Village life of another era comes to life in Santillana del Mar, now a national historic monument. In the quiet plaza near the medieval church, you can watch a herdsman water his cows at an ancient trough beside the public pool where women kneel to scrub their laundry. Handsome 15th century stone mansions, once townhouses of noble families, line narrow cobbled streets; some buildings are open to visitors. The handsome Church of Santa Illana is considered one of the best Romanesque structures in Spain.

**West to La Coruña.** As you continue west, fishing villages and small beach resorts vie for your attention. Historic San Vicente de la Barquera and Villaviciosa retain traditional flavor, and Llanes is surrounded by beautiful sandy beaches.

Largest cities on the Asturian coast are Gijón and Avilés. Along this seacoast you'll want to visit Luanco, where you see old palaces and a lighthouse on Cape Peñas; the sandy horseshoe beach of Salinas rimmed by pine trees; and charming fishing ports at Cudillero, Luarca, and Tapia de Casariego.

West of Ribadeo, coastal cliffs and headlands alternate with a succession of rías cutting deeply into the coast. Handsome glass-fronted buildings face La Coruña's harbor. The Hercules Tower lighthouse, dating from A.D. 2, marks the town's early days as a Roman seaport. King Philip II and the Great Armada sailed from here in 1588.

## The Road to Santiago

If you choose the historic road to the sanctuary at Santiago de Compostela, you follow the trail of countless thousands of medieval pilgrims. They made the long trek across France and northern Spain to pay homage at the shrine of St. James the Apostle (known as Santiago in Spain and St-Jacques in France).

One of the oldest European tourist routes, the fascinating Way of St. James passes medieval towns and monasteries that gave aid and shelter to weary pilgrims.

You can make your own pilgrimage, following "Camino de Santiago" signs. Much of the route follows rural roads through countryside little changed from medieval days. You can linger in cities such as Pamplona, Burgos, and León; visit magnificent urban cathedrals and remote shrines; and explore intriguing fortresses and walled villages atop hills along the way.

The historic road passes south of Lugo, a provincial capital completely encircled by Roman walls. Small squares, historic lanes, arcades, and noble houses add atmosphere to this old city.

Before you start out, obtain a copy of the booklet "The Way to Santiago" from the Spanish National Tourist Office. In addition to *paradores* (government-operated hotels) along this route, you'll find a pair of outstanding hostelries: the Hotel San Marcos in León, formerly a magnificent 16th century convent and still filled with art treasures; and the Hostal de los Reyes Catolicos in Santiago de Compostela, built as a 15th century pilgrims' hospital by King Ferdinand and Queen Isabella.

## Ancient Santiago de Compostela

For more than a thousand years, Santiago de Compostela has been the goal of religious pilgrims who traveled here to visit the tomb of St. James, patron saint of Spain. His feast day on July 25 signals a week-long celebration.

Built between the 11th and 13th centuries with later additions, the soaring baroque cathedral is among the most richly detailed European churches. The ornately carved main façade was completed about 1750. The triple-arched inner portal—the Door of Glory—is a masterpiece of carved granite.

Just inside the main door, you can press your fingertips into grooves worn in the central pillar by countless pilgrims, a traditional rite since the cathedral opened 800 years ago. The cool, dark interior is largely Romanesque, dominated by heavy, thick columns and an ornamented high altar. Behind it, stairs lead down to the crypt.

Diagonally opposite the church is the Hostal de los Reyes Catolicos. A 16th century doorway rises the full height of the three-story building. Inside, it resembles a tastefully elegant museum more than a hotel.

Narrow arcaded streets (called *rúas*) twist and turn through the district. Tall houses from the 15th century, palaces, and old churches line your route. Small plazas surround fountains and statues. Near the large Plaza de la Quintana, the streets teem with university students.

On a hill southwest of the city center, the Paseo de la Herradura (Blacksmith's Walk) loops through Alameda Park, providing views of the city's soaring cathedral towers and red-tile roofs.

## Galicia's unspoiled shores

Southwest of Santiago, four narrow fiord-like estuaries cut deeply into the Atlantic coast. The Rías Bajas carve out a spectacular array of inlets and harbors, beaches and coves, crags and promontories. Modern towns and scattered white villages border the firths. You'll find seafarers' hamlets to explore and plenty of swimming beaches and picnic sites beneath pine trees.

Offshore waters still conceal the remains of Spanish galleons—loaded with gold, silver, precious woods, and other treasures from the New World—scuttled here during battles with the English fleet.

Few towns have a more beautiful setting than Vigo, which Sir Francis Drake plundered more than 250 years ago. Its busy harbor is a regular port of call for ocean liners. Though a modern city, its old section holds special charm, particularly the El Berbés quarter with its flavor of the sea. Offshore are the legendary Cies Islands, once a hideout for raiders and fugitives.

Pontevedra exudes a meditative and aristocratic air; the old monument city dates back to Roman times. To the northwest, a corniche road passes Poyo's monastery and follows the shore to the island resort of La Toja.

Bayona's parador occupies a striking site overlooking the sea. Julius Caesar stopped at this port in 62 B.C. on his way to Britain. In 1493 this small town became the first settlement to learn of the discovery of the New World when one of Christopher Columbus's caravels, the *Pinta*, returned with the news.

# Exploring Country Roads by Rental Car

Planning pays off for venturesome motorists who prefer to set their own pace and itinerary

Driving in Europe gives you a delightful sense of freedom. You can explore any road you fancy, stop where you want, and set your own pace without worrying about schedules. You become an adventurer, probing out-of-the-way places that public transportation doesn't reach.

However, the cost of rental cars and gasoline has soared in recent years, making it more important than ever to plan your trip to gain maximum value for your money.

Major international car rental firms have offices in large cities throughout Europe. You can make reservations before you leave home, charge expenses to a credit card, and have rent-it-here, leave-it-there options on longer rentals. Smaller European firms may save you money if you're making a circle trip out of a major city, but they usually have fewer options and offices. Rates vary by company and country—shop around.

### Making arrangements

Do you plan to spend your entire trip driving in the countryside, or will much of your time be spent in cities? Some travelers use trains between distant locations, then rent a car at each major stop. Short-term rentals are generally more expensive per day than those of a week or longer.

Most car rental companies offer two plans: you can pay a basic daily charge plus a specified add-on amount per kilometer driven, or you pay a higher flat rate with unlimited mileage. Expect extra charges for optional insurance, taxes, and gasoline. Talk to your travel agent about fly/drive trips; these offer flexibility at fixed rates.

Rent the size of car that fits your group, giving some thought to each person's physical size. Be sure that the luggage compartment is large enough to hold your baggage (small bags and soft-sided luggage are more practical than large, unyielding suitcases). Cars with manual transmissions are less expensive than automatics.

The nation in which you rent a car can make a difference in costs. Charges vary from country to country, as do Value Added Taxes (VAT). Several countries reduce the VAT substantially if most of the travel period is spent outside the country.

Arranging credit card payment when you reserve your car saves problems about making a deposit or settling your final bill. Some companies offer prepayment plans, which can save money on currency fluctuations.

Most large cities have car rental offices, but you can avoid the anxieties of city driving by taking delivery of your car at the airport or in a suburban or regional town.

### Before you start out

When you rent your car, you'll need to show your state driver's license. (If you want to obtain an international driver's license, visit the local office of your automobile club before you leave home.) You'll also need to arrange payment—either by credit card or by leaving a sizable cash deposit. If you wish, you can purchase nondeductible liability and property damage coverage.

When you pick up your car, be sure it has a "green card" (it indicates third-party insurance, and must be shown when crossing national borders) and a blue parking disk (for use in city restricted parking zones).

Before you leave the rental agency, be sure you know how to operate the headlights and dimmers, windshield wipers, turn signals, and horn.

Don't try to drive without a good guidebook and detailed road maps showing route numbers, distances, and towns along the way. Tourist offices can provide city maps. Familiarize yourself with international road signs (see page 64) and other highway signs.

Government tourist offices can provide information on national motoring regulations and customs. Seat belts, for example, are mandatory in some nations. Drunk drivers face severe penalties—even imprisonment—in Scandinavia. And in some countries, police are authorized to collect fines on the spot.

Drive defensively. On country roads you'll meet hay wagons, cyclists, even meandering cows and sheep. Rural roads are not always banked, and if you round a curve too fast, you may find yourself headed into a cow pasture.

# special interests

# In Spain

## REGIONAL HANDICRAFTS

Shoppers discover an intriguing array of handicrafts in shops and regional markets. Each provincial center has an official handicraft shop. For a list of these Artespaña markets, write to the Spanish National Tourist Office, or inquire locally at regional tourist information centers.

Among the handcrafted items you'll find are leatherwork, jewelry, ceramics and pottery, embroidery and lace, carpets and rugs, and metalwork.

## SIPPING SHERRY IN JEREZ

The great sherries come from a tiny district in southwest Spain. Jerez de la Frontera, south of Seville, is Spain's sherry capital. Vineyards surround the town.

Visitors are welcomed at *bodegas* (cellars) to tour and sample the different sherries. Most bodegas are open to visitors Monday through Saturday in the late-morning and early-afternoon hours; they are closed on Sundays and holidays. Jerez celebrates a vintage festival during the second week of September.

## RAIL & BUS TRAVEL

The Spanish State Railways System (RENFE) operates an extensive rail system of fast, comfortable trains offering first and second-class service. On long distance trains, passengers must show a seat reservation or boarding pass before boarding the train.

Rail rates are figured by kilometer distance. If you plan extensive rail travel in Spain, you may save money by purchasing a Chequetren ticket, available at RENFE offices or at railroad stations in Spain. Up to six persons can share the ticket, and there is no time limitation on its use.

Bus service throughout Spain is comfortable and well run. Passengers usually board at a cafe, bar, hotel entrance, or street intersection rather than a bus terminal, so be sure to find out exactly where and when to make your bus connection. Even in major cities where there are bus stations, some buses depart from other areas.

## SPECTATOR SPORTS

From mid-March to mid-October, bullfighting is king in Madrid and Barcelona. Bullfights are held in the afternoon, usually at 5 P.M., on Sundays and holidays, and sometimes on Thursdays. In other cities, bullfights are held during local festivals.

In northern Basque provinces, *pelota* or jai-alai has been a favorite sport for generations; now it is gaining popularity in Madrid and other areas as well. From October to June, matches are played daily in principal Spanish cities; in Basque towns the game is played in summer as well.

## TAPA SAMPLING

Meal hours are much later in Spain than in other Western countries. Lunch is served from 1:30 P.M. on; in Madrid, 2:30 or even 3:30 is not uncommon. Few restaurants serve dinner before 9 P.M. The usual dinner hour is 10, though in Madrid and the south, 10:30 or 11 is common.

If you find it difficult to last until mealtime, find a cafe and select from a variety of tempting hot and cold snacks called *tapas.* You can stave off hunger or make a miniature meal on the tiny hors d'oeuvres—from prawns and meatballs to fried mushrooms, cheese, open-faced sandwiches, and slices of sausage. Pair your food with beer or a glass of red or white wine or sherry.

Tapas are displayed and served at *tascas* or *mesones,* traditional Spanish bars. Patrons ease up to the counter and choose from the array. Later they'll stop at another bar to repeat the procedure.

## YOUR CASTLE IN SPAIN

Among Europe's most enjoyable accommodations are Spain's *paradores,* a network of about 70 government-operated hotels scattered across the Spanish countryside. Many occupy historic buildings—renovated castles, palaces, convents, and monasteries—now equipped with private baths and central heating. Other paradores are newly built. Parador restaurants feature regional food specialties.

The government also operates other tourist establishments: *albergues de carretera* (wayside inns) located along major highways; *hosterias* (typical restaurants) decorated in regional style; and *refugios* (mountain shelters) providing accommodations in mountain sports areas.

For a brochure listing the paradores and albergues, write to the Spanish National Tourist Office.

Travelers can reserve a room at any of the hostelries through a central reservations representative: Marketing Ahead, Inc., 515 Madison Avenue, New York, NY 10022.

## CITY HIDEAWAYS

In several Spanish cities, you can discover the charm and character of another era as you wander through the quaint lanes of the old quarter. Wrought iron grilles and pots of blooming flowers adorn whitewashed houses. Behind high gates you'll spy greenery-filled courtyards; often you'll hear the cool sound of a fountain.

To discover these areas, seek out the Judería, the old Jewish quarter, in Toledo and Cordoba, and the Barrio de Santa Cruz in Seville. In many cities the older section is called the Ciudad Vieja, or as in Barcelona, the Barrio Gótico.

## ORDESA NATIONAL PARK

Hikers will enjoy a detour to small Ordesa National Park, high in the Pyrenees in Huesca province.

Reddish sandstone escarpments rise more than 3,000 feet/1,000 meters from the canyon floor, and a hiking trail leads up the valley past waterfalls. You'll find a delightful mix of woods, mountains, rushing streams, and mountain wildlife.

Nearest sizeable city is Lérida, about 120 miles/190 km southeast on the Madrid-Barcelona highway. You can also reach the park by driving east from Pamplona. Just outside the park entrance, the tiny town of Torla has hotel accommodations, a campground, and other tourist services.

**For information on travel in Spain, write to the Spanish National Tourist Office (addresses on page 7).**

# Leisurely Loop in Portugal

Seek out delightful towns, outdoor markets, and country inns as you sample the region's myriad attractions

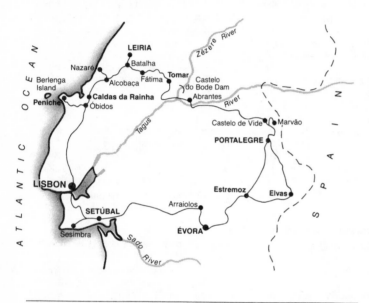

The restful countryside of Portugal delights travelers previously familiar only with its large cities and resorts. Once out of Lisbon, you'll find traffic pleasantly light, except in larger towns. Roads are often lined with greenery and are usually paved, though they sometimes become narrow and twisting as they pass through villages.

One small town after another tempts you to stop. Sturdy castles and protective ramparts are reminders of centuries of warfare and domination. Clustering below each fortress are whitewashed houses adorned with black wrought iron grillwork and blooming flowers. Along the coast you'll see numerous windmills, their sails rotating in the wind.

Crafts such as ceramics, lacemaking, weaving, and woodworking flourish in many small towns. Look for displays in outdoor markets and local fairs, as well as in shops and regional museums. Colorful glazed tiles (called *azulejos*) ornament many churches, public buildings, and patrician homes.

Plan your route to stop in one or more of Portugal's fine *pousadas* (see page 125), country inns renowned for their charm, comfort, and value. On this loop they're located in Óbidos, Castelo do Bode (northwest of Abrantes), Marvão, Estremoz, Elvas, Évora, and Setúbal.

## Exploring the central coast

About 60 miles/100 km north of Lisbon, crenelated walls enclose the enchanting medieval town of Óbidos. Bright geraniums and bougainvillea cascade from stairways and balconies of dazzling-white houses. Churches are everywhere, decorated with painted ceilings and walls of colored tiles. As you walk along the narrow main street, you may see artisans weaving cotton carpets. Donkeys and pedestrians have the right-of-way in streets barely wide enough for a single car. Stroll along the city wall to enjoy views of the town and countryside.

West of Óbidos, the fishing port of Peniche comes to life when the fishing boats unload their catch, and there's a boisterous market on the quay. Boats leave daily for Berlenga Island, an ancient fortress offshore. You can walk the island's shoreline paths, go fishing, explore the cave-hollowed coast by boat.

Another favorite fishing village is Nazaré, known for its wide sandy beach and the colorful traditions of its fishing fleet. Explore the narrow steep alleys of the fishermen's quarter, then ramble along the beach where barefoot fishermen and their families in traditional apparel eke a living from the sea. On this harborless coast, fishermen roll their high-prowed boats down the beach over logs to launch them into the incoming breakers. When the boats return at the end of the day, they must be pulled high on the beach by hand-cranked cables or by teams of Nazaré oxen.

Alcobaça lies inland in a region of fruit orchards and small pottery-making towns. Elaborate tombs, including that of Portuguese King Dom Pedro, are found in the 12th century monastery.

## Ornate monasteries & village crafts

Some of Portugal's most innovative architecture dates from the early-16th century reign of Manuel I. One of the era's artistic masterpieces is the unfinished Batalha monastery, which stands in a green valley. The building's Gothic simplicity is enhanced with such Manueline details as tracery, carved marble arcades, and decorated columns.

As in many Portuguese towns, a historic castle dominates Leiria. Here you'll probably see displays of crafts from neighboring villages—glassware, pottery, woven bedspreads, and willow basketware.

Large crowds of fervent pilgrims visit the shrine of Fátima, particularly on the 13th of the month (largest pilgrimages occur on May 12–13 and October 12–13). Many travel on foot to the shrine, some covering the final distance to the basilica on their knees.

Another interesting site is Tomar, where the Church of the Templars reveals Manueline decoration carried to extravagance. In Abrantes, a maze of flower-filled alleyways leads up to the fortress ruins, where you have a view over the Tagus valley.

## Sampling the vast Alentejo plain

Access to Marvão is difficult, but you'll be glad you made the effort. Anchored atop a granite peak near the Spanish border, the town is a delight. Narrow alleys lace the village below the fortress. From atop the still-intact ramparts, you look down on the town, across to Spain's jagged mountains, and over the Alentejo plain.

Nearby Portalegre gained wealth and fame through its tapestries, woven here since the 16th century. You can make weekday visits to the tapestry workshop, located in the former monastery, to see handwoven tapestries made and displayed.

Stretching southward is the flat, sunburnt Alentejo, its vast grain fields occasionally broken by groves of cork oak or olive trees or a flock of grazing sheep.

In the Alentejo pottery center of Estremoz, wares are arrayed on the main square at the Saturday market. Nearby in the small regional museum, you can learn about the Alentejo and its people.

Detour east of Estremoz to Elvas, where elaborate 17th century fortifications still guard an ancient fortress. Walk about the town to see its impressive defenses and attractive squares. An aqueduct built in the 17th and 18th centuries still brings water to Elvas.

Allow a full day to explore Évora, one of Portugal's most interesting cities and the market center of the Alentejo. A walled town since the Roman era, Évora faded under the Visigoths and in 715 was occupied by the Moors. Dazzling-white houses, balconies, hanging gardens, and arched alleyways enhance its Moorish character. From a rich past, it retains a Roman temple and many handsome medieval and Renaissance buildings.

Perched atop a hill on the Alentejo plain, Arraiolos is known for its brilliantly colored wool carpets executed in simple designs.

## South of Lisbon

The landscape becomes greener as you return to the coast. On the approach to Setúbal, scattered olive trees, rice fields, and vineyards come into view.

This busy port facing the wide Sado estuary is a prosperous industrial center, particularly since completion of the bridge from Lisbon across the Tagus. Setúbal's fishing fleet numbers more than 2,000 boats, and you may detect the pungent aroma of sardines coming from large canneries near the docks.

The fishing village of Sesimbra clings to steep hills that tumble to the sea. Drying laundry hangs from windows of the white houses, and fishermen still gather along narrow twisting streets to mend nets and exchange stories. After the fleet returns in late afternoon, the day's catch is auctioned on the beach.

On weekdays you can visit the Bacalhôa *quinta*, a large Portuguese country estate near the Lisbon-Setúbal road. Its 15th century architecture shows Moorish and Florentine influences rather than the fanciful Manueline style. You'll enjoy strolling through the quiet formal gardens and viewing arcaded chambers tiled in pictorial azulejos.

Nazaré fishermen mend nets along wide, sandy beach. Since town has no harbor, high-prowed boats are pulled onto beach.

In outdoor market in Estremoz, handmade ceramic dishes are spread on ground to entice passing shoppers.

# Enjoy Markets & Festivals in Minho

In northwest Portugal, families preserve traditional customs and crafts of an earlier era

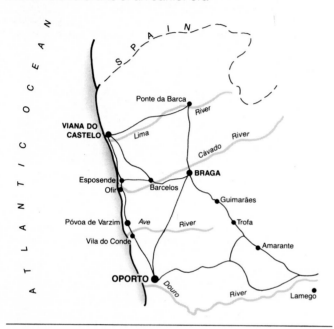

**Smiling vendor weighs fruit in outdoor market. You'll find festive bazaars in country towns throughout Portugal.**

Tradition remains strong in Portugal's northwest corner. In fishing villages and small inland towns, rural families follow customs and practices passed down from earlier generations.

At colorful outdoor markets, you can purchase regional handicrafts made in the time-honored ways. These include lace and embroidery, handwoven fabrics, pottery and ceramics, cane and rush articles, carved wood objects, and decorative metalwork.

Local celebrations are occasions for energetic dancing and singing. Among festivals of special interest are the Barcelos pottery fair in early May, the lace-makers' procession in Vila do Conde about June 23, and the procession and blessing of fishing boats in Póvoa de Varzim in mid-August. Viana do Costelo stages the region's most famous folk celebration, a 3-day festival in mid-August. Religious festivals in Braga on June 23 and 24 and Guimarães on the first Sunday of August are celebrated with processions, folk dancing, and fireworks.

Rail and bus service link the main towns. From Oporto, trains travel inland to Braga and Guimarães and north to Póvoa de Varzim and Viana do Castelo.

## Along the Costa Verde

Pine forests shelter peaceful beaches along the Costa Verde. Seaside resorts at Vila do Conde, Póvoa de Varzim, and Ofir alternate with simple villages where the day's highlight is the return of the fishing boats.

Shuttle lace-making is the traditional craft at Vila do Conde, a resort amid pines at the mouth of the Ave River.

Part fishing port and part elegant resort, Póvoa de Varzim borders a magnificent golden sand beach. At its southern end, you'll find the fishermen's quarter, where family members keep busy working on boats, mending nets, preparing fresh fish to dry in the sun, or assembling piles of seaweed (to be used later as fertilizer).

Beyond the fishing village of Apúlia stretches the long sandy beach of Ofir-Esposende, a relaxing coastal resort on the Cávado River.

Viana do Castelo flourished during the 16th century, when it developed a prosperous fishing trade with the Hanseatic cities. Handsome buildings from that era dot the old town. Gardens border the Lima River.

You can return to Oporto along an inland route through Braga, the capital of Minho province. Surrounded by mountains and valleys, Braga is rich in history and religious tradition. Processions take place here during Holy Week and on other religious holidays. Crafts people sell their wares each Tuesday at Braga's market.

Thursday is market day in the pottery town of Barcelos, a busy agricultural center on the Cávado River. Museum displays are located in the old palace.

Founded in the 10th century, Guimarães is a prosperous commercial city and craft center. You'll enjoy the town's historic buildings and attractive old quarter.

Craftswomen make net and lace in the village of Trofa. During good weather, they often display their wares beside the road.

# Lofty Retreat of Royalty

Fragrant green forests and cool mountain breezes have attracted royalty and inspired poets

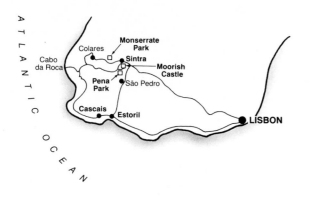

Tucked against the slope of a densely wooded mountain range northwest of Lisbon, lofty Sintra was the favorite summer refuge of Portugal's kings for six centuries.

Today you can enjoy the fresh, cool mountain climate and enchanting scenery that attracted Portuguese royalty and inspired poets such as Lord Byron, who called Sintra "a glorious Eden." You can tour royal palaces and even live like a king in the venerable Seteais Palace, a stately home now converted into a small luxury hotel.

Frequent suburban trains make the 17-mile/28-km run between Lisbon (Rossio Station) and Sintra. Guided excursions depart from Lisbon for Sintra and the Costa do Sol. In Sintra, horse-drawn carriages transport visitors up the hills to nearby attractions.

## Royal palaces rise on verdant hills

Royal palaces, a mysterious old Moorish Castle, and a pair of botanical gardens are special attractions. Half-hidden villas look down on the village of Sintra from the wooded hills.

Twin conical chimneys rise above the tile roofs of Sintra's royal palace. João I built the original palace here in the late 14th century, but it was Manuel I who enlarged and embellished it in the early 16th century with fountains and sunlit courtyards, glazed tiles, and Moorish

windows. Take a look at the prints and paintings in the museum library, then walk around town to see the same sights today.

The road climbs south in a series of hairpin curves to the old Moorish castle, originally built in the 7th and 8th centuries. Towers guard its perimeter wall. A wild and lonely place, it rises from a rocky spur and provides sweeping views from Sintra to the sea.

Crowning one of the highest peaks in the Sintra range is Pena Palace, built by King Fernando II in the mid-19th century around the remains of a former monastery. Combining Gothic towers and Moorish minarets amid a curious variety of architectural details, the building is enhanced by its lonely setting. Period furnishings decorate the interior. From atop the tower you have an awesome view of the entire region from Lisbon to the Atlantic coast.

Surrounding the palace is a large botanical park, ornamented with ponds, fountains, and grottoes. From Pena Park a marked path leads to the hilltop cross.

Motorists can make a loop around the slopes of the range. Fragrant, green eucalyptus and pines cover the slopes, where shifting winds propel the mists and clouds. Mountain rainfall encourages a forest floor of ferns. In spring, mimosa blooms with abandon and wildflowers brighten grassy slopes. In the folds of the hills, you'll discover hidden gardens and superb vistas.

Side roads lead to a Capuchin monastery, where monks' cells have been carved from the rock, and the Peninha chapel. The mountains end at Cabo da Roca, Europe's westernmost point, where a lighthouse crowns the sheer cliff above an angry sea.

You can return to Sintra through Colares, a small town known for its wines. Monserrate Park is landscaped with magnificent trees and plants from around the world.

On the second and fourth Sundays of each month, a lively fair takes place in São Pedro village south of Sintra.

Twin conical towers of Sintra's royal palace add distinctive accent to this wooded hill town northwest of Lisbon.

# The Sunny Southern Coast

In the winterless Algarve, bask on a beach beside the sea or explore Moorish-style towns and fishing ports

An exotic Moorish flavor tinges the Algarve, Portugal's sunny southern coast. In this winterless land, blinding-white towns face south toward Africa, their flat-roofed buildings and tall lacy chimneys outlined against the brilliant blue sky.

Blending old cultures with new development, the region blooms with deluxe resorts, golf courses, casinos, and marinas. Warm temperatures and wide, golden beaches lure sun lovers.

Separated by hills from the dry Alentejo plain, the coastal region is one vast subtropical garden where flowers bloom prolifically in the glinting sun. Climbing the gentle slopes are huge orchards of fig and apricot trees, olive and orange groves, carob and cork trees. In January, almond trees burst into bloom, veiling the landscape in snowy splendor.

From Lisbon it's a 35-minute flight or a 4 to 5-hour drive to Faro. Express trains link the capital and coast in about 6 hours. Local trains serve the large coastal towns from Lagos east to Vila Real de Santo António.

## Along the sun-drenched coast

The Algarve is Portugal's garden, a maritime province enjoying a subtropical climate. Though tourists arrive in ever-increasing numbers, fishing dominates many coastal towns; occasionally you'll happen upon a lively fish auc-

**Fishermen return to Sagres harbor in midafternoon, pull dories onto beach, and sell fish right from their boats.**

tion. Moorish architecture adds a distinctive touch and recalls five centuries of occupation.

The Algarve's main highway connects the region's major towns, wending east from the Sagres Peninsula to the Spanish border. Spur roads lead down from the highway to resorts and the sea.

Capital of the Algarve is bustling, colorful Faro. Its recapture from the Moors in 1249 marked the end of Arab power in Portugal. City life revolves around the busy harbor area, a district enhanced by wide avenues and shaded city gardens. Shops and patterned mosaic pavements border the Rua Santo António.

South of the harbor lies the peaceful old quarter, encircled by a wall of ancient houses. Enter the old town through a handsome gateway, the Arco da Vila, and stroll along narrow streets toward the cathedral. Faro's beach is about 6 miles/9 km from town, connected to the mainland by a bridge.

East of Faro are small towns so Moorish in appearance you could easily imagine yourself in North Africa. Visitors are drawn to the attractive fishing port of Olhão by its lively fish market, as well as by the white, cube-shaped houses separated by narrow alleys. Best views of the old district are from the belfry of the parish church or the bridge over the railroad at the entrance to town. Similar in appearance to Olhão, Fuzeta also has a good beach.

Encircled by gray stone ramparts, Tavira rises at the foot of a hill facing a river estuary. One of the coast's oldest towns, it has a bridge over the river dating from Roman times. From the castle, you can look over the town with its peaked roofs and numerous churches. Tavira is the Algarve's primary tuna fishing center. In summer, fishermen set out at dawn in Phoenician-type boats to fish in the traditional way—sometimes leaping into the water and battling the huge fish in order to hoist them aboard.

Pine trees border a pleasant sandy beach at Monte Gordo, a coastal village that has become a popular seaside resort.

From the ancient fortified castle of Castro Marim, you gaze across the Guadiana River and facing border towns to the ocher-colored Spanish plain.

One of the largest Algarve ports, Vila Real de Santo António borders the west bank of the Guadiana River facing the Spanish town of Ayamonte. Black-and-white mosaic paving radiates from the town's main square, and lovely gardens line the Portuguese bank of the river. Cars cross the Guadiana by ferry.

## Sandy beaches & lively resorts

West of Faro lie the major resorts—lively Albufeira, the fishing port of Portimão, celebrated Praia da Rocha, and Lagos on its magnificent bay. Smaller hideaways include elegant Vale do Lobo and the fishing villages of Quarteira and Armação de Pêra. All along this coast, sandy beaches nestle beneath reddish gold cliffs, inviting swimmers and sunbathers.

One of the most attractive little towns in the Algarve, Albufeira has an excellent beach and good facilities for tourists.

The fishing fleet adds color to the delightful port of Portimão, curving along a bay. The town is one of several Algarve fish canning centers.

Brightly colored *carrinhas* (open carriages) drawn by mules transport travelers between Portimão and the best known of the seaside resorts, Praia da Rocha. A favorite of visitors in both winter and summer, the resort faces the sun at the mouth of the Arade River. Cliffs eroded in abstract shapes rim the coast. Santa Catarina Fort commands the entrance to Portimão Bay and offers a view point over the Praia da Rocha's golden beaches and clear blue sea.

Lagos combines attractive beaches with the activities of a fishing port. A statue of Prince Henry the Navigator stands in the large square between the harbor and old town, a reminder of the era when fleets of Portuguese caravels sailed from this harbor on voyages of discovery and commerce.

## The windswept Sagres Peninsula

Beyond Lagos is the bleak and lonely Sagres Peninsula, haunted by the spirit of Prince Henry the Navigator, who lived on this isolated outpost in the 15th century and dreamed of finding a sea route to the riches of India.

With the leading mariners, cartographers, and astronomers of the day, he tested navigational theories and improved instruments which were put to practical use during long voyages. His experienced navigators ventured ever farther, upgrading maritime charts, discovering new lands, and establishing trading posts.

Buffeted by unceasing Atlantic gales, his old navigation school still stands on the arid, treeless headland. Try to plan your visit to see the movie which traces the main events during this era of great discovery; an English version is shown daily at 3:45 P.M.

A surfaced road skirts the Sagres headland to Cape St. Vincent. Ships from all parts of the world pass this promontory.

## Inland towns & wooded mountains

For a different glimpse of the Algarve, drive inland. On country roads you'll pass plodding donkeys laden with saddlebags and carrying riders dressed in somber black.

Estói has a lovely 18th century palace, set in a park of formal gardens, fountains, and lakes.

The lively market town and handicraft center of Loulé is renowned for the varied openwork chimneys atop its white houses.

Continue toward Silves, one of Portugal's oldest communities. Red sandstone walls of the Arab castle dominate the town, a reminder of the days when this was the Moorish capital of the Algarve. After you've walked along the castle's battlements and viewed the two huge underground cisterns, stop east of town for a look at the unusual Portuguese cross.

North from Silves or Portimão, you drive up an orchard-covered valley into the mountains. The road climbs beneath eucalyptus and pines up the slopes of the Fóia, highest point in the range, to a view point with superb vistas over southwestern Portugal.

## A European Bonus

# Hobby or Study Trips Add Holiday Interest

Build your vacation plans around a favorite sport or hobby, or study a new skill or subject

If you're seeking new travel experiences, plan your European holiday with a special focus. Adventurous and outdoor-oriented voyagers can participate in a wide range of active vacations and special-interest holidays.

Try a new sport or skill or enjoy a familiar one in fresh surroundings. Foreign government tourist offices can provide information on outdoor holidays and on numerous short study courses in a broad range of interest areas. Or mold your itinerary around one of your hobbies—such as art appreciation, food and wine, gardening, Roman monuments, or unusual railroads.

You can also use your time abroad to learn more about a country's culture or to study the local language. Many short courses are offered by European schools and by "study abroad" programs sponsored by U.S. universities and colleges.

### Enjoy a new or familiar sport

If you thrive in the outdoors, why not enjoy your favorite sport in a new environment? Perhaps fishing is your idea of fun; if so, you'll find some of the world's best trout and salmon waters in Scotland and Ireland, or you could inves-

tigate mountain streams in Austria and Yugoslavia.

Travelers who are happiest astride a horse can write to tourist offices for information on riding instruction, pony trekking trips, and equestrian holidays.

If you prefer to spend your days on the water, you can enjoy sailing, cruising, canoeing, kayaking, and river rafting holidays in many countries.

Visiting golfers can play the historic courses of Scotland, where golf was born centuries ago.

Skiers have a choice of downhill or cross-country excursions in the various Alpine and Scandinavian countries. You can stay in an elegant or informal resort or ski cross-country from hut to hut. Mountaineering schools offer instructions and expeditions for both novice and experienced climbers. Walkers and hikers explore on foot everywhere; short group trips or long-distance excursions are available. Cyclists can rent bicycles for day touring or longer trips; tourist offices can provide route suggestions.

### Hobbies guide your travel plans

If you plan your journey around a favorite hobby, it adds enjoyment and leads you to other like-minded travelers. You can travel independently or join a special-interest tour. Your travel agent and the various government tourist offices can provide suggestions.

To learn more about a country's foods and wines, join a wine-tasting or restaurant tour or sign up for a series of cooking classes abroad. Gardeners can obtain new ideas at outstanding demonstration and estate gardens. If you enjoy ceramics, weaving, or another craft, investigate opportunities to visit workshops or study your craft abroad.

You can enjoy trips on narrow-gauge and steam railways and paddle-wheel steamboats, explore the Roman heritage in Britain and France, tour historic castles and houses, make brass rubbings, visit the *ateliers* of famous painters, go cave exploring, attend music festivals, visit war museums, join photography tours, go hang gliding or ballooning.

### Take a course or learn a language

An increasing number of travelers use their time abroad as a learning opportunity, taking language classes or delving into a country's culture. Among topics you can study are history, geography, fine arts, drama, music, literature, and archeology. You can also learn about national social programs, industries, and agriculture. Travelers take courses on topics ranging from music and craft classes to woodcarving and folk painting.

Government tourist offices can provide information on courses offered for English-speaking visitors. Many U.S. colleges and universities also sponsor "study abroad" programs for travelers as well as full-time students.

For sources of information on foreign study, write to the Communications Division, Institute of International Education, 809 United Nations Plaza, New York, NY 10017.

# special interests

# In Portugal

## HANDICRAFTS & FOLK ART

Regional handicrafts reflect the variety of cultural differences within Portugal. Many have a utilitarian use; others are ornamental or have a religious inspiration.

You'll discover folk art piled in cheerful disorder in local markets and fairs and arranged in attractive displays in shops. Handcrafted articles include painted and glazed earthenware and pottery; carved woodwork; quilts and blankets; lace and embroidery; articles of wicker and straw; metalwork in iron, copper, brass, and tin; delicate filigree work; items made of cork, skins, and leather.

You can see handicrafts from throughout Portugal on display in Lisbon's Museum of Popular Art near the Belém Tower; it's open daily except Mondays and holidays. For information on regional crafts, write to the Portuguese National Tourist Office.

## FERRY TRANSPORT

Visitors to Lisbon can appreciate the city's charms from the Tagus River on one of the fast ferries linking the city with other riverside towns.

Passenger and car ferries and hovercraft service link Setúbal with Tróia (and with Sesimbra in summer).

Along the Algarve coast, river ferries operate at Faro, Tavira, Portimão, and Vila Real de Santo António.

## HISTORICAL TRAINS

Portuguese Railways (CP) still operates two historic steam trains for tourists. Inquire locally regarding times of operation.

The Historical Train runs on the narrow-gauge railway (Tâmega line) between Livração, Amarante, and Arco de Baúlhe.

The 19th Century Train runs on wide-gauge tracks, mainly on the Minho line, between Oporto and the northern frontier at Valença.

## LISBON'S OLD DISTRICTS

Oldest and most picturesque of Lisbon's bairros is the Alfama, a maze of narrow streets lined by venerable mansions and marked by attractive churches. Eight centuries of history are distilled in this delightful old quarter.

Walk these lanes in early morning when the fish market is open on Rua de São Pedro, or in late afternoon when everyone is outside on the streets and squares. In June the alleys are lively during festivities of the "People's Saints" when singers and dancers perform in the squares. Other colorful old Lisbon districts are the Mouraria, Madragoa, and Bairro Alto.

In restaurants specializing in Portuguese cuisine, you'll often hear the fado songs sung to guitar accompaniment.

## GETTING AROUND LISBON

Travelers in Lisbon use the city's characteristic trams and buses as well as a modern underground railway to get around this hilly city. Fares vary according to number of transport zones traveled and means of transport used. A funicular climbs the Calçada da Gloria slope to the Alcântara view point.

If you plan to spend several days in Lisbon and want to use surface public transport, you can buy a Tourist Ticket at any of the City Transport Company's information kiosks.

## RELAX IN A POUSADA

Portugal's first pousada (meaning a resting place or inn) was founded in the 12th century by a Portuguese queen to offer pilgrims "a roof, a bed, and a candle." Today accommodations are much more generous, and the warm hospitality continues.

Operated by the Portuguese Tourist Organization, these inns are located in towns, mountain areas, and in the countryside. Some are in converted historic buildings such as castles, palaces, and monasteries; other pousadas have been specially built.

To maintain the welcoming atmosphere, the pousadas are relatively small—from 5 to 28 rooms. Inns are furnished in Portuguese style, and local foods and wines are usually on the menu.

Since pousadas are popular with Portuguese as well as overseas travelers, it's wise to make reservations regardless of the season. For more information, write to the Portuguese National Tourist Office.

## FOLKLORE & MUSIC

Portuguese folklore becomes most expressive during religious pilgrimages and folk festivals. For information on events, write to the Portuguese National Tourist Office.

Throughout the country, groups of young entertainers in regional dress perform the songs and dances of old Portugal—the quick-stepping fandango of Ribatejo, the spritely corridinho of the Algarve, dances of the fishing people of Nazaré and Póvoa de Varzim, the nostalgic fado of Lisbon, lively viras and malhões of Minho, and many others. Check with local tourist offices for information on performance locations.

## FOOD & WINES

Portugal's regional food specialties reflect the variety in geography and climate and the influence of other cultures. Each part of the country has its favorite dishes, which you can sample in pousadas and other restaurants featuring regional cuisine.

You'll find many excellent Portuguese wines, which are produced in various regions of the country. Oporto is the home of the famous port wine, brought down the Douro River from the eastern mountains for aging. On weekdays you can visit the wine lodges in the city's Vila Nova de Gaia quarter on the river's south bank to sample port and learn how it is made.

For information on Portuguese foods and wines, write to the Portuguese National Tourist Office.

**For information on travel in Portugal, write to the Portuguese National Tourist Office (address on page 7).**

# Island Hopping in Denmark

Roam the gentle countryside of Hans Christian Andersen and savor historic Danish seafaring towns

Uncrowded Funen is Denmark's garden island, a tranquil land brightened by hollyhock-splashed cottage gardens and half-timbered farmhouses, square-towered country churches and elegant old manor houses. Red Danish cattle graze in wildflower-dotted pastures and plod placidly home in the evening. Off Funen's south coast lie some of Denmark's most delightful islands.

The countryside of Hans Christian Andersen is at its prettiest in summer, when the wheat stands golden yellow, the oats green, and mounds of drying hay mark the meadows. April, May, and June are the months of least rainfall; later in summer you may have to dodge rain showers more often. The marine climate never gets extremely hot, and there's always a breeze.

Express trains link Copenhagen and Odense, the largest town on Funen; a spur line extends south from Odense to Svendborg. Buses serve the main towns. Bridges link Funen's south coast with the islands of Tåsinge and Langeland; ferries travel to Ærö and the smaller islands.

Though you'll find hotel accommodations in most towns, consider spending a night or two in a Danish *kro* (country inn) or as a guest on a farm.

## Join the cycling Danes

In Denmark practically everyone rides a bicycle—except the foreign tourist. Cyclists enjoy Funen's low, gently undulating countryside and its everchanging wayside scene. You'll pedal through wooded areas and along the coast, visiting old villages and elegant country estates. You can stop for a picnic, a chat with a friendly farmer, or a cool glass of lager.

In Odense and other large towns, cycle shops and some railway stations rent bicycles by the day or week. If cycling appeals to you, contact the Danish Tourist Board for information on a variety of cycling tours departing from Svendborg and looping through the southern islands. You pedal independently at your own pace along a preselected route, but arrangements for bike and equipment rental, lodging, meals, and ferry passage are handled for you.

## The town of Hans Christian Andersen

Odense, Funen's largest town, is best known as the birthplace of Hans Christian Andersen, Denmark's great writer of fairy tales. The Odense River flows through town, emptying into the sea some 14 miles/22 km to the north.

According to tradition, Hans was born in 1805 in the house at Hans Jensensstræde 39, the son of a cobbler and a washerwoman. Here you'll see mementoes of his life and writings, including his writing desk, top hat, and famous umbrella. He spent his childhood in the humble house at Munkemöllestræde 3 (now also a museum); in one small room, the family lived and slept, and Father Andersen plied his cobbling trade.

Houses from the 16th and 17th century have been preserved on Montestræde, and other old houses can be found in Overgade. Rail buffs enjoy a visit to the Danish Railway Museum to see historic equipment.

In summer you can take a boat ride on the tree-lined Odense River; check at the tourist office for departure times. Paths border stretches of the river.

In a wooded riverside site south of Odense is Funen Village (Den Fynske Landsby), a delightful collection of buildings reconstructed as a typical Funen settlement of the 18th and 19th centuries. You'll see thatched farmhouses, half-timbered cottages, mills, and other structures characteristic of the era. Open daily from April through September (Sundays in winter), the village can be reached by bus from Odense. In midsummer, Andersen's stories are dramatized in the village's outdoor theater.

## Funen's south coast

From Odense, roads lead south to Svendborg and Fåborg on Funen's south coast.

One of Denmark's most attractive castles lies just off the main road south of Ringe. Mirrored in its encircling moat and reached by drawbridge, towered and turreted Egeskov Castle resembles a proper fairy-tale palace. Built about 1550 as a private fortress during a period of civil war, the rosy brick castle appears to rise directly from the water. The building is not open to visitors, but you can enjoy its parklike gardens and visit a museum featuring antique cars and planes.

The old sailing town of Svendborg is still devoted to commerce and the sea. Funen's second-largest town contains a regional museum, Anne Hvide's Gård at Fruestræde 3; the old Church of St. Nicolas dedicated to the patron saint of sailors; and a zoological museum containing Danish birds and mammals.

Surrounded by wooded rolling hills, Fåborg overlooks its own fiord. In 1728 fire damaged the old city, but many of its houses were spared. Only one of the town gates remains of the original walled city. A museum in the tall belfry contains an excellent collection of paintings by Danish artists.

West of Fåborg at Horne is an unusual round church, the only one of its type on the island. It was once both church and fortress, with walls 7 feet/2 meters thick, but today only the core of the building remains. About 1 mile/ 1½ km north of Horne, the 500-year-old Kaleko water mill has been turned into a museum.

Thatched farm buildings blend with Langeland's golden fields. Cyclists find little traffic on these southern islands.

## Island hopping in the southern isles

On the southern coast, Svendborg and Fåborg are jumping-off towns for the islands south of Funen. From Svendborg you can reach Tåsinge and Langeland by bridge, but you'll need to take a ferry to Ærö and smaller islands in the archipelago.

Main ferry routes link Svendborg and Ærösköbing, Fåborg and Söby, Marstal and Rudköbing. Motorists traveling on weekends and during vacation periods should reserve ferry space to avoid delay (see page 141).

**Tåsinge.** An idyllic island of billowing grain fields and thick beech groves, Tåsinge has few villages breaking its flat horizon.

Thatched roofs add a pleasant touch to many of Troense's whitewashed and half-timbered houses. Denmark's days of naval glory are recalled in a pair of maritime museums in the town's old school and in the 17th century castle of Valdemars Slot.

At Bregninge, stop at the windmill for a superb view.

**Langeland.** Largest of the archipelago islands, Langeland is linked by bridge to Tåsinge. Attractive beaches draw swimmers and sunbathers.

In Rudköbing, the island's main town, you'll find charming old houses lining Brogade and Östergade. The road north passes Tranekær Castle, built as a royal fortress about 1200, and Egelykke Manor.

**Ærö.** Ferries transport travelers to Ærö, most captivating of the islands. Bus service connects Ærösköbing with Marstal and the fishing village of Söby.

The old seafaring town of Marstal, home port of many of Denmark's ships, has the tang of tar and salt-

Children walking down Ærösköbing street are dwarfed by tall hollyhocks. Pastel colors brighten many island houses.

water. Displays in its museum recall the era when some 400 ships used to sail from here.

Delightful Ærösköbing is a national treasure. Quaint old houses line cobbled streets lighted by gas lamps. You can mail post cards in a 1749 post office and see an unusual collection of ships in bottles. The 18th century church has interesting carvings on its pulpit.

# Fascinating Rail Trip across Norway

Traversing valleys, forests, mountains, and fiord country, this route offers an exciting look at Norway

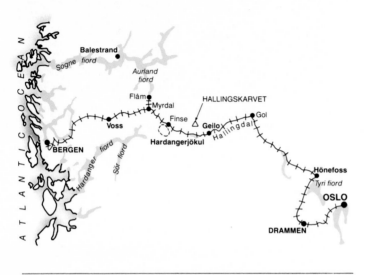

From mountaintop above Bergen, you look down on attractive city and its harbor. Many fiord trips depart from this port.

One of Europe's most scenic rail routes climbs across Norway's mountainous spine, linking the country's two largest cities—Oslo and Bergen. During the fascinating 6½-hour trip, the train wends from agricultural valleys through pine forests and up into the bleak tundra and icy mountains, then dips into western Norway's beautiful fiord country.

Completed in 1909 and totally electrified, the railroad is an engineering feat. More than 60 miles/100 km of track lie above timberline in country covered by snow most of the year. Passing waterfalls and glaciers, trains go through about 200 tunnels and 18 miles/29 km of snowsheds. Several of Norway's famous ski resorts are located along the rail line; skiing lasts from Christmas through April at most of them.

For an exciting finish to your journey, get off the train in Myrdal, take the short but spectacular ride on the unique Flåm rail line, and continue on to Bergen by fiord steamer.

## Over the top of Norway

Leaving Oslo, the train heads for the lakes, woods, and hills of Nordmarka, where Oslo families go on country outings. Later you pass through the Hallingdal district, where Norwegian peasant culture still survives.

West of Geilo, one of Norway's major resorts, the railway enters the high mountain zone, crossing near the base of Hallingskarvet, an impressive mountain wall about 21 miles/34 km long. Near Finse, the Hardangerjökul glacier comes into view. High snow fences and covered snowsheds shield the tracks, a necessity at this elevation. Sod-roofed farm buildings and storehouses dot the tundra.

Just before Myrdal, look for one of the trip's best sights: a view down more than 1,000 feet/300 meters to the Flåmsdal, a huge ravine yawning at the foot of towering mountains. West of Voss the train enters fiord country, giving you glimpses of some of Europe's most spectacular scenery between the many railway tunnels.

## A train that stops for photographers

In Myrdal you change to the steep (to 55°) Flåm rail line, shortest and most scenically breathtaking of Norway's mountain railroads.

In about 12 miles/20 km, the railway descends to the town of Flåm on Aurland fiord. It drops 2,800 feet/850 meters, passes through 21 tunnels, and completes a circle inside a mountain tunnel to reach the valley. Emerging from the tunnel, the train crosses the thundering Kjosfoss Falls and stops so that passengers can take photographs, then continues down the valley to the village at the edge of the fiord.

After spending the night in Flåm, you continue the next day by ferry to Bergen (changing ships in mid-fiord) along the beautiful Sogne fiord. The meshing of boat and train connections allows travelers going from west to east (Bergen to Oslo) to make the fiord excursion from Bergen to Flåm, take the rail trip up to Myrdal, and still catch a late-afternoon train into Oslo—all on the same day.

# Dalarna, the Heart of Sweden

In the farming district around Lake Siljan, learn about folk culture and enjoy outdoor sports events

Midsummer mist fails to dampen spirits of this Dalarna nuptial party. Bridal pair wears traditional wedding costumes.

Swedes call Dalarna the heart of Sweden. In summer and winter, they come here on holiday, drawn by the province's scenery, outdoor sports, and rural folk culture. Most of the principal resorts—Leksand, Tällberg, Rättvik, and Mora—rim Lake Siljan.

This is a land of lakes and fir forests, separated by narrow cultivated valleys speckled with bright red farm buildings. It is also the nation's oldest industrial center— Dalarna's mineral wealth financed Sweden's imperialistic adventures several hundred years ago. You can visit Falun's open-pit copper mine—operated since 1300—and adjacent museum from May to August.

Peasant culture still thrives in Dalarna. Farm women often wear traditional dress to Sunday church services. Rural fiddlers play for local dances, and crafts such as weaving and woodcarving remain popular.

You'll learn more about Dalarna farm life at several open-air museums around Lake Siljan. Groups of wooden farm buildings typical of an earlier era show handcrafted details like carved gables and decorative folk paintings.

Swedes celebrate Midsummer Eve enthusiastically on the weekend nearest June 23, and visitors join in the fun. In towns along Lake Siljan, events begin with the raising of a Maypole decorated with greenery and flowers. Dancing and outdoor activities continue all night.

Skiing in Dalarna lasts from Christmas through March. Winter visitors also find skating and curling rinks and slalom runs; you can join a sleigh ride or follow ski trails to chalets in the nearby mountains. Dalarna's major midwinter event is the Vasa cross-country ski race from Sälen to Mora, an event attracting some 10,000 competitors and even more spectators.

Trains travel from Stockholm to Mora in 4½ to 5 hours, with stops in Borlänge, Leksand, and Rättvik. Local buses also connect the province's main towns. In good weather, many natives bicycle along rural roads.

## Around Lake Siljan

Attractive resort towns border Lake Siljan's shoreline. One of the oldest settlements is Leksand, where the church is built on the site of a pagan temple. In early days, parishioners traveled to church in long, oar-powered "churchboats"; the tradition is celebrated on the first Sunday in July when crews from various lakeside parishes compete in the churchboat races. Another July event is the 10-day run of *The Road to Heaven*, an open-air miracle play based on folk traditions with music and dancing.

Tällberg occupies a magnificent site on the lake's southeast shore. The home of the late Swedish artist, Gustaf Ankarcrona, is now a museum where you can see works by folk artists.

At Rättvik's Gammelgård open-air museum, you see an old Dalecarlian farmstead with buildings decorated in rural folk art. Folk dancers and musicians entertain twice weekly in July and early August.

Mora is closely associated with Sweden's most famous painter, Anders Zorn. You can visit the Zorn Museum, which contains many of his best paintings as well as Dalarna handicrafts and rural art. The home of this impressionist painter is also a museum. Near the lake, about 40 timber buildings typical of Swedish rural architecture are grouped in Zorn's Gammelgård.

# Scandinavia's Land of the Midnight Sun

Visit Lapp villages and join rugged outdoor activities when you travel north of the Arctic Circle

**Lapp trader displays handicrafts for tourists—Lapp slippers, reindeer skin handbags, and other small articles.**

Europe's last wilderness lies north of the Arctic Circle—the vast land of the Midnight Sun.

Spectacular vistas of snow-capped mountains and the fiord-indented coast are punctuated by sparkling lakes, tumbling rivers, pine and birch forests, and wild tundra in the interior. You can visit encampments where Lapps tend herds of grazing reindeer, and join in a host of outdoor activities.

The long day of the Midnight Sun—when the sun never sets—arrives in late May and lasts until mid-July near the Arctic Circle. On the weekend nearest Midsummer, outdoor celebrations occur all over Scandinavia.

Early in September, the first frosts create a brief explosion of vibrant color inland. Trees and shrubs glow in clear hues of yellow, red, and russet. Colors often emerge overnight and vanish a few days later.

Winter brings a different mood, when snow blankets the northern hills and tundra. Cross-country skiers arrive, and Lapps gather for local reindeer markets.

## Traveling in the far north

Once you decide to head north of the Arctic Circle, you'll find a wide choice of transportation. If you use only surface transport, however, the vast distances eat up valuable time. Often you can combine several modes of travel to advantage.

Scandinavian Airlines and Finnair serve major cities north of the Arctic Circle. In late spring and early summer, visitors who want a glimpse of the northland can make overnight round-trip Midnight Sun excursions from Stockholm and Helsinki.

Throughout the year, coastal steamers cruise north from Bergen along Norway's spectacular fiord coast, past North Cape to Kirkenes; they stop briefly at coastal towns to deliver passengers, mail, and freight. In summer, cruise ships also make the coastal run.

Rail lines head north from Stockholm by way of Boden and Kiruna to Narvik on the Norwegian coast;

from Oslo to Trondheim and Bodö; and from Helsinki to Rovaniemi and Kemijärvi.

In the far north, a system of connecting bus lines offers the best way of getting around. Local buses fan out from the main bus and rail routes to remote areas.

If you're driving, you'll find most roads are graveled, though some are oiled; potholes often mar the road. Efficient ferries transport vehicles across fiords. Best months for driving are from late June through September (spring thaw makes some roads impassable until mid-June).

Good tourist inns and hotels dot the towns and main routes. Hotels and holiday villages have been built in favorite recreation areas. Tourist inns aren't luxurious, but they're modern, clean, centrally heated, and moderately priced. Since the region has limited accommodations and a short season, you should make reservations well in advance.

## Along Norway's fiord coast

The majestic scenery of Norway's fiord coast has attracted travelers for years. Vast forests, deep fiords, shimmering lakes, plunging waterfalls, and snow-capped mountains provide awesome panoramas. For many visitors the important destination is North Cape, Europe's northernmost outpost. It's a lonely cliff rising nearly 1,000 feet/about 300 meters above the Arctic Ocean at 71° North latitude.

You can make the trip north by coastal steamer from Bergen or travel by bus or car on the Arctic Highway. From early June to mid-September, the Nord-Norge-Bussen (sometimes called the "Polar Express") makes a 4-day run from Fauske to Kirkenes, with overnight stops at Narvik, Sörkjosen, and Lakselv.

If you plan to drive, allow 6 travel days between Trondheim and North Cape. You'll leave your car (or the bus) at Repvåg, board a ferry to the fishing village of Honningsvåg, and continue by bus to North Cape.

A warming Gulf Stream moderates Norway's coastal climate. Ferries and fishing boats enliven port activity. New buildings rise in the small northern towns, many of which were bombed or burned during World War II. In fishing villages, tidy wooden houses are painted bright blue, orange, and yellow and have lace curtains at the windows.

Bodö and Hammerfest, both rebuilt since World War II, are thriving fishing ports. Narvik, terminus of Sweden's iron-ore railway, is an important ice-free shipping port. Tromsö has been the jumping-off place for expeditions into the Arctic and to the North Pole; you can see objects from these trips at the Arctic Museum, which also has a Lapp collection.

## Lapp villages dot the northern tundra

Stretching across the northernmost regions of Scandinavia, the wild tundra of Lapland is inhabited mainly by Lapps, a nomadic and self-sufficient people with their own language, cultural traditions, colorful red and blue apparel, and handicrafts. Most Lapps have given up the nomadic life, but some still follow the reindeer herds.

Reindeer provide the Lapps with food, skins for warm clothing, bones and antlers for implements. Highlight of the Lapp year is the annual winter reindeer roundup.

Among the more accessible Lapp settlements are Karasjok and Kautokeino in Norway; Jokkmokk, Gällivare, and Jukkasjärvi in Sweden; Rovaniemi, Enontekiö, Kilpisjävri, Inari, and Utsjoki in Finland. Some towns have museums that trace the Lapps' history, show how they live, and display their handicrafts.

## Summer activities in Lapland

Spring appears suddenly in Lapland. In May the first flowers peek through melting snows, and rivers thunder with ice floes. From first thaw to first snowfall, Scandinavians devote nearly every spare waking hour to outdoor activities—fun that you can share.

Hikers find an excellent network of trails in the highlands and across the fells and tundra. The season begins after Midsummer and lasts into September. Insects appear in hordes as the snow recedes, so remember to bring repellent.

Fishing is excellent in Lapland's lakes and rivers and in the Swedish highlands. Guided fishing and hunting trips are available, with air taxi service to remote areas. You can fish for salmon in several rivers or go deep-sea fishing from Hammerfest. Travelers shoot the rapids on Norway's Alta River and in Finland's Kuusamo district (east of Rovaniemi), and make boat trips on some of the larger lakes.

A minor gold rush started here nearly a hundred years ago. If you like, you can pan for gold in the Karasjokka River, upriver from Karasjok on Norway's Finnmark plateau, or in remote tributaries of Finland's Lemmenjoki and Ivalo rivers west of Ivalo.

An interesting day trip is the train ride between Kiruna and Narvik on the scenic "iron-ore route." Ore is mined in Kiruna (visitors welcome June to August) and shipped by rail to the Norwegian port of Narvik. Since the railway provides the only access to some scenic areas of the Swedish highlands, numerous tourist centers have sprung up along the rail line.

## Winter above the Arctic Circle

In winter, drifts of snow transform Lapland's hills, lakes, and birch-studded tundra. Temperatures drop far below freezing, but no one goes into hibernation.

Reindeer roundup time is December and January, when Lapps bring their herds to local markets. Cross-country skiing draws an increasing number of visitors; the season lasts through April, and spring skiers enjoy long days beneath the Midnight Sun.

Travelers seeking a new outdoor experience can join a guided "reindeer safari," exploring the Lapp wilderness by reindeer-drawn sleigh. Most excursions are held in March. For more information, write to the Finland Tourist Board (address on page 7).

# Open-air Museums Show Village Life

Enjoy traditional architecture, entertainment, and crafts in outdoor folk villages

In many European countries, open-air folk villages preserve the architecture and life style of an earlier time. Many museum towns are rural in nature, but some recreate town life of a century or two ago.

Visit a folk museum and you may see farm buildings complete with animals, thatched cottages or sod-roofed log cabins, timbered brick houses or plank-sided dwellings. Many buildings have been furnished in period style, including utensils and tools. Shops often announce their business with interesting wooden or wrought iron signs.

Sometimes you can watch artisans working at old-time crafts; some museums have adjoining craft shops. In summer, costumed entertainers occasionally perform folk songs and dances.

Most open-air museums welcome visitors only from April or May to September or October, but a few stay open the year around. The ones listed below are just a sampling of those available. Others are listed in the index. Check local tourist offices for additional folk museums and the dates and hours of any that you plan to visit.

### See a different side of Britain

Near Coalport in the Severn valley, birthplace of the Industrial Revolution (see page 21), Blists Hill Open-Air Museum preserves furnaces, brick and tile works, a coal mine, a section of the Shropshire Canal, and other industrial monuments of this important era.

At Beamish, northwest of Durham, an open-air museum depicts social and industrial life in northeast England around 1900. You visit furnished cottages, a railway station, and workshops; see equipment displays; and ride a clattering electric tramcar.

You can visit Cogges Farm Museum in the tiny Oxfordshire hamlet of Cogges, near Witney. The Edwardian farm goes back at least to the 11th century Domesday Book; some buildings date from the 17th century. You'll see an old cobbled dairy, a magnificent barn, ox byres and pigsties, stables, and sheds sheltering old farm carts.

Learn about the life and culture of Wales at the Welsh Folk Museum at St. Fagans, on the western outskirts of Cardiff. Typical buildings have been brought to this 100-acre site from all over Wales, and resident artisans demonstrate traditional Welsh country crafts.

### Rural & ancient dwellings in Ireland

Houses from all areas of the Shannon region have been moved to Bunratty Folk Park west of Limerick. Look at agricultural machinery in a courtyard and watch crafts people at work (see page 29).

Replicas of Celtic and medieval lake dwellings, typical of those found in Ireland from about 600 B.C. to the Middle Ages, have been built on the grounds of Craggaunowen Castle, about 10 miles/16 km northwest of Shannon Airport. Celtic and medieval art is housed in the tower.

### Old-time villages in the Low Countries

North of Arnhem in a large wooded park, the Netherlands Open-Air Museum contains numerous farm buildings, shops, old Dutch houses, windmills, and bridges transported here from various parts of the country.

Life in a Zuider Zee fishing village is depicted in Enkhuizen's Zuider Zee Museum (see page 43).

At Schoonoord in Drenthe province, buildings of De Zeven Marken Open-Air Museum illustrate life in Drenthe villages about 1900. You'll see turf huts, Dutch farm buildings, a smithy, clogmaker's shop, bee farm, and sawmill.

Belgium's large open-air museum at Bokrijk is located about 57 miles/92 km east of Brussels, between Hasselt and Genk. Ancient Flemish houses surround a triangular village green, and you'll see a small 12th century church. Sheep graze in the fields. The nature reserve also includes an arboretum and garden, lakes, and deer park.

In Luxembourg, visit a wine and folklore museum at Bech-Kleinmacher, near Wellenstein in the Moselle wine district. It is housed in the 350-year-old Possenhaus, a vine-grower's dwelling.

### Scandinavia preserves its past

Vintage dwellings and farm buildings have been preserved in many Scandinavian districts.

**Denmark.** Best known of Denmark's open-air museums is the Old Town in Århus. About 60 houses and shops were brought here from all parts of the country and set up along cobblestone lanes. Furnished buildings show how Danish urban life developed between 1600 and 1850.

North of Copenhagen in the suburb of Lyngby, representative Danish farm buildings, windmills, and country houses have been assembled on an 85-acre rural park to represent various Danish districts and periods.

Iron Age villages have been reconstructed on two sites: on a heather-clad moor around Flynder Lake at Hjerl Hede, in northern Jutland about 10 miles/16 km south of Skive; and at the Oldtidsbyen at Lejre, a research center about 6 miles/10 km west of Roskilde in North Sealand. Visitors see how people lived and worked in prehistoric times.

**Norway.** The excellent Norwegian Folk Museum at Bygdöy, just west of Oslo, has a vast collection of more than 150 old wooden buildings and a 12th century stave church. Dwellings are grouped to represent different districts; one section is a reconstructed 18th century town.

The folk culture of the Gudbrandsdalen, one of Norway's most prosperous country districts, is emphasized at Maihaugen, north of Oslo on the outskirts of Lillehammer.

Town life in past centuries is the theme of Gamle Bergen, located near the entrance to Bergen's harbor. Old buildings from the town have been relocated along cobblestone streets and alleys. Houses are furnished in early 19th century style.

Trondheim and Tröndelag Folk Museum is located outside Trondheim at Sverresborg fortress. More than 60 buildings are grouped to depict farm settings, old Trondheim with merchants' houses, and a Lapp village.

**Sweden.** Old Sweden comes to life in Stockholm's lively Skansen, where more than 100 buildings from all over the country have been assembled. Costumed entertainers perform and crafts people work here in summer. The museum features a Lapp camp and reindeer enclosure.

Sod-roofed rural buildings and elegant manor houses from throughout southern Sweden have been reconstructed in Lund's Kulturen. Vying for your attention are rune stones and Viking implements, quaint stores and cottages, an old wooden church, and a farm complete with goats and geese.

**Finland.** Just a short bus ride from central Helsinki is Seurasaari Island, where old peasant buildings and manor houses from all over Finland have been relocated.

Turku's unusual Handicrafts Museum is located in a group of wooden houses, survivors of a disastrous 1827 fire that destroyed most of the town. In several dozen small shops, you see how craftsmen lived and worked in the 19th century; in summer, crafts people demonstrate tools and techniques used 150 years ago.

Northeast of Lappeenranta at Imatra, only 6 miles/10 km from the Russian border, you can visit a Karelian farmhouse museum. North of the Arctic Circle, learn about Lapp culture at Inari's open-air museum.

## Germany's museum villages recall other eras

Farmhouses of northern Germany have been gathered at Ostenfelder Bauernhaus, in the North Friesland fishing port of Husum, and at Freilichtmuseum des Bauernhausvereins Lehe near Bremerhaven.

Lower Saxony peasant houses—which shelter people and animals under the same roof—can be seen at Wilsede, a village in the Luneburg Heath reserve that allows only horse-drawn vehicles. More typical Lower Saxony dwellings stand at Cloppenburg, southwest of Bremen; houses, farm buildings, a church, and mill of the 17th and 18th centuries have been gathered on this 40-acre site.

Shelters on log pilings, typical of those built by prehistoric lake dwellers, have been reconstructed at Unteruhldingen, on the shore of the Bodensee. A small museum on shore displays items found during the excavations.

## Rural dwellings depict Swiss country life

Examples of Swiss regional architecture have been moved to the Ballenberg Swiss Open-Air Museum northeast of Lake Brienz. A 20-minute bus ride from Brienz, the museum is set on a forested site with a small lake. Houses and farm buildings are furnished in country style.

## A Spanish village in Barcelona

The Pueblo Español (Spanish Village) was built on the slopes of Montjuich mountain for Barcelona's 1929 World's Fair, but its exhibits and gardens were so popular they have been maintained. Buildings along village streets and squares show the great diversity of the country's regional architecture. You'll also see displays of regional costumes and demonstrations of Spanish folk crafts.

# Three Baltic Holiday Islands

Runic stones, fortified churches, windmills, and sandy beaches attract vacationers to these historic isles

A trio of Baltic islands off Sweden's southeast coast offer a respite from mainland activity. Long-time favorites of Scandinavian vacationers, the islands' charming old towns, rich history, sun-drenched beaches, and varied scenery intrigue visitors. Most people spend their summer holidays here, arriving between late June and mid-August. Bornholm hosts a summer music festival in late July and early August, featuring concerts in island churches. In early July, Gotlanders stage their Stangaspelen—athletic games dating back to Viking times. Outdoor concerts and a pageant opera also take place on Gotland during July and August.

The warm sunny days of autumn can be even more pleasant. Walkers find plenty of interesting routes and destinations, and cyclists enjoy the level, traffic-free island roads. Swimmers usually enjoy the sea until late September.

The Danish island of Bornholm and Swedish Gotland can be reached by plane or car ferry. Buses serve island towns, and rental cars are available. A long bridge across the Kalmarsund links Öland to the Swedish coastal city of Kalmar.

Island accommodations range from comfortable hotels in the larger towns to inexpensive pensions and seaside guest houses near the swimming beaches. On Bornholm, many families rent small holiday chalets. Gotland has several holiday villages built near the coast in various parts of the island. Scandinavian tourist offices (addresses on page 7) can provide more information on island accommodations. Since these islands are popular holiday destinations, make advance arrangements for a summer visit.

## Bornholm, an old Viking stronghold

Once a Viking bastion, the Danish island of Bornholm lies in the Baltic about 105 miles/170 km southeast of Copenhagen and some 22 miles/35 km off Sweden's south coast. Rönne, the island's thriving capital, is 30 minutes by air from Copenhagen. Car ferries reach the island in 7 hours from Copenhagen, 2½ hours from Ystad, Sweden.

Runic stones, fortified round churches, and castle ruins are reminders of less idyllic times. Bornholm was controlled by Sweden and later by the Hanseatic city of Lübeck before passing to the Danes about 1660.

Black-shingled, conical roofs top Bornholm's famous round white churches, fortified hundreds of years ago against pirates who plundered the coast. Religious services took place on the ground floor; in times of trouble, the people took refuge in the fortified upper chambers. Handsome 14th century Biblical frescoes often decorate the beams. Largest of the churches is at Österlars, south of Gudhjem. Others are located at Nyker and Nylars, both near Rönne; and at Olsker, south of Allinge.

Since Bornholm is relatively small and most towns border the coast, you can combine island attractions into a circular loop. Rönne, Gudhjem, Svaneke, and Neksö have interesting old sections. You'll want to visit at least one of the round churches and sample the varied coastal scenery.

When you've had enough sightseeing, you can walk in the countryside, sail or fish off the coast, or relax on sandy beaches. Bornholm has some of the most attractive bicycle routes in Denmark; for more information on island cycling, write to the Danish Tourist Board (address on page 7).

Displays in Rönne's museum feature island history, shipping, and bird life. Follow the coast road north to Hasle and the eroded cliffs of Jons Kapel, then continue on to mysterious Hammershus, where you can walk amid the ruins of one of Denmark's largest medieval castles.

Near the island's northern tip are Sandvig and the neighboring fishing port of Allinge. Paths traverse pine-covered hills, and you can see a large group of ancient rock engravings.

Quiet Gudhjem is an enchanting gem. Colorful cottages—many of them half-timbered or thatch-roofed—nestle against the hillside, each with a small garden overlooking the sea. You can visit a herring smokehouse to learn about one of Bornholm's main industries. Good beaches edge the nearby coast, and pleasant walks follow the wooded cliffs.

Continue to Svaneke and Neksö, a pair of attractive port towns on the east coast. Turn inland to explore the wooded Paradise Hills and, north of Åkirkeby, the forest of Almindingen, where walkers enjoy many delightful paths. You can survey the entire island from atop 516-foot/157-meter Rytterknægten mountain. On the south coast, beaches and sand dunes rim the sea near Dueodde, and megalith tombs can be seen at Arnager.

## Gotland prospered in Hanseatic days

Sunny Gotland lies about 60 miles/100 km off Sweden's east coast, about a half-hour by air and 700 years in time from Stockholm. Visby, the island's capital, rose to glory in the Middle Ages as the cultural crossroads of Scandinavia and a key trading center of the Hanseatic League. However, the island has been inhabited since the Stone Age, and farmers plowing their fields still occasionally uncover an ancient weapon, tool, or coin.

Largest of the Baltic islands, Gotland is about 75 miles/120 km long and 30 miles/50 km wide. Much of its land is undulating limestone plateau, lushly green in the interior with rugged cliffs edging the west coast. Woolly sheep graze everywhere. This is the warmest of Sweden's provinces; its Mediterranean climate lasts well into October and roses bloom until Christmas. The island's swimming beaches are among the best in Scandinavia.

Medieval Visby calls itself the "city of ruins and roses." The magnificent city wall, built in the 12th and 13th centuries, is largely intact and surrounds the town on all but the sea side.

Inside the walls, narrow half-timbered houses roofed in red tile line cobbled streets. Sudden glimpses of flowers, fountains, and tumbled cathedrals delight the eye. You'll see remnants of Visby's medieval wealth—merchant's impressive stepped-gable houses along Strandgatan, the main street during Hanseatic days; the old Apothecary; and St. Mary's Cathedral, the only one of the town's 17 medieval churches still in use.

Gotland's Fornsal is one of Europe's best provincial museums, devoted to the island's rich cultural history—mysterious picture stones and Viking rune stones, coins and jewelry from various eras, ancient weapons and relics—and its medieval religious art.

In the countryside you'll see dozens of ancient churches built during the great medieval commercial era; many are still in use. Most of the churches are covered with unusual ornamentation, and interiors are well preserved. Many contain some artistic or architectural treasure—paintings, crucifixes carved of wood, stained-glass windows, stone sculptures.

Gotland also has prehistoric and Viking remains—tumuli, fortresses, and burial grounds. The island's natural features include unusual limestone sculptures called "raukar," shaped by the Baltic's waves and winds, and the stalactite caves of Lummelunda.

Daily flights from Stockholm's Bromma Airport reach Visby in about 35 minutes. Car ferries leave the mainland from Nynäshamn (a short commuter run from

Black conical roof tops Österlars Church south of Gudheim, largest of Bornholm's handsome fortified churches.

Stockholm) and Oskarshamn. From June to late August, ferries also sail to Gotland from the coastal town of Västervik and from Grankullavik on the northern tip of Öland.

## Windmills mark Öland's skyline

Less heralded than Gotland, Öland lies just off Sweden's southeast coast. Scattered along its skyline are numerous windmills, giving the long island (90 miles/145 km) an unusual profile.

Borgholm, on the western coast, is the island's largest town and tourist center. Overlooking it from a commanding site is Borgholm Castle, one of Sweden's largest and most beautiful castle ruins. You can walk among the arches and along the ramparts of this medieval fortress, which was gutted by fire in 1806.

Solliden, a summer residence of Sweden's royal family, is located within easy walking distance of Borgholm. Sheep and cattle graze inside the imposing ruins of Gråborg Fortress, whose high thick walls once enclosed a large Iron Age stronghold.

An ancient forest of gnarled oaks covers the island's northern tip. Southern Öland's landscape is dominated by the desolate Alvar, a treeless limestone plateau.

# Exploring in Finland's Lake District

In this forested land of lakes, sightsee by steamer from waterside towns or settle in for a longer stay

In lake-studded southeast Finland, boating on a tree-rimmed lake is a relaxing way to spend a sunny day.

Umbrellas shield produce stalls in Savonlinna's open-air market. Shoppers also come to greet friends and exchange news.

Finns and visitors alike enjoy Finland's outdoor pleasures—lakes, forests, sunshine. One of the most scenic regions where you can get close to nature is the eastern lakes district, accessible by plane or train from Helsinki.

Strewn through the thick forests of southeast Finland are thousands of lakes connected by numerous interior rivers. From June through August, excursion boats depart from lakeside towns, cruising through the beautiful maze of islands and waterways. Lake steamers, hydrofoils, and motorboats leave from Lahti, Lappeenranta, Savonlinna, Kuopio, and other towns.

Summer visitors see the lake district best by combining various kinds of transport—train, plane, bus or car, and boat. An aerial view increases your appreciation of the region's many lakes and extensive forests.

Major towns in the region offer comfortable accommodations for short visits, or you may wish to relax as many Finns do, staying in a fully equipped—sometimes luxurious—log cabin in one of the holiday villages. Here you'll spend your days swimming, fishing, canoeing, and hiking. Sailors can charter yachts by the week at Lappeenranta and Savonlinna.

From January to mid-March, winter sports enthusiasts travel to Lahti and the Kuopio district, drawn by excellent cross-country trails, downhill and slalom runs, ski jumping, and *skijoring* (skiers towed by a horse or vehicle). International athletes gather each March to compete in Lahti's winter games.

## Along Lake Päijänne

From Helsinki, it's a 1½-hour train ride to Lahti. The town is situated at the southern end of lakes Vesijärvi and

Päijänne, second largest (to Saimaa) of Finland's lake systems. Gateway to central Finland, Lahti is a modern industrial town, proud of its city hall designed by Finnish architect Eliel Saarinen.

Steamers and motorboats travel north to Jyväskylä along the 70-mile/110-km waterway. Cottages are scattered on Vesijärvi's shores and islands. Proceeding through the canal lock connecting the two lakes, you have a view of the Salpausselkä Ridge, a prominent natural landmark formed during the Ice Age. As you continue north, scenery grows more wild; rocky shores and forested ridges rim Päijänne.

Bordering the north end of the lake is Jyväskylä, an important woodworking center and university town, which stages an annual summer arts festival. Near town at Saynatsalo is a civic center designed by renowned Finnish architect Alvar Aalto.

## Exploring the Saimaa lake region

Some of Finland's most scenic countryside is encompassed by the vast Saimaa lake system northeast of Helsinki. Over the centuries, the lands along Finland's eastern border have been a pawn between nations, and many events in Finnish history are entwined with their evolving fate. From Savonlinna, Lappeenranta, or Mikkeli, you can cruise amid wooded islands in this labyrinth of beautiful lakes, canals, and rivers.

Heart of the district is Savonlinna, reached from Helsinki by train (6 hours) or air (30 minutes). From here, you can travel in various directions to cover the district.

Various excursions combine boat travel with other transportation. You can take day trips or plan to stop off in various ports and board another steamer in a day or two. Some excursion boats cruise the waterways for several days, their passengers sleeping and eating aboard.

**Lappeenranta.** At the south end of Lake Saimaa—only about 10 miles/16 km from the Soviet Union's border—is the excursion center of Lappeenranta. Express trains cover the 140 miles/225 km from Helsinki in about 3½ hours; it's a 30-minute trip by air.

In the old part of town, you'll see ruins of the ramparts and fortifications. You'll want to visit the morning market in the heart of town, then stop at the South Karelia Museum near the harbor (closed Mondays). For a good view over the town, lake, and nearby islands, ride the elevator to the top of the water tower.

Boat trips cruise north through the Saimaa lake system; one—Oy Saimaa Lines, Ltd.—travels the Saimaa Canal, crossing into the Soviet Union and on to Vyborg (visa required for travel to the U.S.S.R.).

**Savonlinna.** Founded in 1639, Savonlinna is the oldest city in eastern Finland. Built on several islands and a cape jutting into the lake, the attractive resort enjoys a superb location and a quiet natural park in the heart of town.

Its best known landmark is Olavinlinna fortress, a well-preserved medieval castle built on a small island guarding the Kyronsalmi Straits. The town grew up on islands surrounding the fortress. Built about 1475, Olavinlinna was a bastion that protected the eastern frontier of the Swedish kingdom (which ruled Finland until the early 1800s) against attacks from the east and supported colonists who moved here to develop the land. Guided tours in English are available. In July the castle courtyard serves as a stage for the Savonlinna Opera Festival; other music and dramatic events are also performed here.

During the era when this region was ruled by Russia, wealthy families from St. Petersburg (now Leningrad) traveled to the holiday and health resort of Savonlinna. Casino Park, its baths, saunas, and other modern spa facilities are built on one of the town's islands.

Other interesting places to visit are Savonlinna's cathedral, built in 1879, and the lively open-air Savo Market, centrally located near the harbor.

**Excursions from Savonlinna.** Southeast of Savonlinna is Punkaharju, a famous Ice Age ridge forming a narrow causeway between lakes Puruvesi and Pihlajavesi. Now a national park, Punkaharju is accessible from Savonlinna by bus, train, or (summers only) boat.

In Kerimäki, about 14 miles/23 km northeast of Savonlinna, take a look at Finland's largest wooden church (open June to mid-August). Built more than 600 years ago, it will hold 3,300 people. From Kerimäki, boats transport visitors to the Hytermä nature reserve and museum islands, where a large folklore collection is on display.

Another excursion leads to Rauhalinna, a 20-room Byzantine-style wooden manor house. Built by the Russians about 1900, it overlooks the lake from a wooded site about 10 miles/16 km east of Savonlinna.

Steamers cruise southwest from Savonlinna through Saimaa waterways to Lappeenranta or Mikkeli; other boats travel north to Kuopio and northeast to Joensuu.

## North to Joensuu & Kuopio

If you cruise north from Savonlinna to Joensuu, your steamer will call briefly at ports along the shores of lakes Haukivesi and Orivesi. You can see the Orthodox convents of Lintula and Uusi-Valamo, moved here from the Lake Ladoga area when that part of Karelia was ceded to the U.S.S.R. following World War II. If you like, you can go direct to Joensuu from Helsinki by train (6 to 7 hours) or plane (45 minutes).

The only sizable town in the North Karelia region, Joensuu is proud of its Saarinen-designed town hall.

About 50 miles/80 km north of Joensuu is mountainous Koli, a scenic holiday center on the west shore of Lake Pielinen. Most visitors take the train to Vuonislahti, on the lake's eastern shore, then board a motorboat to cross the lake to Koli; you can also take a local bus.

Gaining in popularity as a holiday center, Koli offers excellent canoeing on the Pielisjoki River, well-marked footpaths, and other attractions. From the 1,000-foot/300-meter summit, hikers enjoy superb views.

An important Finnish ski center, Kuopio retains strong remembrances of old Finland, particularly of the Karelia region which was ceded to the Soviet Union. You'll want to visit Kuopio's colorful market, the Orthodox Cathedral, and Vainolanniemi peninsula and park. You can enjoy a town overview from the Puijo hilltop tower. Mementoes of Orthodox Karelia are displayed in an ethnological museum on the outskirts of town.

# Winter Visitors Join in Holiday Festivities

Off-season travelers enjoy folk celebrations, Christmas and pre-Lenten events, winter sports

When the summer crowds depart, Europe settles back to relax and enjoy itself. Travelers in the off-season find a different holiday experience on the Continent.

During the mellow days of autumn, woods turn from green to gold. Harvest and wine festivals dot the calendar.

Winter visitors enjoy numerous folk celebrations, fairs, and markets—but these are events geared to residents rather than tourists. A new arts season begins in autumn, featuring an impressive array of concerts, opera, ballet, and drama in major cities across Europe. In the mountains, snow signals the beginning of another ski season.

In the winter months, you'll find faster and more cheerful service, less waiting in line, and time to relax and enjoy your surroundings without being disturbed by tourist crowds.

Some countries and cities offer special promotions to entice winter visitors.

## Skiers flock to the high mountains

Late-autumn snows mark the beginning of the winter sports season, and Alpine resorts get ready to welcome the ski crowds. Famous resorts garner most of the publicity, but there are many excellent lesser-known resorts—with correspondingly lower rates. Travel agents and transatlantic airlines can provide information on ski packages.

Experienced skiers find challenging downhill runs on famous Olympic slopes. Cross-country skiing is increasingly popular, and you'll find trails in many areas. If you want to enjoy other winter sports as well, there are ice-skating rinks, ski jumps, bobsled and toboggan runs, and facilities for curling, ice hockey, ice boating, and *skijoring* (skiers towed by horse or vehicle). Nonskiers enjoy rides in horse-drawn sleighs, snow hiking, trips by cable car, sunbathing on terraces of Alpine restaurants, and lively *après-ski* activity.

Or you can head for the Pyrenees or the mountains of Scandinavia. Cross-country skiing is the popular activity in Scandinavia, and you can go ski touring from hut to hut.

Germany alone has more than 300 winter sports resorts in the Bavarian Alps and in wooded mountainous districts such as the Harz Mountains, the Black Forest, and the Bavarian Forest. In Switzerland, cross-country skiers enjoy good trails everywhere. Spain's Sierra Nevada range near Granada attracts skiers who spend the morning on the slopes and the afternoon swimming and sunbathing on the nearby Costa del Sol.

You can skate all winter on Holland's artificial ice rinks. When a hard frost sets in, everyone turns out to skate on the frozen lakes and canals in a scene resembling a painting by Brueghel.

## Christmas markets & traditions

Yuletide is a special season everywhere. Most European countries have traditional celebrations, and you'll find the season as festive and joyous abroad as it is at home.

**Christmas markets.** In a number of German and Austrian towns, the opening of the *Christkindlmarkt* signals the start of the holidays. Families come to see trees decorated in twinkling lights and to buy Christmas ornaments and other decorations, toys, gingerbread men and Christmas confections, Advent calendars, and other surprises.

Largest of the German Christmas markets is in Nuremburg; others are held in Cologne, Frankfurt, Munich, Rothenberg, West Berlin, and other cities. Austria's major Christmas fair is in Vienna; you'll also find them in Salzburg and other Austrian towns.

During the holidays in Rome, families enjoy a festive Christmas market in the Piazza Navona.

**Festive traditions.** Spending Christmas in London? Join in the carol singing around the tall Christmas tree that always stands in Trafalgar Square. Pantomime plays—a mixture of pantomime and fairy tales or nursery rhymes—are presented in some West End theaters to the delight of both adults and children.

In Belgium, Holland, and northeast France, children

put out their shoes on the night of either December 5 or 6 for St. Nicholas to fill with toys and candies that night. (December 6 is the birthday of St. Nicholas, Bishop of Myra in Asia Minor in the 4th century, who started the practice of Christmas gift-giving.) In the French province of Lorraine, children parade through Nancy, Metz, and Épinal.

Zürich brings out its bright red Fairy-Tale Tram. Aglow with electric lights, it tinkles and jingles down the Bahnhofstrasse. On board, the motorman is dressed like St. Nick in scarlet suit and white whiskers; a storyteller dressed as the Christmas Fairy entertains children with Christmas stories and carols while their mothers shop.

In southern France, celebrating Christmas is a public affair with medieval church pageants, torchlight street processions, and festive dinners at country inns. A parade of costumed pilgrims carrying lighted candles traditionally crosses the valley from Arles to Les Baux.

Italian churches prepare elaborate Nativity scenes (*Presepi*) which remain on display until January 6.

## Pre-Lenten & Easter festivities

In many European countries, the pre-Lenten Carnival (or *Fasching*) season is a time of great revelry.

**Fasching celebrations.** In Vienna, New Year's Eve marks the beginning of Fasching, the period during which the city is at its merriest. Beneath crystal chandeliers, dancers waltz until dawn at a series of festive balls.

During Carnival season, processions of Belgian children and costumed and masked adults make their way through many towns. Goose races are held in the Antwerp polders, and Lenten bonfires light up the Walloon countryside of southeast Belgium.

Mainz and other German towns in the Rhineland and Baden-Württemberg celebrate *Fassnacht* with parades of children and adults, fancy-dress balls, and outdoor dancing. Market women in Munich's Viktualienmarkt close stalls early on Shrove Tuesday and dance around the square. In the Black Forest, residents celebrate the Alemannic (Old High German) *Fasnacht* carnival.

Carnival parades are held in Lucerne and many other Swiss cities. In Basel, the celebration is held on the Monday following Ash Wednesday; it begins about 4 A.M. with *Morgenstraich* (crack of dawn) processions and lasts through evening masked balls.

A procession of spectacular floats is the highlight of Italian *Carnevale* festivities in Venice.

**Holy Week.** Great outbursts of religious fervor and splendor mark the Holy Week celebrations in Spain. In Seville, traditional processions take place every evening during Holy Week. Robed penitents precede the *pasos* (floats) representing Biblical scenes; bands playing funeral marches bring up the rear. Dense crowds line the routes. Similar somber observances occur in many Spanish cities.

**Greek Easter.** In Greece, Easter is the year's most important holiday. Three weeks of pre-Lenten festivities followed by 40 days of Lenten fasting culminate in a full week of Easter celebrations. Good Friday is a time for candlelight

processions; other religious services are held on Holy Saturday night and Easter Sunday, followed by a week of feasting, dancing, and singing.

## Good-bye winter; hello, spring

In northeast Yugoslavia, the Slovenian town of Ptuj bids farewell to winter in February with a historical pageant involving hundreds of costumed people wearing grotesque masks.

Ireland celebrates the birthday of its patron saint with a week-long St. Patrick's festival and parades in many towns. Limerick hosts an international band festival, and high-stepping musicians parade through the town on Sunday.

In small Austrian villages, *Märzenfeuer* (March fires) light up the slopes to scare away the evils of winter.

Biggest spring festival in Switzerland is *Sechseläuten,* a 2-day April ritual in Zürich traditionally marking the end of winter and the beginning of spring. It features two sizable parades; lots of parties (especially by members of ancient guilds); and the public burning of the Böögg, a huge effigy of a snowman that represents Old Man Winter.

Farming traditions are preserved in Austria with *Zweigsegen,* the blessing of new growth, and *Kornaufwecken* (waking up the crops) when boys carry bells through the village as soon as days begin to lengthen—even though there may still be snow on the ground!

Spring is a joyous season in Spain, celebrated with fairs and *romerías* (pilgrimages to a local shrine followed by a picnic party). Seville blossoms with its April Fair, highlighted by equestrian parades of costumed riders and their ladies, dancers performing classic *sevillanas*, cattle-dealing, and a vast street fair.

Maypoles decorated with greenery and ribbons are erected in many German and Austrian villages on May 1, and villagers join in dancing and merrymaking.

# Relax for a Few Days with a Farm Family

Join in farm chores, eat with the family, go to market, take short trips to nearby destinations

Instead of sightseeing as a tourist, why not pause in your travels and live with a European farm family for a few days as a paying guest?

On a farm vacation you'll gain much: the opportunity to experience the rural life of a country, a healthy and relaxing change of pace, a chance to get acquainted and share ideas with people of another culture, and a great way to beat the high cost of traveling.

And you'll like what you lose, too—the inconveniences of traveling. Forget about a nightly search for lodgings, tedious repacking, transportation annoyances, and impersonal accommodations. Farm holidays are especially popular among families traveling with children.

Usually you stay in rooms right in the farmhouse and take your meals with the family. Some farms offer a separate cottage with its own cooking facilities so you can come and go as you please.

## Finding your farm accommodations

You can live on a farm in Belgium, Britain, France, Germany, Ireland, Scandinavia, and Switzerland. Write to the appropriate government tourist office for information (addresses on page 7). Rural families in other countries also accept paying guests, but you generally can't find out about them until you're on the scene overseas.

You can also make arrangements through one of the organizations which coordinate home-based holidays in Europe. Visitors become paying house guests—staying not only with families in rural areas of the country selected but in towns and villages as well.

## Sharing accommodations with the family

Is a farm holiday right for you? Not if your idea of a vacation is luxurious accommodations or an array of cosmopolitan diversions.

The farmhouse can be anything from a simple house on a real working farm to a country manor. Living arrangements are comfortable, but family life is down-to-earth. You'll enjoy a warm welcome, a clean room with a comfortable bed, delicious hearty food, and a good time—but you may have to share the bathroom with the family.

You'll usually have hot and cold running water in the room itself. Some accommodations are furnished in regional style. Comfort is basic but adequate.

Breakfasts, and often other meals, are included in the basic price. Most farms take only a few guests at a time in order to preserve the family atmosphere.

Unless you can communicate easily in the local language, make sure that at least one member of the host family speaks English. A foreign language phrase book and dictionary will help you get your basic needs understood, but it's pleasant to be able to communicate and exchange ideas more fully.

## Your days in the country

Pick an area where you have access to transportation and several nearby destinations to visit. Usually you can arrange to rent a car, motorbike, or bicycle for your explorations.

You'll soon find yourself slipping into the rhythm of rural life, awakened in early morning by the sounds of household and farm activity. After breakfast, you can go on a leisurely walk in the country, fish for trout in a nearby stream, or settle down with a good book. If you're interested, you can watch or lend a hand with farm chores—collecting eggs, tending sheep, milking cows, repairing fences, preparing and planting the land.

From your farm base, you can make easy day trips to nearby towns or attractions. Enjoy midday hospitality at country inns or picnic in the countryside, then return to the farm in time for the evening meal and family sociability.

A highlight of the week is the farmers' market. Farm families head into town to purchase fresh produce and other foods; it's a sociable occasion to greet friends and exchange news. Produce stalls and "mobile market" vans fill and overflow the town's central square with a tempting array of vegetables, fruit, dairy products, meat, fish, and staples. Sellers also may offer herbs and spices, cut flowers and bedding plants, live animals, clothing, and other household goods.

# special interests

# In
# Scandinavia

## TRANSPORTATION TIPS

Rail travelers can purchase the Nordturist Rail Pass to explore Scandinavia in economical fashion. Good for 21 days, the pass allows unlimited first or second-class rail travel and free or discounted ferry passage on many routes. Bus services supplement air and rail service and enable travelers to reach many remote destinations.

Focusing on one country? Inquire from the appropriate tourist office (see page 7) about special discount passes.

In Copenhagen, Oslo, and Stockholm, tourists can purchase cards good for one to four days of unlimited metropolitan area transportation and free or reduced admission to many city attractions.

Car ferries provide important motoring links on many routes, particularly among Denmark's scattered islands. To avoid delays, reservations are recommended on the busier routes, particularly during the main summer travel months.

## COTTAGES, CHALETS, CABINS

When Scandinavian families go on holiday, they usually head for the sea, the lakes, or the mountains. Often families or groups of friends stay in modern "self-catering" cottages and cook for themselves.

Cottages, chalets, and log cabins can be rented by the week in all the Scandinavian countries. Accommodations range from luxurious cottages to rustic mountain huts. Some are grouped in holiday villages, where sports facilities and various leisure activities may be provided.

Many cottages are situated beside a lake or near the sea; use of a boat (and in Finland, a sauna) is often included. You may be able to rent bicycles or canoes nearby. Cottages are furnished with cooking and dining facilities and utensils, heat, and some bedding (bed linens and towels are not usually included).

Since these vacations are popular with Scandinavians, it's advisable to book accommodations well in advance for peak seasons—from mid-May to early September, Christmas, Easter, and the February school holidays.

## WALKING & HIKING TRIPS

Visiting hikers are welcome to join the Scandinavians on the paths and hiking trails. You can take short walks near mountain villages, stroll through deep forest, join organized guided day trips, or embark on an ambitious hiking expedition.

Marked paths cover all regions of Norway, Sweden, and Finland, ranging from short day walks to long-distance trails across mountains and moorland. Some routes have overnight shelters a day's hike apart. Many scenic areas of Denmark also have planned hiking routes.

Write to the government tourist offices for information on hiking routes, maps, trail accommodations, and guided excursions.

## FARM HOLIDAYS

Farm vacations give visitors the experience of living with a Scandinavian farm family. Usually you stay in the farmhouse; all meals are included in the cost. Some farms have individual cottages or apartments with electric stoves and refrigerators for families wishing to do their own cooking. On Finnish farms, you'll frequently have free use of a rowboat and access to a sauna.

## SCANDINAVIAN DESIGN

Shopping in Scandinavia is a feast for the eyes. Designers combine function with beauty, blend design with bright colors. Quality is the most striking feature of Scandinavian products. You'll be tempted by many tastefully designed articles for the home—glass and crystal, rugs and textiles, china and ceramics, furniture, silver and stainless and pewter, and handicrafts of all kinds.

Each capital city has a permanent design exhibition with a selection of the best of the country's arts and crafts. In Copenhagen, visit Den Permanente, at Vesterbrogade 8 near the central rail station; in Oslo, stop at the Forum, Rosenkrantzgate 7; in Stockholm, the permanent exhibition is Form Design Center, Sveavägen 17; in Helsinki, stroll through the Finnish Design Center, Kasarmikatu 19.

## WHAT'S YOUR HOBBY?

Combine a relaxing vacation in Scandinavia with your own favorite sport, hobby, or interest. Government tourist offices and local information centers in Scandinavia can help you enrich your travels.

You can join mountaineering treks, riding and cycling trips, and guided hikes.

If you thrive near the water, inquire about canoe safaris or sailing opportunities. If you prefer to be a passenger, you'll find numerous day sightseeing cruises on Scandinavia's lakes, harbors, and canals. Longer trips include Sweden's fascinating Göta Canal route and voyages by coastal steamer or cruise ship along Norway's fiord coast (see page 37).

You'll find not only art and history museums but exhibitions of folklore and handicrafts, industrial tours, and special-interest collections. Homes of several famous musicians and artists are open to the public.

Tourist offices can guide you to music festivals, opera and ballet, outdoor theater and concerts, and folklore programs.

## SEEKING FAMILY TIES

If your ancestors came from one of the Scandinavian countries, you'll find official help in searching for family roots. Tourist offices can suggest how to proceed and what information will be most useful.

Sweden has established the Swedish Emigration Museum in Växjö; its research staff has compiled an impressive record on emigration of Swedes to America beginning about 1850. The museum has a wealth of information about Swedish genealogy and artifacts concerning the migration.

Denmark celebrates its friendship ties with America annually on July 4 at Rebild National Park near Ålborg. Many Danish-Americans come to join in the festivities.

**For information on travel in Scandinavia, write to the tourist offices of Norway, Sweden, Denmark, and Finland (addresses on page 7).**

# Index

## PHOTOGRAPHERS

**Inga Aistrup/National Travel Association of Denmark:** 135. **Neville Armstrong:** 23 top. **Tom Baker:** 66. **Dave Bartruff:** 58 top, 98, 113, 119 top, 120. **Harry Basch:** 17, 32. **Morton Beebe/Image Bank:** 34 top, 103, 112. **Johan Berge/Norway Travel Association:** 128. **Kathleen N. Brenzel:** 119 bottom. **Bob/Virginia Brunner:** 105. **Bullaty/Loweo/Image Bank:** 104. **Richards E. Bushnell:** 122. **Jack Cannon:** 31, 33, 82, 87 top, 90. **Ron Carlson:** 129. **J. Colombaris/Image Bank:** 95 bottom. **Grant Compton/Image Bank:** 15 top, 89. **Ken Cooperrider:** 114, 130. **Anthony Edgeworth/Image Bank:** 40. **Richard Fish:** 34 left. **Scott Fitzgerrell:** 15 bottom. **Shirley Maas Fockler:** 127, 136 bottom. **Cornelia Fogle:** 18, 26, 47, 50 top, 55 bottom, 58 bottom, 63 bottom. **Lee Foster:** 42, 48. **Fremdenverkehrsverbad Hallstatt:** 74 top. **Jon Gardey:** 24, 95 top. **Larry Dale Gordon/Image Bank:** 106. **F. Grehan/Image Bank:** 71 top. **Richard Gross:** 88. **Keith Gunnar:** 55 top. **Bruce Hayes:** 57, 74 bottom, 79, 80. **Kess Photo:** 10, 87 bottom. **Russell Lamb:** 111. **L. Linkhart:** 56, 96, 97. **Milt & Joan Mann:** 50 bottom. **Steve W. Marley:** 23 bottom, 25. **Ruth Mason:** 121. **John Norall:** back cover. **Mary Ord:** 9 bottom. **Tim Ord:** 9 top, 16. **Richard Rowan:** 136 top. **William Rubenstein:** 63 top. **Cynthia Scheer:** 39 bottom. **Siegel/Swiss National Tourist Office:** 71 bottom, 72. **Nikolay Zurek:** 39 top, 49.